History Teaching and Historical Understanding

Edited by
A. K. Dickinson and P. J. Lee

HEINEMANN
LONDON

Heinemann Educational Books Ltd
LONDON EDINBURGH MELBOURNE AUCKLAND TORONTO
HONG KONG SINGAPORE KUALA LUMPUR IBADAN NAIROBI
JOHANNESBURG LUSAKA NEW DELHI KINGSTON

Cased edition 0 435 80290 9
Paper edition 0 435 80291 7

First published 1978

Published by
Heinemann Educational Books Ltd
48 Charles Street, London W1X 8AH
Printed in Great Britain by
Biddles Ltd, Martyr Road, Guildford

Contents

Contributors

B. Barker: Head of History and Director of Studies
Sir Frederic Osborn School
Welwyn Garden City

Asa Briggs: Provost of Worcester College
Oxford

A. K. Dickinson: Lecturer in Education with special reference
to the teaching of history
University of London
Institute of Education

A. D. Edwards: Senior Lecturer in Education
University of Manchester

A. Gard: Head of History
The Boswells School
Chelmsford

I. Goodson: Research Fellow in the Centre for Contemporary Studies
University of Sussex

P. J. Lee: Lecturer in Education with special reference
to the teaching of history
University of London
Institute of Education

Preface

The impetus for this book has been provided by the rapid growth of new ideas, or the development of older ones, which has recently characterized the public discussion of history teaching. It is not easy to say how far these ideas have changed history teaching: we suspect that for many pupils, school history is the same as it was for their parents, and that the outward show of history on the move conceals more cautious and even hostile reactions among some teachers. The hostility is not justified, and the still all-too-frequent lecturing and note-giving which masquerades in some schools as history teaching is an affront both to real teachers and to history. But perhaps after all some caution is not so reprehensible: teachers are hard-headed and hard-working, and if they detect rash enthusiasm and zealous confusion in some manifestations of 'the new history', it may be worth pausing to reflect upon their doubts.

It is our hope that this book represents both a pause for reflection, and a further step along the road to a different kind of history teaching. The first three chapters are concerned with matters that have received a great deal of attention in recent years, but on which much remains to be said. In the first chapter Dickinson, Gard and Lee discuss a theme which has been central to almost all the (manifold) interpretations of 'the new history', the use of evidence in history teaching, and re-examine some of the underlying issues. One of the most important recent contributions to thinking about history teaching has been Historical Association pamphlet TH35, in which Jeanette Coltham and John Fines set out a suggested framework of objectives for the study of history. Gard and Lee, in the second chapter, argue that it is time to re-assess this pamphlet, and in so doing cast doubt on the ease with which an objectives approach can be applied to history. The cautious reception which teachers have sometimes given to the offerings of curriculum reformers is discussed by Goodson, who also suggests more effective strategies for future progress.

The next five chapters all examine questions which have received relatively little attention. Their central theme is *historical understanding*, and it is a basic premise of this book that explanation, interpretation and imagination must be taken much more seriously than has so far been the case. The pivotal chapter is Edwards' account of language in history, which breaks new ground in an area which (after Bullock) is just beginning to attract notice. In Chapter 5 Lee discusses one aspect of historical understanding, and develops an analysis of the thinking it demands from children. This analysis is the basis of the pilot study described by Dickinson and Lee in Chapter 6. One of the more controversial innovations in history teaching is the history game. In the seventh chapter Barker shows that the thinking which inspired history games suggests a broad range of methods intended to increase children's understanding, and offers some practical examples. At the end of this section Dickinson tackles the awkward subject of examinations, and argues that they too must encourage historical understanding.

Finally, as a postscript, Asa Briggs describes recent developments in history after school, developments which have probably all influenced school history, but which could hardly yet be said to have been assimilated in schools. This is not surprising, for historical practices and understanding are still rapidly developing, and as Briggs shows, it is not easy to assess their significance when professional opinions are themselves divided: history teachers in these circumstances need more time to consider the implications for teaching of these changes. The developments sketched out by Briggs should perhaps be regarded as important matters demanding further consideration, rather than a list of new features for immediate incorporation into school history.

We hope that this volume will be a contribution to the continuing development of history teaching, and that it may play at least a small part in widening the current debate. That it has appeared at all is in no small measure due to Mr Jonathan Burnett, who freed us from our teaching commitments at Alexandra Park Comprehensive School for several weeks at a difficult stage in the book's compilation, and especially to Miss Fuz Bagum whose untiring and unstinting help in the preparation of the manuscript enabled us to meet a timetable we had thought impossible. We should like to take this opportunity of expressing our thanks.

1. Evidence in History and the Classroom

A. K. DICKINSON   A. GARD   P. J. LEE

PART I.   INTRODUCTION

The perennial debate on the appropriate role of primary source material in school history, initiated by M. W. Keatinge in 1911, has been vigorously reawakened by the protagonists of the 'new history'.[1] They have claimed that primary sources of one sort or another can be used in the classroom not only to stimulate interest and to illustrate themes or events but also as evidence. G. R. Elton has led the counter-attack, asserting that much of what is wrong with the teaching of history in schools stems from a mistaken belief that school history should aim to produce research scholars.[2]

Elton's thesis is that, ideally, schools should concentrate on encouraging interest and some grasp of the magnitude of the past, undergraduate studies should promote analytical thought, and then properly equipped scholars will emerge at the postgraduate level. According to this thesis the main aim of school history below the sixth form should be to give children a desire to learn about the past. Sixth-form courses themselves might include a 'look at original sources' but priority should be given to the study of 'some part of the history of a student's own country' and ensuring that each pupil acquires 'some vision of ages not his own, some ability to sink himself in minds and circumstances very different from those with which he has been equipped by the accident of birth'.[3] Some of the principles enunciated by Elton have been a feature of traditional school history, with its emphasis on a chronological précis of human actions from ancient times to the recent past, followed by a more detailed study of selected periods in the upper forms. Such courses were designed to give all pupils a sense of perspective and to give older children an insight into the depth as well as the breadth of the past. But they had two very undesirable characteristics: they concentrated excessively on introducing pupils to their national heritage, and on treating history as a body of received information to be accepted and memorized, a view reinforced by most examinations. Primary source material generally had a limited role, being used occasionally to stimulate curiosity, interest, even awe, or to illustrate particular points.

Although some of Elton's principles have been features of traditional school history, others do not fit that model. He emphasizes that knowledge of the past is important in its own right, as well as being a prerequisite for the more developed awareness of history as a discipline. Implicit in his account is a notion of teaching an 'appreciation' of history, an awareness of the differences of societies remote from the pupils' own. This conception of history teaching goes beyond the usual characterization of traditional history as a corpus of received information, drawing its inspiration instead from undergraduate history courses, but Elton is unable adequately to develop it because he wants to emphasize the discontinuity between school and university history.[4] The role of primary source material in such a study would be mainly to stimulate and to illustrate. This appears to be the same as the role ascribed to it in traditional history teaching, but source material as illustration fits much better with the notion of history as appreciation. The use of sources in this way already implies a minimal attempt to get children to *see* them as evidence for past events or ways of life. It is important to distinguish this from the stronger sense in which one may try to get children to *use* sources as evidence, and from the mistaken view that such materials tell us something about the past regardless of the extent of our knowledge.

Recently there has been a great deal of support for the idea of using primary source material in the stronger sense. Many teachers believe that school history should give children a practical introduction to the historical mode of enquiry. Children are plied with documents, statistics, potsherds, etc. in the hope of teaching them the skills of the historian. J. Chaffer, quoting R. Wake, has said of this trend: 'Today the method of the historian is everywhere argued as the model for teaching the subject. As a discipline history appears ideally suited to a Nuffield approach, for it has long been seen as essentially a process of enquiry: "there are no historical facts, only evidence".'[5]

This notion of school history has a welcome emphasis on inquiry, on pupils finding out about the past. But some of the statements of its advocates have at times been misleading. Turner, for example, seems to see evidence as a special category of objects, failing to distinguish between the various senses in which one can speak of pupils using sources, and conflating such activities with the relatively simple ancilliary skills of history.[6] The same sort of imprecision is manifested by John Fines, who passes unconcernedly from talking of 'archives' to talking of 'documents' as though they were the same, finally referring to 'evidences':

Fourthly, comes the most important question of all: what are *archives*? Must we restrict ourselves to handwriting? The co-ordination with museums has already been noted, but we need to bring in printed works, drawings, photographs and cine film, tapes and gramophone records. *Documents* need not be on paper, nor in crabbed handwriting: one document I sometimes use in teaching is a rubbing of a metal plate attached to the bridge at Sturminster Newton in Dorset: it tells how those who damage the bridge will be transported for life. Many older teachers are frightened of foreign phrases like 'teaching kits', and feel that these are merely 'bags of tricks'. Many of them are, but if we are to use *evidences* in our teaching they must not all be of one kind, and if we don't like other people's teaching kits then we must make our own. (Our emphasis.)[7]

Neither 'archives' nor 'documents' in general are necessarily 'evidence'. They may count as evidence, but that is a question of the purpose for which they are being used by the historian or, in schools, of whether children learn to see them as such. Archives, of course, are in any case the official records of institutions, not just any documents. This apparently minor point is of some importance if one is claiming to teach 'historical skills', in which case the nature and provenance of documents cannot be so lightly treated.[8]

Another problem is that the view of skills advanced by the protagonists is often a narrow one. Paleography is frequently mentioned and is indeed a prerequisite of the historian's study of some documents. But it is an ancilliary skill rather than a way of thinking central to history. Clearly such skills have their place, but it is also necessary to distinguish between them and the ways of thinking which are central characteristics of the historical mode of enquiry.

The assertion that the concrete nature of historical materials will help children to find out about the past also merits careful examination. Marilyn Palmer has advanced this argument, and the materials she mentions are certainly concrete — archaeological finds, historical buildings, models, pictures and charts, and original documents.[9] But what makes them *historical* materials is our historical understanding of them, and that is *not* concrete. This means that if we are to succeed in using primary sources for anything more than arousing interest then our children must understand them as saying something about the past. It is tempting, but misleading, to ignore this fact and to assume that children are automatically getting closer to 'real' history if they are given primary sources.

There is clearly a need to distinguish some of the different ways in which primary source material may be used in the classroom. The underlying assumption of recent debates has been the necessity to teach history as a 'mode of inquiry' rather than as a 'body of knowledge'.[10] It is therefore important to try to get clear what is inherent in the historian's use of his evidence, and what implications this may have for the use of 'sources' in school history.

PART II. EVIDENCE IN HISTORY

Any discussion of history teaching must commit itself to an account of certain features of historical activity, or condemn itself to vagueness and irrelevance. We must emphasize, however, that in Part II we are not attempting a balanced characterization of historical inquiry, or even a relatively complete account of particular aspects of it. Quite apart from the arrogance involved in assuming that we are equipped for such a task, it would entail considerations far beyond the scope of this chapter. Our aim is the much narrower one of picking out aspects of these activities in order to elucidate the concept of historical evidence.

Fortunately historians have not been silent on the practice of their craft, and indeed J. H. Hexter has set out 'a primitive sketch' of what is done by 'almost all historians who have contributed anything to the advancement of men's understanding'.[11]

> In his study of some part of the record of the past a historian discerns . . . a clue . . . to some pattern of human activity that to the best of his knowledge other historians have not perceived or have misunderstood. For any of a hundred reasons he decides to follow up on the clue. In order to do so, he carefully studies or restudies that part of the record and looks into other parts of it that he thinks may provide him with additional evidence to enlarge his understanding. When he believes that he has gone as far into the matter as the subject is worth and understood it as well as his talents and the time at his disposal permit, he writes about what he has found out.[12]

Of course the relationship betwen the practice of history and evidence of the past is continuous and reciprocal, and therefore fundamental to each of the aspects of historical activity picked out here. But although it is strictly impossible to separate these aspects into *temporally* distinct elements, they provide convenient phases of history for the purposes of discussion. There is the starting point of the inquiry, with the 'record of the past' and the historian's 'clue'. There is the following up of the clue, entailing study and restudy of the record and the search for additional evidence to enlarge understanding. And finally there is writing about what has been found out. We will therefore take each phase in turn, and attempt to sketch out some features which seem central to recent discussion of history teaching.

1. The Starting Point: Questions and Evidence

In the main historians have been more concerned with the processes by which investigations are successfully prosecuted than with specific comments on their beginnings.[13] Under these circumstances it is natural to turn to G. R. Elton's detailed and forthright description of historical practice:

> Historical research does not consist, as beginners in particular often suppose, in the pursuit of some particular evidence which will answer a particular question; it consists of an exhaustive, and exhausting, review of everything that may conceivably be germane to a given investigation.[14]

The historian must certainly make one initial choice, of main area of study or line of approach. But after that (if he is worth considering at all) he becomes the servant of his evidence of which he will, or should, ask no specific questions until he has absorbed what it says.[15]

Elton weakens this latter prescription a little, but re-affirms his basic contention: 'At least, his questions remain general, varied, flexible. . . . The mind will indeed soon react with questions, but these are the questions suggested by the evidence. . . .'[16]

It must be recognized, of course, that in this account Elton is as much concerned to refute certain kinds of relativism as to describe historical practice. He wants to deny that the historian's choice of questions 'artificially limits his choice of material — that he finds in the evidence that for which he looks'; and he is clearly right to insist that selection is not in itself vicious or distorting, but a necessary precondition of any inquiry in any discipline.[17] However, in pressing this case he goes further than is needed to meet the relativist argument. In particular, by passing so lightly over the 'one initial choice', and by seeming to insist that the historian ask no 'specific questions' until he has considered 'all the evidence . . . the total of historical material which may conceivably be relevant to his enquiry' he distorts an otherwise admirably lucid account of the beginnings of historical research.[18]

Making an initial choice is not just a matter of picking out a neatly packaged chunk of the past with its evidence securely attached. To choose 'an area or line of approach' is to choose to ask certain questions and not others. It means, if a historian is writing (say) constitutional history, deciding what range of human activity falls within that category, or illuminates it. It means deciding whether to ask legal and formal questions, or to cast a wider net. It means examining an aspect of the past as a set of relatively static institutions, or broadening the inquiry to find out how the machinery worked. Such decisions and the questions which follow them in an important sense prescribe the evidence. Without questions there can be no *evidence*: it is questions which turn mere detritus into evidence for the past. And because anything in the world is potentially evidence for the past, it is a tall order to require historians to eschew 'specific questions' until 'all the evidence' is known. Elton draws back slightly from this extreme position: he concedes that for a historian to consider 'the total of historical material which may conceivably be relevant to his inquiry' is 'in many circumstances . . . an impossible counsel of perfection'.[19] But he treats this as a contingent matter, whereas if his account is to be taken literally it must be a *necessary* shortcoming. And in reality it is not a shortcoming at all.

If a desire to defeat relativist dogmas persuades Elton to minimize the importance of a historian's 'initial choice' and to distort the concept of evidence, it is clear that the central core of his argument, the interplay between evidence and a historian's questions, and the tentative nature of early questions, is a fundamental feature of history. This interplay is continuous: questions and evidence are extended and retracted together. There appears to be a paradox here, for it is impossible to say what evidence is available until a question has been asked, and it is impossible to ask meaningful questions without *some* knowledge of the evidence available. Questions will obviously be modified by what evidence there is, and it is easy to see from this why a professional historian is tempted to say that the latter can 'all' be known. A professional knows what questions have been asked, and what evidence has been employed in answering them. In his long training he learns *pari passu* what questions to ask and what evidence he can call upon. Because he knows what questions are worth asking, he has a good idea of what evidence there is; because he has a wide knowledge of what historians have found it possible to treat as evidence, he knows what questions are likely to be worth asking. The paradox is resolved with the recognition that questions do not arise out of the blue, but in a continuous public tradition of inquiry. It is the strength of Hexter's account that he recognizes that historical investigations begin in a context: the context of the public activity of the community of professional historians. Thus Hexter's historian 'discerns . . . a clue . . . to some pattern of human activity that to the best of his knowledge other historians have not perceived or have misunderstood'.[20] To say that professional historians know what questions are worth asking is not to assert that such questions are fixed and unchanging, or that there is *no* disagreement among historians about worthwhile questions. It is to say that questions can be judged against shared standards: such shared standards having their origin in common conceptions for assessing the current condition of any particular area of historical knowledge. There are always new questions, but professional historians share a considerable measure of agreement on the *kinds* of question that are worth asking, and hence on the evidence, which can then be treated, in effect, as a stockpile or heritage of objects. This, however, is the special prerogative of the professional: it remains true that evidence is *not* a special category of objects, or a determinate stockpile, but anything which can be used to help answer a question about the past.

Historical investigations begin in the context of a public tradition of inquiry. Hexter uses his own work as an example:

Some two decades ago, broad though loosely connected reading about the fifteenth and sixteenth centuries in Europe persuaded me that the most widely accepted accounts of what was going on at the time had a number of defects. Their correction would entail a fairly drastic restructuring of views long current . . . about early modern Europe. Of a half-dozen or so defects three are especially relevant here.

1. Because of the influence of Jacob Burckhart's great work, *The Civilization of the Renaissance in Italy,* historians saw through Italian spectacles too much of what happened in trans-Alpine lands from 1450 on. I thought that a more serious consideration . . . of the Netherlands-Burgundian principality . . . would provide some correction of this overly Italianate perspective.

2. Middle-class French historians . . . and Marxist historians . . . had de-emphasized the role of the aristocracy in the Western

European monarchies during the period that concerned me. From what I could make out . . . the aristocracies of the Western European lands were not having such a bad time of it in those days.

3. The traditional picture of the relation of the aristocracy to rulers of the countries of Western Europe was actually two pictures, radically divergent one from the other. One portrayed the nobleman as a tame, cowed courtier, financially dependent on royal favour. . . . The other portrayed him as a treacherous feudal magnate ever in search of a chance to revolt in order to diminish the royal power. . . . This Jekyll-Hyde character suffered from inherent incredibility. Moreover, it ran counter to what my reading suggested: that between rulers and aristocracy the ordinary relation was a symbiosis, ambivalent and shaky on both sides. . . . [21]

A glance at the beginning of many papers in the historical journals, or at the introductions or prefaces of a great many major historical works, will confirm Hexter's account. Take, for example, G. E. Aylmer's introduction to *The State's Servants*. His 'original idea in 1949-51' was

to relate the larger long-term development of English central administration (on more or less 'Toutian' lines) to the history of the Civil War, Commonwealth and Protectorate. It was the lack of an adequate framework of reference for what administration had been like before the Civil War, which turned my study towards the reign of Charles I. Of course the question does not look the same now as it did twenty years ago. . . . Other people's work, both published and in progress, has profoundly affected what I have tried to do. . . .[22]

A historical investigation may proceed from wider or narrower, more or less sharply defined questions. Such questions, as Elton insists, will often be tentative, and will be modified by the evidence. Even the 'one initial choice' is in practice often tentative: it does not prescribe a tightly demarcated area of study once and for all, but shifts (sometimes markedly) in the course of a historian's investigation. This is clearly illustrated by Aylmer's introduction.[23] But whether tentative or firm, wide or narrow, it is impossible to understand the origins of any historical investigation without reference to its context in an ongoing tradition of inquiry.

It is this character of history as a public form of knowledge which mediates the *changes* in what is taken to be worth asking in history, and hence historians' conceptions of what evidence there is. The changing history of the English or French Revolutions (of 1642 and 1789), the increasing influence of economic theories on economic history, and the changing emphasis in constitutional history or history of education, all testify in different ways (and on different scales) to the continuous reconsideration of possible questions in history. The 'same' piece of evidence can answer to different questions, but different questions can open up the possibility of regarding new items as evidence. Sometimes it is a matter of new techniques, sometimes of new ways of looking at 'the record of the past', and sometimes of new evidence; but it is the standards tacitly or explicitly accepted by the community of professional historians which determine what shall qualify and what shall not. These standards are not fixed or arbitrary, but derived from concern for truth and evidence presupposed in asking any serious question about the past.[24]

It is, therefore, in the current condition of history that any historical investigation has its origins. The choice of an 'area of study', a 'line of approach' or a particular question all involve a complex relationship between accepted historical knowledge (however tentative and even transient), procedures and standards, and 'the record of the past'. A historian coming 'to the record of the past with . . . a mind empty of the knowledge of the past' and of the public traditions of history enshrined in common ways of working would 'surely condemn himself to a life of nearly total futility, redundancy, and error': he would not be a historian at all.[25]

2. Following up the clue

The historian '. . . studies and restudies that part of the record' (i.e. the part relevant to 'the pattern of human activity' he believes he has discerned) 'and looks into other parts of it that he thinks may provide him with additional evidence to enlarge his understanding'.[26] Hexter's sketch indicates the overlap between the issues involved in the beginnings of a historical investigation and those implicit in following it through. For the first problem facing Hexter's historian is where to look, a question which has already been examined in one context in the previous section.

Where to look? The professional historian may be tempted to regard this as a spurious problem. The problem is not so much where to look, as what to do with what you find. But in so far as this is true, it conceals the real nature of the professional's competence: he has a thorough knowledge of what, in practice, might *be* evidence. We are not referring here to knowledge of 'basic sources'. Obviously an important part of the professional's competence lies in knowing where and how potential evidence is stored, and having a wide knowledge of what historians, in the practice of their trade, have come to regard as 'the sources'. This brings us back to the point already discussed in the previous section: namely, that it is easy for a professional to regard evidence as a kind of stockpile of objects. For certain objects (documents, buildings — anything may qualify) have been as it were built into the fabric of the public corpus of historical knowledge as the evidence on which that knowledge rests. Hence those objects are already, in that sense, evidence, even if the particular historian so regarding them has never used them as such. (Perhaps if the notion of 'sources' were reserved for potential evidence viewed in this way, confusion would be avoided.)[27]

It is not, however, this knowledge of *sources* which concerns us here, but the understanding on which that knowledge must rest: an understanding of what potential evidence a given form of life may create. Underlying this understanding in its turn is a detailed knowledge of the past society which produced (and deposited) the material which the historian now chooses to regard *as* evidence. Thus even to know what might provide evidence already entails considerable knowledge and understanding of a period.

How to understand the evidence which *is* available? It is almost a commonplace that evidence cannot speak for itself: 'History . . . depends not only on the surviving record of the past, but on what historians bring to it.'[28] Paramount among the things historians bring to the record (after the questions which turn it into evidence) is a knowledge of how it arose, of what part it had in the society which produced it. This is not just a matter of assessing specific evidence for bias or reliability, but of *understanding* it at all. This understanding is prior even to deciding into which of the historian's two basic categories the evidence falls: 'that produced specifically for his attention', or 'that produced for some other purpose'.[29] It involves understanding what that evidence *meant* in the world from which it survives. F. W. Maitland's *Domesday Book and Beyond* remains one of the best examples of this kind of understanding in action.[30] From the outset Maitland makes it clear that the fundamental problem is to understand what Domesday Book *was*:

> At the present moment, though much has been done towards forcing Domesday Book to yield its meaning, some of the legal problems that are raised by it . . . have hardly been stated, much less solved. . . . If only we can ask the right questions we shall have done something for a good end. . . .
>
> To say that Domesday Book is no collection of laws or treatise on law would be needless. Very seldom does it state any rules in general terms, and when it does so we shall usually find cause for believing that this rule is itself an exception, a local custom, a provincial privilege. . . . But further, Domesday Book is no register of title, no register of all those rights and facts which constitute the system of land-holdership. One great purpose seems to mould both its form and its substance; it is a geld-book.[31]

In the pages which follow this passage Maitland begins to show what a geld-book is: he tells the story of how William came to have the information which makes up Domesday Book collected.[32] It is only as Domesday Book comes to be understood in its context that it can be understood as evidence which reflects back on that context.

Some of the fiercest disputes in history originate in a failure to understand the significance of an institution in its own society, and such a failure can vitiate the use made of that institution as evidence. (The 'counting of manors' controversy in the history of England in the seventeenth century might fall into this category.)[33] Once again we are forced to recognize that before there is any possibility of a historian using the record of the past as *evidence*, he must already have a knowledge of the society in which it originated: a knowledge and understanding of a particular period.

Given that the record of the past is understood, how reliable is it as evidence? How far is it in a position to tell the historian anything? Is it the product of an attempt to deceive — maybe not the historian, but some contemporary? How far (if it is *intended* as a record) is it biased?[34] These questions draw attention to two aspects of the historian's activity. In the first place he is equipped to make a critical use of evidence by a process of training. It is possible to set out a list of some of the important questions the professional may ask of his evidence: for example,

> . . . what is the history of the document, how did it come into my hands? What guarantee is there that it is what it pretends to be? Is the document complete? Has it been tampered with or edited? . . . Who was the author? What was he trying to do? What were his sources of information? What was his bias? How far was he likely to have wanted to tell the truth? . . . Am I quite sure that I know what the words used meant to the writer?[35]

But learning that these (and others) are the questions to ask does not constitute learning to ask them. It is not a matter of having a check list, but of developing certain attitudes, standards and understandings in the course of exercising judgement under the supervision of an experienced practitioner: in other words of acquiring understanding in the framework of a public tradition.

In the second place, the exercise of critical judgement upon evidence in particular cases itself depends on detailed prior knowledge of the workings of a past society. Even in the (relatively) straightforward case of bias, knowledge of the writer, the circumstances in which he wrote and of a whole background of beliefs and ideas is presupposed. Here again we encounter the paradox: knowledge in history is acquired only through evidence, but only where there is prior knowledge of the past can any particular piece of evidence be used as such.

The resolution of this paradox lies in recognizing once more that history is an ongoing public tradition. Historians do not labour in solitary confinement, but come to their evidence with a range of accepted knowledge, standards and procedures based on the work of their colleagues down the years. This shared knowledge is not fixed and unchallengeable, but equally it is not a matter of *faute de mieux* knowledge or profitable short cuts. The works of other historians are not just second-best sources of information, but part of a common framework in terms of which historical questions, interpretations and evidence are given meaning. It is not simply information which is at issue here, but a whole way of looking at the world.

3.   Writing history

The immense variety of forms which history can take precludes easy generalities about writing history. There are, however, two interrelated aspects of history which are relevant to our purpose here: the notion of 'the second record' introduced by Hexter; and the possibility of historical objectivity.[36]

By 'the second record' Hexter means 'everything that historians bring to their confrontation with the record of the past'.[37] 'Potentially . . . it embraces the historian's skills, the range of his knowledge, the set of his mind, the substance, quality and character of his experience — his total consciousness.'[38] Each historian's second record differs from that of every other historian: it is '. . . personal, individual, ephemeral, and not publicly accessible'.[39] But

> Every time a historian . . . moves from the record of the past to a historical assertion *about* the past he is drawing on his second record, claiming that he has and, if necessary, can produce from his second record grounds for his assertion that the first record means what he says it means. In this way he makes some part of his second record, hitherto private and inaccessible, open to criticism and evaluation.[40]

Hexter stresses the personal and private, and minimizes the public aspects of the second record, because he wants to say that a historian may legitimately draw upon a much wider range of his experience in doing history, than can a social scientist working in his own domain. In particular the historian is not limited to what has been incorporated into the public, relatively formalized, knowledge of a discipline: he may equally call upon his private and personal experience and common-sense knowledge. This, Hexter argues, explains an important facet of historical writing, the use of 'translational' and 'psychedelic' (literally 'mind-expanding') language.[41] This kind of language is a means of helping people to entertain, to contemplate, a way of thinking to which they may be unaccustomed, or which may even be antipathetic to their own most fundamental assumptions.

> As a result of the impact of the translational and psychedelic language on their second record, readers indeed learn things about what happened in the past that they could not learn otherwise; that impact actually achieves an expansion of the readers' understanding.[42]

Because the historian cannot know what is in the second records of his readers he will be uncertain whether his translational and psychedelic rhetoric communicates what it is intended to communicate, and so must rely on '. . . his experience of previous good and ill fortune in like situations and . . . his sense of the sort of rhetoric that would affect his own second record in the particular case that concerns him.'[43]

Hexter's account is illuminating and important, but his concern to mark off history from social science leads him to exaggerate the importance of the subjectivity of the second record. A historian's second record must include his experiences *qua* historian, which will include the shared understandings and procedures characteristic of a public form of knowledge. It must include everything from his basic assumptions (that there *are* certain items which may be regarded as part of the record of the past, and can be used as *evidence* for that past) to his detailed historical knowledge. Hence the historian is in a better position to know what is in the second records of at least a vital part of his audience (other historians) than Hexter allows. Such knowledge extends far beyond the 'boundary rules of logical discourse' which Hexter is prepared to recognize as shared ground, and indeed this is implicit in his inclusion in the second record of the historian's 'skills' and the 'range of his knowledge'.[44]

Moreover, while it is true that the private and personal cannot be ruled out, in so far as it is employed in writing history it must become public.

Hexter seems to miss this point in warning that although 'By laying down restrictive rules as to what historians may properly draw on from their second records, it is possible to reduce considerably the effective and practical differences among historians in this respect . . .' such restrictive rules are undesirable.[45] The issue, however, is not *what historians draw on* from their second records, but *how they use what they have found.* A distinction between the context of discovery and the context of validation is useful here.[46] Strategies for *discovery*, and ideas for new interpretations can come from anywhere: it does not matter how private and idiosyncratic their origins may be (although Hexter himself disposes of the idea that they could all or even mainly derive from some purely private mental life — see the passage quoted on p. 8 at the end of our first section, 'The Starting Point'). But discoveries and interpretations asserted as fact must be justified in publicly accessible ways; in the context of *validation* we cannot appeal to private experience. In practice, Hexter recognizes the distinction. Thus, if Hexter found the key to his interpretation of More's *Utopia* in his own experience, the argument which supports that interpretation is public and accessible. The fact that he felt it necessary to use 'translational' and 'psychedelic' language in order to modify and extend his readers' second records merely emphasizes this. For

> However fully persuaded I may be of the actual similarity of More's anxiety and mine about our families, about his perception of the dimensions of sin and mine, I cannot argue that my experience *proves* anything about his, because of course it does not.[47]

What Hexter's discussion *does* raise is the interesting question of how far the absence of certain kinds of experience may *impoverish* the second record, and so a historian's strategies for making sense of the past. How important is it, for example, that a military historian has never been engaged in any form of active combat?[48] It may be that some ways of seeing evidence will not be open to a man of limited experience, but it is by no means clear that experience must be first-hand (not vicariously gained through studying history). Some forms of present experience may indeed be prejudicial to understanding the past. It seems likely that a relatively underdeveloped second record — lacking in direct *and* vicarious experience — may have implications for history teaching; that question will be raised in Part III. The general issue, however, is too large for proper examination in this chapter. In any case we are forced back again to the basic distinction: the origin of a historian's strategies for interpreting evidence is one thing; whether those strategies result in valid interpretations is quite another.

Here, of course, we are already beginning to get involved in questions of historical objectivity, and in the context of this chapter it is possible only to make a few general observations which have some implications for history teaching. Objectivity in history does not depend on the certainty of historical knowledge, any more than objectivity in natural science depends on the certainty of scientific knowledge. (On that criterion there could *be* no objectivity.) Nor does it depend on historians agreeing about everything, although if there were no measure of agreement objectivity would not be possible. Common assumptions about the possibility of making sense of the past, about the possibility of regarding parts of the world as evidence for that past, and about the procedures for validating historical knowledge, are a precondition of objectivity. The marks of this measure of agreement are evident in historical writing: the careful and accurate use of footnotes and quotation marks, the citation of evidence, justification of interpretations, and the relation of new work to what has gone before.[49] It is in this openness of historians' writing to inspection and criticism, and in these shared procedures and understandings of a common enterprise, that the possibility of historical objectivity exists.[50]

Throughout the account we have given in Part II, two themes stand out:
 (i) history is not something undertaken privately, begun from scratch by each individual, but is an ongoing public form of knowledge with its own shared understandings, procedures, and standards;
 (ii) historical knowledge and the process of historical inquiry cannot be divorced.

These two themes have important implications for history teaching. But criteria taken from a brief sketch of one aspect of historical activity are by themselves insufficient, for to assume that nothing may be done in the classroom which may conflict with the practices of professional historians is to beg precisely the question at issue. In Part III we will discuss the place of source material, whether regarded as evidence or as something less, in the wider context of teaching history.

PART III. EVIDENCE IN THE CLASSROOM

We have seen that two main types of claim are made for the use of source material in the classroom: the historical and the pedagogic. In the latter claim the concreteness and immediacy of the material as *objects* is assumed to have a direct parallel in the intellectual operations entailed in treating it as evidence. This ambiguity has already been referred to in Part I. The basic assumption of the first type of claim is that children should be taught a mode of inquiry, as opposed to a body of knowledge, and that this involves the use of source material by children. Even a slight change in emphasis produces major shifts in the scope of this claim: for example it may be held that children using sources are (i) doing what historians do,[51] (ii) simulating the historian's craft,[52] or (iii) learning to do what historians do. These assertions have their negative counterpart in the argument that children should do nothing false to the practices of historians.[53]

Are any of these positions tenable? It was argued in Part II that history is a complex intellectual activity in which the origins of an investigation, its prosecution and its public communication all involve both knowledge of the past and of the current condition of inquiry. If such a view is accepted, assertion (i) is either pretentious 'claptrap' or an imprecise statement of something more modest.[54] The trouble with 'simulation' in assertion (ii) is that it is simply ambiguous, although in his later handling of the question William Lamont, whose phrase it is, clearly has in mind an activity more like (iii) than (i).[55] The notion of *learning* to do what historians do (iii) is also imprecise. It could be taken as in some sense training professional historians and thus as a possible preliminary to 'doing what historians do'. But we can speak of children learning to do what historians do in a limited sense, without involving a conclusion in which children become fully fledged historians in their own right. Thus it is possible to speak of children learning some of the attitudes and methods of the historian through limited practice at working with source material. This is a much more modest and qualified claim which would not be in conflict with the fundamental points in our discussion of historical evidence, and might be thought to play a valuable part in history teaching, provided that we reject the negative notion of not doing anything false to the activity of historians. It *may* be a necessary prerequisite of learning history that certain activities in some respects conflicting with the strict canons of professional practice occur in schools. (The prior selection by the teacher of materials to 'suggest' problems, and even to suggest or make likely particular answers, would be examples of this. So would history games.)

The limits of what is possible for children in learning to do what historians do is recognized in an ambiguous way by the idea of 'historical appreciation', briefly mentioned in Part I. What we describe as 'appreciation' of history stresses understanding of history in its own terms, as part of a child's general education, just as the appreciation of literature aims to impart a genuine understanding of and interest in literature in its own right, without attempting to produce professional writers or critics.[56] However, the very term 'history' is ambiguous as between the past and our study of the past. There is thus a potential ambiguity in the idea of 'appreciation' of history: are we concerned to teach an appreciation of the past or of the discipline? The traditional view has very much emphasized the former, but the tension between the two possible interpretations is frequently apparent. Elton's prescriptions for sixth-form teaching exemplify this:

> It is right that all history courses should include some part of the history of the student's own country, because he will be better able *to acquire some grasp of the techniques required for the understanding of the past* if he starts from relatively familiar ground. (Our emphasis.)[57]

It seems to us that these ideas need to be developed, that is that teachers should be concerned to impart an appreciation of the discipline as well as of the past. If we concentrate on the past and take the discipline as 'given', children are unlikely to acquire any notion of history as an ongoing activity, and without this it would be impossible to speak of a form of knowledge.[58] But an understanding of the ongoing activity of historians requires that children should have some understanding of what historical evidence is, gained through practical experience of working with evidence themselves. We must therefore turn to a consideration of what this involves, and what it is possible to do.

It is customary to distinguish between the use of pictures, cartoons and documents as *illustration* and as *evidence*. Such a view is too simple. In its place we shall attempt to set out a number of logical phases in the handling of historical materials. These suggested phases are *not* temporally isolated, nor are they developmental stages. They simply represent a tentative conceptual categorization for purposes of discussion.

(i) *Pictures of the past.* This is a pre-evidential phase, in which potential evidence is used by the teacher or the pupil as if it afforded direct access to the past. Hence a Canaletto of London in the eighteenth century is treated as though it were a window opening onto the past, making it available for direct inspection. (Children are particularly prone to regard newsreel material in this way.)

(ii) *Illustration.* In this phase potential evidence is used to illustrate some historical assertion or interpretation: the 'fact' or interpretation is presented as a 'given', and the potential evidence merely accompanies it; the former is not *derived from* the latter. For example a Cromwellian proclamation on public order may be used to show puritan ideas on morality. Yet for a child to grasp that something may illustrate an assertion in this way already implies a minimal understanding that it is possible to see things *as evidence* for the past, and that it is upon such evidence that historians' assertions depend. What we have here is in fact the beginning of a continuum, stretching from the *relatively* simple and passive seeing *as* evidence to the complex interpretative activity of the professional historian.

(iii) *Evidence for particular inferences.* The third phase involves not simply seeing something *as* evidence, but knowing *how* something can be evidence, in a more developed way, involving increasing knowledge of the society which produces the evidence, and knowing how the historian might check it: the kind of scrutiny he would subject it to, the criteria he would use—the questions discussed by Kitson Clark for instance. Thus a pupil who has already studied a good deal of fourth- and fifth-century Roman history, presented in the course of his work with extracts from Gildas and the Kentish Chronicle describing the arrival of Hengist in Britain, who from these sources describes the arrival of the Saxons in terms of their employment as *foederati* by the British, is already relating the documents as evidence to late Roman society. To go on to raise questions about the documents asking, for instance, what Gildas' view of the situation was, and how he knew what had happened, is already to have some idea of assessing evidence. Relating evidence to its context and testing the evidence are not separable activities, they are interdependent (how could evidence be tested without knowledge of its context?) and are learned *pari passu*. This phase also involves a wider range of questions than those confined to the examination of a single document, and these questions too will be developed step by step with increasing grasp of the evidence, and with the growth of knowledge. In their turn questions demand the *selection* of appropriate evidence, and in a limited way this may also be part of phase (iii).[59]

(iv) *Evidence for interpretations and histories*. There is no clear-cut division between this and the preceding phase: phase (iv) involves essentially the same understandings and procedures, used here not in dealing with limited assertions, but in complex interpretations of evidence within the framework of history as a public form of knowledge. This is in fact the kind of activity we have already discussed in Part II.

The problem of evidence in the classroom could be said to be fundamentally a matter of how best to get children to some level of competence in phase (iii). At its highest, this may well involve the production of some limited but 'original' local history, although to assume that this is more demanding than a first-rate but less 'original' study of some aspect of national history would be a mistake.[60] More precise claims of what children are capable of require further empirical research. At present psychological evidence with any bearing on this issue is very slender, and in any case without a specifically historical conceptual framework (perhaps of the sort discussed above) it is difficult to see how one could examine what children can actually do.[61]

The achievement of this phase (iii) competence, whatever else it requires, does not demand a syllabus of source material alone: indeed such a syllabus would be profoundly unhistorical.[62] We have already argued (Part II) that some context of historical knowledge is a condition of understanding evidence; a study limited to sources would ignore this, and also the fundamental character of history as a public form of knowledge. Learning to use historical evidence involves a continuous process of handling historical material under supervision and in a wider context of historical knowledge; it may include highly selected exercises with very limited goals. A teacher may introduce his pupils to phase (iii) activities with relatively modest extracts, and without attempting to inculcate every historical 'skill' or 'attitude' at once. Pupils may be learning genuine features of historical inquiry without ever seeing an 'archive teaching unit'. This is not to deny the value of such units, nor of more ambitious exercises. Tony Edwards' discussion in the *Handbook for History Teachers* very clearly illustrates the range of activities which may legitimately be employed.[63]

Because of the relationship between evidence and historical knowledge, the gradual development of children's understanding must go hand in hand with the acquisition of knowledge of the historical context which produced that evidence. Increasing knowledge of context involves the development of children's 'second records' (see Part II). Through increased knowledge of the society which produced the evidence, through increased historical knowledge generally, and through greater experience of the ways in which inferences can be made from, and assertions checked against evidence, children are building up their limited second records. They do not come blank to the study of history, but bring their own experience and preconceptions to it, and, initially at least, their judgements of evidence are likely to reflect this.[64] That is not to say that children's own experience and preconceptions are undesirable, and are to be kept out of history; they have no other starting point. It is rather that this experience is widened and developed by their study of history. (This is after all one of the fundamental reasons for the inclusion of history in the school curriculum.) It is partly through such development of their second records that they become more competent in using evidence. Once again it is evident that the dichotomy between learning historical content and learning history as a mode of inquiry is both theoretically misconceived and misleading for practice.[65]

We have confined our discussion in this paper to some aspects of the place of evidence in history and the classroom, because it has been a central feature of the recent debate on history teaching. There is, of course, much more to teaching history than this: it involves imagination, explanation and understanding, too, and failure to give adequate attention to these might result in an orthodoxy of 'sources' as distorted as the orthodoxy of 'facts'. But whatever omissions there may be in current thinking, if it serves to change pupils' perceptions of history, it will have accomplished a great deal. There clearly remains a long way to go when children can still write like this: 'You could not pick any arguments with [my answers to] questions one and two because they had come off the sheet that the teacher had written'.[66] If we can make this sort of response even slightly less frequent the debate will have been worthwhile.

NOTES

1. Keatinge, M. W., *Studies in the Teaching of History*, Black, 2nd edn., 1921.
2. Elton, G. R., 'What Sort of History should we Teach?' in M. Ballard (ed.), *New Movements in the Study and Teaching of History*, Temple Smith, 1970.
3. ibid., pp. 228-9.
4. ibid., pp. 224-5, p. 229.
5. Chaffer, J., 'What History Should we Teach?' in R. Ben Jones (ed.), *Practical Approaches to the New History*, Hutchinson, 1973, p. 48.
6. Turner, T., 'Training the Student and Teacher' in R. Ben Jones (ed.), op. cit., pp. 27-9.
7. Fines, J., 'Archives in School', *History*, Vol. LIII, No. 179, October 1968, p. 256.
8. See Margaret Bryant's comments on a similarly casual treatment by other writers: 'Knowledge about the nature of the historian's sources is often inadequate. [One recent article], for example, appears to define a "true archive" as an original document or perhaps a reproduction preserving as far as possible its appearance and immediacy. But surely it is nothing of the sort? An archive is distinguished from a mere record or from other types of material or written document by its *function* — it arose from an administrative process, of which it formed a part, and it was preserved and consulted in the course of further administration. The disclosure of this administrative process is one of its most important uses as evidence.' (Bryant, M., 'Documentary and Study Materials for Teachers and Pupils: Part III, Practices: Research or Claptrap?' in *Teaching History*, Vol. II, No. 5, May 1971, pp. 42-43.) Miss Bryant's own treatment of the place of evidence in the classroom is characteristically perceptive. See also note 54 below.
9. Palmer, M., 'Using Stimulus Material', in R. Ben Jones (ed.), op. cit., p. 88.
10. See Lamont, W., 'The Uses and Abuses of Examinations' in M. Ballard (ed.), op. cit., particularly pp. 200-1, for a persuasive example of this point of view. Lamont makes a similar case, more carefully argued, and expanded to include an excellent sketch of imagination in history, in 'How Far Beyond Beginnings?' in W. Lamont (ed.), *The*

Realities of Teaching History, Chatto and Windus, 1972. While there are ambiguities in Lamont's accounts, they remain, with the work of Bryant, Edwards (see note 63) and Rogers (see note 53), the most cogent arguments for what is loosely called 'The New History'. A less enthusiastic but very precise account of 'sources' in the classroom is in Burston, W. H., *Principles of History Teaching*, Methuen, 2nd edn., 1972, pp. 39-47.

11. Hexter, J. H., *The History Primer*, Allen Lane, 1972, p. 97.

12. loc. cit.

13. See Kitson Clark, G., *The Critical Historian*, Heinemann Educational Books, 1967; or Bloch, M., *The Historian's Craft*, Manchester University Press, 1954. This investigative process is examined below pp. 8-10.

14. Elton, G. R., *The Practice of History*, Sydney University Press, 1967, pp. 66-7.

15. ibid., p. 62.

16. loc. cit.

17. ibid., p. 62.

18. ibid., p. 66. See Bloch, M., op. cit., p. 64 for a brief and caustic comment on a more simplistic view than Elton's, but one which shares some features of Elton's account.

19. loc. cit. For the range and variety of historical evidence see Bloch, M., op. cit., pp. 66-8.

20. Hexter, J. H., op. cit., p. 97.

21. ibid., pp. 263-4.

22. Aylmer, G. E., *The State's Servants*, Routledge and Kegan Paul, 1973, p. 2.

23. For another example, see Namier, L., *The Structure of Politics at the Accession of George III*, Macmillan, 2nd edn., 1957, pp. ix-xi.

24. The practical operation of these standards is lucidly described by Elton, G. R., op. cit., *passim*, 1967.

25. Hexter, J. H., op. cit., p. 113.

26. ibid., p. 97.

27. For examples of professional knowledge as knowledge of sources, see Elton, G. R., op. cit., *passim*, 1967.

28. Hexter, J. H., op. cit., p. 106.

29. Elton, G. R., op. cit., 1967, p. 77. See also Bloch, M., op. cit., pp. 60-2.

30. Maitland, F. W., *Domesday Book and Beyond*, Cambridge University Press, 1897, and reissued in Fontana Library, Collins, 1960. For further examples see Elton, G. R., op. cit., 1967, pp. 78-9; or Kitson Clarke, G., op. cit., pp. 65-7. Articles in historical journals often illustrate this feature of history. See, for instance, Stephens, J. N., 'Bede's Ecclesiastical History', in *History*, Vol. 62, No. 204, February 1977.

31. Maitland, F. W., op. cit., Fontana edn., 1960, pp. 24-5.

32. ibid., pp. 25-30.

33. See Tawney, R. H., 'The Rise of the Gentry, 1558-1640', *Economic History Review*, XI, 1941, and 'The Rise of the Gentry: a Postscript', *Economic History Review*, 2nd Series, VII, 1954; and Cooper, J. P., 'The Counting of Manors', *Economic History Review*, 2nd Series, VIII, 1956.

34. See Elton, G. R., op. cit., 1967, pp. 74-7; and Kitson Clark, G., op. cit., Chapters 8 and 9, for discussion of the critical use of evidence.

35. Kitson Clark, G., op. cit., pp. 62-3.

36. Hexter, J. H., op. cit., Chapter 4.

37. ibid., p. 103.

38. ibid., p. 104.

39. loc. cit.

40. ibid., p. 106.

41. ibid., p. 139.

42. ibid., p. 141.

43. ibid., p. 144.

44. ibid., p. 143, and p. 104.

45. ibid., p. 104.

46. This distinction is borrowed from philosophy of science, and while it is useful for a discussion of *some* of the issues involved in 'the second record', has only a limited application in history.

47. ibid., p. 131.

48. See the review by Brian Bond of J. Keegan, 'The Face of Battle', Jonathan Cape, 1976, in *History*, Vol. 62, No. 204, February 1977, p. 81.

49. But objectivity does not *consist* in this measure of agreement. See Hamlyn, D. W., 'Objectivity' in R. F. Dearden, P. H. Hirst, and R. S. Peters (eds.), *Education and the Development of Reason*, Routledge and Kegan Paul, 1972, pp. 246-59.

50. For a survey of some basic distinctions in the notion of objectivity in history see Walsh, W. H., *An Introduction to Philosophy of History*, Hutchinson, 3rd edn., 1967, pp. 93-116. Blake, C., 'Can History be Objective' in P. Gardiner (ed.), *Theories of History*, The Free Press, 1959; and Passmore, J. A., 'The Objectivity of History' in W. H. Dray (ed.), *Philosophical Analysis and History*, Harper and Row, 1966, are valuable philosophical discussions. A 'constructionist' view is put by Goldstein, L. J., *Historical Knowing*, University of Texas Press, 1976, pp. 183-216. Elton, G. R., op. cit., 1967, reasserts a historian's basic assumptions.

51. See Ben Jones, R., 'Towards a New History Syllabus', in *History*, Vol. 55, No. 185, October 1970, p. 395: 'Documents compel the candidate to prove himself an historian', or ' . . . the project . . . (uses) primary sources . . . so that the candidate may stand upon his own feet to be judged an historian'. Turner, T. S., op. cit., p. 26, misquoting Lamont, says that children 'should be given a genuine opportunity of "becoming their own historians" . . .'.

52. Lamont, W., 'The Uses and Abuses of Examinations' in M. Ballard (ed.), op. cit., pp. 200-2.

53. See Rogers, P., *Some Philosophical Aspects of Curriculum Construction with Special Reference to History*, unpublished Ph D thesis, University of Glasgow, 1975, pp. 407-8. In note 38 (p. 408) he does admit limitations 'due to psychological and sociological factors', but concludes: 'While professional practice cannot be attained in full, its attainment remains the only proper ambition and guide.' One guide, certainly, but *only* one. *Unattainable ambitions* can be a poor guide to educational *practice*. We have some reservations about the position Rogers takes in his thesis on the place of evidence in the classroom, but would add that the thesis is one of the most important pieces of work to appear on the subject in the last fifteen years, and has forced us to examine very carefully our own stance on several issues. See notes 58 and 59 below.

54. Bryant, M. ('Documentary and Study Materials for Teachers and Pupils: Part II Theories and Practices', in *Teaching History*, Vol. I, No. 4, November 1970) quotes W. B. Stephens' resounding review of archive teaching units: ' . . . to compare the mature work of historical research with the exercises conducted by children from limited and preselected material of this kind is the sort of clap-trap that brings the scholarship of educationists into doubt.' (*Journal of the Society of Archivists*, Vol. 4, No. 1, April 1970, p. 84.) It is the strength of Margaret Bryant's own paper that she sets her discussion firmly in an educational context.

55. Lamont, W., 'How Far Beyond Beginnings' in W. Lamont (ed.), *The Realities of Teaching History*, Chatto and Windus, 1972, pp. 170-1.

56. Compare Elton, G. R., 'What sort of History Should we Teach?' in M. Ballard (ed.), op. cit., pp. 228-9.

57. loc. cit.

58. Rogers argues that it is impossible to speak of knowledge at all if those for whom it is claimed have no understanding of its grounds. This is an interesting and powerful

argument, resting on what is often held to be one of the basic criteria of knowledge. (If I am to be said to *know* something, it must be the case, among other things, that I have good grounds for what I believe.) It is not clear how far Rogers wants to push this claim, and it may be argued that no professional historian could conceivably have 'good grounds' for every assertion he makes if this means he must examine all the evidence relevant to his assertion at first hand. But if Rogers is prepared to allow professionals recourse to secondary works, and is content to insist that children must have an under-standing of the *kind* of grounds on which historical knowledge rests, his point is extremely important. (Rogers, P., op. cit., pp. 116-17, pp. 393-4, and p. 408.)

59. Pupils may be given tasks which require them to select appropriate evidence from broadly pre-selected materials. (That is, the materials will not *all* be relevant to the particular questions, for which further selection is then required.) Rogers has argued that *representative* selections of material should be used in this way: 'there is no reason whatever why a reputable selection of evidence on a suitable topic cannot be presented to children . . .' given ' . . . a properly prepared introduction from the teacher'. Rogers takes Elton's *Tudor Constitution* as a paradigm of selection as 'a microcosm of the evidence', but this involves problems about the relationships of evidence to questions, of the kind we discussed in Part II. (Rogers, P., op. cit., pp. 448-9.) However, provided it is understood that this selection from pre-selected material is part of a process of *learning* to do what historians do, and not *doing* what historians do, it is clear that such activities may be an important part of achieving competence in phase (iii).

60. 'Original' in inverted commas because it will still have to fit into a wider framework, even in asking questions not so far asked about a particular area. This raises issues too large to enter into here, about the relation of one historian's work to another's, and about 'originality' in history generally. (But we do not wish to appear to belittle local history.)

61. There is a brief discussion of the problems posed for history by existing theoretical and developmental frameworks in Part I of Chapter 6 by A. Dickinson and P. J. Lee, (pp. 94-9).

62. See Lamont's carefully balanced comment (Lamont, W., 'How Far Beyond Beginnings' in W. Lamont (ed.), op. cit., 1972, pp. 170-1). We would stress the historical impossibility, rather than the impracticality, of such courses.

63. Edwards, A. D., 'Source Material in the Classroom' in W. H. Burston and C. W. Green (eds.), *Handbook for History Teachers*, Methuen Educational, 1972.

64. This connects with the 'impoverishment' of second records referred to in Part II. Of course, children's second records will be in some respects 'impoverished', and this may lead them to make false assumptions about the range of human behaviour (among other things). But this is something which must be discovered in each case: it is obviously a gross error for teachers to assume that it is necessarily true with reference to any *particular* historical context.

65. Turner, T. S., op. cit., p. 26, exemplifies this: 'Method, therefore, in its widest connotation, comes first and knowledge takes second place'. Lamont seems at times to come close to accepting this dichotomy too (particularly in 'The Uses and Abuses of Examinations' in M. Ballard (ed.), op. cit., pp. 200-1), but in 'How Far Beyond Beginnings' (in W. Lamont (ed.), op. cit., 1972, p. 167) he describes it as 'up to a point, a false antithesis'. It is still, however, merely that 'the skills *developed* will have to be *exercised on an area of content*' (our emphasis). This is a curious way of putting it: the 'skills' only make sense in the context of historical knowledge; they are not learned independently of it and later applied. (See Part II.)

66. Response of a second-year girl (in an urban comprehensive) to an invitation to suggest possible weaknesses in her answers to questions on a passage about Henry II. (See Part II of Chapter 6 particularly pp. 99-100.)

2. 'Educational Objectives for the Study of History' Reconsidered

A. GARD   P. J. LEE

PART I.   INTRODUCTION

The emergence of the curriculum reform movement in the 1960's, the development of 'Nuffield science', the 'new maths' and, perhaps most important of all the growth of various schemes of integrated or inter-disciplinary work in 'the humanities', gave further impetus to the long tradition of critical appraisal of history teaching. A widening range of history teachers became involved in re-thinking what they were doing and in questioning some aspects of traditional school history. Products of this concern were a widespread interest in the use of evidence in history teaching, experiments in new types of syllabus, and a concern for more valid forms of assessment, often reflected in the establishment of Mode 3 examinations for CSE and GCE 'O' Level. Thus Coltham and Fines' Historical Association pamphlet *Educational Objectives for the Study of History*, published in 1971, came on the scene at an opportune moment when there was a widely felt need for a solid theoretical basis for this process of re-thinking.[1]

This pamphlet has certainly been valuable in provoking discussion. It quickly gained currency and influence as a major contribution to the 'new history': R. Ben Jones wrote in his editorial introduction to the essays in 'Practical Approaches to the New History', published in 1973, that '. . . its influence is writ large on the essays that follow'.[2] Readers of *Teaching History* will recognize that the same could be said of many contributions to that journal.[3] The pamphlet has been specifically recommended to teachers considering the AEB 'A' Level history pilot scheme.[4] With its increasing influence over the last five years, and the importance of some of its assumptions, the time has come for a critical re-appraisal.

While our chapter is critical, it should not be thought that we are against the general aspirations for school history that Coltham and Fines are trying to articulate. We are in sympathy with them in so far as they stress the participation of the pupil in learning history, point out that pupils do not come *tabula rasa* to history but have their own 'fund of personal knowledge and experience', and treat history as a way of finding out about the past rather than as a body of received information. Our contention is that the way in which Coltham and Fines attempt to articulate these aspirations, and the confusions in their paper, have seriously misleading results.

We will look first at the framework of Coltham and Fines' paper, considering its validity on its own terms (Part II), but a more fundamental issue is the validity of their notion of an educational objective in history (Part III). Finally, and perhaps most important of all, in Part IV we will examine some of the assumptions about historical imagination, interpretation and evidence embodied in the substantive contents of the various categories laid down by their framework.[5]

PART II. THE FRAMEWORK

Coltham and Fines' framework incorporates a range of assumptions about learning and history which cannot be allowed to pass unchallenged and thus by default to set the limits of the discussion. It is therefore a necessary prerequisite of more substantive treatment of Coltham and Fines' ideas that the assumptions of the framework itself receive close attention.

There are four main divisions in the Coltham and Fines framework:

Section A: Attitudes towards the Study of History.
Section B: The Nature of the Discipline.
Section C: Skills and Abilities.
Section D: Educational Outcomes of Study.

These sections are themselves sub-divided, but there is in addition a further set of distinctions which is recurrent throughout the taxonomy, and is used to mark off Section A from the rest, namely the classification of 'behaviour' as conative, affective or cognitive.

There are a number of major structural weaknesses in this framework, four of which we wish to examine here. First, the classification of 'behaviour' as conative, affective or cognitive is confused and misleading. Second, the sectionalization set out above entails at least an inadequate distinction between parts of B and C, if not simple redundancies. Third, the framework either produces or reinforces a tendency to throw together quite different levels and kinds of activity under a common label (e.g. 'analysis' or 'synthesis') as if they were unitary skills. Finally, the framework is claimed to exhibit certain sequences in 'logical' (or sometimes 'developmental') order. It is not clear what is involved in these claims, and the order actually employed is difficult to interpret either as 'logical' or 'developmental'.

The classification of behaviour as conative, affective and cognitive appears to do little real work in the taxonomy, and one is tempted to regard it as merely the muted echo of American precedents. However, in Section A: *Attitudes towards the Study of History*, it has to bear a certain amount of weight. Unfortunately the classification is largely vitiated from the outset by the apparent interchangeability of the notions of 'affective' and 'conative' behaviour. On p. 5 in the general introduction we are told that 'Section A is concerned principally with the *affective* aspects of the learners' personalities', but at the beginning of that section the authors maintain that 'the three behaviours in this section are all *conative* (or *willing*) behaviours' (p. 6, our emphasis). Matters are not clarified by the statement on p. 8 that 'The three behaviours in Section A have in common, not only their *affective* nature — the *conative* effort, the willingness to act in these ways — but also the necessity that they appear at all ages and stages . . .' (our emphasis). There is then a general confusion between affective and conative behaviour throughout Section A. Nevertheless, it is obviously intended that what marks off Section A is its concern with this conative (or affective) 'behaviour'.

It is the specific analysis given of conative behaviours in Section A, however, which calls the whole operation in question. The 'three behaviours' referred to above in the quotation from p. 6 are 'Attending', 'Responding' and 'Imagining'. Now the curious thing about this selection is why 'Imagining' should have been singled out as 'conative', since almost any of the behaviours listed later in the taxonomy — memorization, comparison, explanation, etc. — might equally be said to be conative. Coltham and Fines maintain that it '. . . demands conative effort on the part of the learner to enter into, as it were, "the shoes" or "the skins" of people met only through such evidence as a description or portrait' (p. 7). No doubt in some sense imagining demands that the subject 'wills' his imagining — but then so do explaining and memorizing and comparing. 'Willing' is merely a necessary prerequisite: when one carries out any activity (other than involuntary movements) one can be said to have willed it. Nor can one say there is something special about historical imagining — as opposed for example to explaining — which makes it impossible to compel another to do it. This appears to be the force of the argument on p. 6 that 'The individual acts of his own volition, indeed, no one can force another to be attentive, responsive, or imaginative in the sense intended here.' In the case of *both* explaining and imagining one can make pupils fulfil the minimal requirements of the activity against a certain reluctance, and in *both* cases real resistance makes such attempted compulsion pointless. 'Imagining' is not peculiar in this respect. This mistake arises because of a more fundamental one: Coltham and Fines fail to analyse their own concept of 'Imagining'. The description of imagining given on p. 7 (quoted above) already indicates that it should be classified as a *cognitive* activity. We discuss this issue below (Part IV), but here it is worth noting that the attempt to classify imagining as conative leads to a thoroughly confused account. Thus quite different descriptions of the connections between sections are given in the introduction to the framework, where the cognitive activities are said to depend on the affective (p. 5), and later, where 'Imagining', allegedly a *conative* behaviour, is said to be '. . . dependent on encounters with the material of history (Section B) in increasing amount, and on some forms of ability in handling this material (Section C)' (p. 8), which the authors have themselves described as *cognitive* behaviours (p. 5).

What, then, can be salvaged from Section A and the classification of behaviour on which it rests? Of course there *are* attitudes which are important to the study of history, which the teacher would wish his pupils to acquire, for example, caution towards sweeping generalizations about the past.[6] But attitudes are to be specified in terms of their cognitive content. Caution is not a generalized intellectual paralysis, but involves—for instance—recognition of the complexity of human behaviour and the difficulties of specifying what in the past are to count as examples of the 'same' phenomenon. That this does not fit Coltham and Fines' classification of attitudes as conative and affective behaviour is borne out by the inclusion of just such an attitude as an example of their cognitive category of 'Judgement' (p. 21): 'Uses caution and admits doubt in interpreting material'.[7] Thus one is left simply with the requirement that history teachers should intend children to enjoy their history and to undertake historical activities willingly rather than grudgingly. In the oddly archaic language of certain schools of psychology, one could say that the 'behaviours' listed in Sections B, C and D all require prior 'willing'. More sensibly they might be said to have a conative *aspect*. If it is really thought necessary one could list a few examples of signs that activities were being undertaken willingly. Having said that, one has exhausted Section A. It has either been collapsed into the other sections, or alternatively reduced to an introductory note: namely that an overall objective will be the willing performance of the activities in Sections B, C and D.

The difficulties raised for Section A by Coltham and Fines' classification of behaviour are matched by ambiguities and redundancies in the main scheme of sectionalization. These are particularly obvious in Sections B and C. Section B is entitled 'The Nature of the Discipline', and contains a sub-section on 'Organizing Procedures', and Section C is entitled 'Skills and Abilities'. Several similar headings occur in both: for example in each category we find evaluation, analysis and synthesis. Indeed it seems that most of the 'Organizing Procedures' could—if one accepted the usage of Coltham and Fines—be described as 'skills': take for example (e) on p. 13:

> (e)   Recognition of any gaps in the evidence, and pursuit of appropriate action by e.g. further search, extrapolation forwards or backwards from collected evidence. . . .

What is the rationale for the distinction between these sections?

In their introduction to 'Organizing Procedures' (p. 12) Coltham and Fines explain that

> The main argument for this arrangement is that only as he masters the relevant skills will the learner come to know what historical method is (learning by doing). It could also be argued that only if he is aware beforehand of the nature of the skill which he is aiming to master—

if he has received at least a description of the activity—can he be
expected to undertake it purposefully and be able to repeat the
procedure on different material.

This is corroborated later when a 'product' is defined as '. . . the result of
applying skills (Section C) in the manner set out in [Organizing
Procedures] . . .' On the basis of these remarks it would seem that the
distinction is that while under 'Organizing Procedures' they are concerned
that pupils should *know* what skills a historian uses, under 'Skills and
Abilities' they are concerned that pupils learn to *employ* these skills
themselves, and indeed we find that the list of objectives under 'Organizing
Procedures' begins 'knows that the following are the main procedures to be
applied to primary and secondary source material . . .' (p. 12).[8]

   This division is paralleled by the separation of 'Information' from
'Abilities'. In Section B, sub-section 1, on p. 11, the authors give a whole
list of names and terms to be recalled:

   names of constituent elements of the whole range of human behaviour
   (curiosity, hatred, fear, affection, jealousy, ambition, thought, belief);
   names of particular places, people, or groups of people associated with
   specific events. . . .

This list is quite separate from 'Memorization', 'Comprehension' and
'Judgement and Evaluation', which appear as 'Skills and Abilities' on
pp. 17-21.

   Even if it were consistently maintained, the attempt to divide
'Organizing Procedures' and 'Information' from 'Abilities' displays three
serious weaknesses. First, learning the names of certain historical activities
(even if it were intelligible as a separate intellectual task) would amount to
a somewhat arid acquisition. And this applies equally to the recall of
names and places. It is true that the authors tell us that these items of
information are to be recalled 'in context'. This is quite inadequate
however, when the framework creates such a sharp dichotomy between
'knowing' and 'abilities'. The point is not that a pupil should be able to
recall in some unspecified 'context' that William the Conqueror landed in
England in 1066, but that if we are to say that this is something he *knows*,
this knowledge must involve the ability to apply it (for example in
constructing a narrative or in answering questions posed by some piece of
evidence new to him).[9]

   Second, Coltham and Fines seem to be claiming that one cannot learn
what an activity is without doing it, and that one cannot do it without
knowing in advance what it is. (See p. 12 quoted above, p. 24.) If they
mean that it is impossible to learn a practical skill without being given in
advance the rules which define that skill, they are simply wrong. Children
learn how to talk grammatically, for example, before they are aware of the
rules of grammar. If they mean that learning proceeds more efficiently
where some formulation of the rules is available, then this comes down to
an argument for bringing these two aspects of learning—knowing the
rules, and learning how to perform the activity which conforms to
them—together. The attempt to keep them apart in any case breaks down.

Concluding their account of 'The Nature of the Discipline' (which includes 'Organizing Procedures') they remark that 'Overall the only important objective is that learners shall proceed to independent operation in all the sections described here . . .' (p. 16). To talk of 'independent operation' is to imply more than just the ability to recite the names of historical activities.

The third weakness helps to explain the difficulties in which Coltham and Fines find themselves here. It is significant that in the passage from p. 12 already discussed (quoted p. 24) they slip from talking about *skills*, to *historical method*, and finally to *activities*. The notion of a skill is an ambiguous one. Craftsmen have skills: a mastery of certain ways (rule governed) of doing a limited and generally predictable range of things, which is largely gained through practice, often under the supervision of a master. Such skills can be improved by continual practice of roughly the same routines. History undoubtedly involves skills of this kind, and Coltham and Fines mention some: 'Uses the alphabetic system to locate items speedily', for example (p. 17). But skills of this kind are very different from those activities which characteristically involve more complex kinds of intelligent thinking, and the grasp of interrelated principles; and it is therefore highly misleading to treat 'skills' as a generic term for all mental abilities, and hence to trade on the convenience for an 'objectives' approach of the more restricted notion.

Precisely the same ambiguity arises in Coltham and Fines' attempt to divide historical 'behaviours' into unitary categories suitable for an objectives approach. 'Skills and Abilities' are divided into a number of categories, such as 'Reference Skills', 'Memorization', 'Analysis' and 'Synthesis', which are in themselves obviously very different levels of skill. More important, each of these skills is treated as unitary, that is the various examples given under 'Analysis', 'Synthesis', etc. are seen as being the same skill manifested at different levels. But an examination of their examples shows that they are in fact quite different skills. Thus on p. 18 under 'Comprehension' they include both 'Gives the gist of material read' and 'Formulates question(s) to be asked about and of the evidence'. Under 'Analysis' (p. 19) we find 'Can name separate parts of an object orally' and 'Identifies bias/point of view/value judgement in a piece of evidence or secondary source material'. 'Synthesis' (p. 20) links 'Can combine time indicators with sequence of events' and 'Constructs an accurate and vivid picture of conditions of life at a particular point in time'. It is true that the *word* 'Analysis', for example, could with some licence be applied both to the ability to name the different parts of a suit of armour, and to the identification of bias in the Anglo-Saxon Chronicle's account of William the Conqueror, but it simply does not follow from this that the same skill is involved. Coltham and Fines are assuming that behind the use of a single word like 'Analysis' there must be one single type of activity, which in this case they appear to identify as something similar to chemical analysis ('Separating a whole into its elements' — p. 19).

On this dubious foundation Coltham and Fines base their contention that the pupil can practise the same historical skills at any level.

. . . within a category, there are different levels of difficulty; the detection of bias (. . . Analysis) may not be very easy for younger learners, but some aspects of analysis — e.g. identification of component parts — are certainly within the competence of the youngest learner, given material comprehensible to him. (pp. 22-3)

Indeed the general tenor of the pamphlet suggests that in doing *any* of these things the pupil is in a real sense doing the same as a historian does. While we would not want to deny that this may sometimes be the case, this is a very large claim, which their own examples do nothing to substantiate. The objectives framework here as elsewhere obscures and distorts fundamental distinctions.

Finally, in several places in the pamphlet Coltham and Fines order their objectives in what are claimed to be developmental or logical sequences. For instance on p. 15 the assertion is made that there is a 'Logical order in the procedures as set out on pp. 12 and 13. This claim is not evident from the examples referred to. Consider for example the following sequence:

(a)   Exploratory examination of a single piece of evidence or single product.

(b)   Collection and examination of all evidence from primary and/or secondary sources relevant to an interest, and from other disciplines if appropriate.

(c)   Establishment of nature and actual framing of questions (or selection of one from among possible questions) to be asked of the evidence. (p. 12)

Clearly the earlier stages of this sequence are not logically necessary for the later ones. Nor can it be said to embody a psychological order, charting the actual process of historical enquiry. The idea that one could collect all the relevant evidence without having framed any questions betrays an odd notion of the way historians work.[10]

Again, in Section D ('Educational Outcomes of Study') Coltham and Fines claim that each sub-section (i.e. 1. 'Insight', 2. 'Knowledge about Values', 3. 'Reasoned Judgement') '. . . describes a developmental sequence related in each case to a particular aspect of the study of history' (p. 27). It would seem that they mean a developmental sequence in each sub-section, composed of the examples they give, rather than a single sequence composed of the series of three sub-sections. Thus under 'Insight' (p. 25) we have:

Comments sympathetically on recounted behaviours not normally acceptable in own culture.

Entertains ideas offered by people of different belief, culture, opinion, generation, etc. from own.

Examines such ideas with detachment.

Acknowledges change as a normal and continuing part of the human situation.

No attempt is made to elucidate the alleged sequence or its relationships to different aspects of history, and it is difficult to see what such a sequence could be. Are sympathetic comments developmentally, logically, or in any other sense prior to entertaining ideas—and if so, upon what are the sympathetic comments supposed to be based?[11]

PART III.   HISTORY AND EDUCATIONAL OBJECTIVES

Coltham and Fines have a very specific list of conditions for deciding what is to count as an educational objective. An educational objective

(I)   . . . describes . . . what a *learner* can do as a result of having learned . . .

(II)   . . . describes what an observer . . . can see the learner doing . . .

(III)   . . . indicates what educational experience [the learner] requires if he is to achieve the objective.

In particular the authors stress that they are not talking about '. . . very general aims—e.g. to understand the ideas of others . . .', and that they are not '. . . referring to aims concerned with the teacher's behaviour—e.g. to encourage a concern for the past' (pp. 3 and 4—authors' emphasis).

It is strange that the appearance and widespread acceptance of a fully-fledged 'objectives' treatment of history should come just as critics of this approach are winning serious attention. Most of the general problems of the objectives approach which have recently been debated are raised again by the Coltham and Fines' taxonomy. If one attempts to define all educational activities in terms of such objectives the danger is that content will be seen in purely instrumental fashion as a means of bringing about the required behaviour. For complex and sophisticated forms of understanding to be translated into precise sets of observable behaviours would, if possible at all, require an extremely detailed specification. As Stenhouse has observed, with particular reference to the study of works of art, 'All too often, unless the specification of objectives is more detailed and sophisticated than anyone seems able to make it, the result of [the] recipe, "the planning of content and methods to achieve the objectives", is the use of methods to distort content in order to meet objectives.'[12] Furthermore, since the objectives scheme specifies particular behaviours as products of 'educational experiences' it is likely to emphasize end products rather than the processes of thought involved, and, as Eisner has pointed out, it cannot take account of creative or original thought without becoming so general as no longer to fit its own criteria.[13] These issues are particularly important in the context of evaluation, where an objectives approach is often claimed to make some sort of measurement possible; it would seem doubtful whether this is so unless one concentrates on the attainment of relatively simple skills even though these may have nothing to do with the learner's mastery of the discipline one is attempting to teach. How far should such simple but observable attainments be preferred to a perhaps fragmentary and incomplete learning of complex forms of understanding?

A major difficulty in discussing objectives arises from an ambiguity in that notion which Coltham and Fines' detailed specification does not resolve. They are at pains to stress that an 'objective' is not to be equated with just *any* relatively general intended goal. It is therefore tempting to take them to be insisting on strictly 'behavioural' objectives, a conclusion which is reinforced both by their frequent reference to 'behaviours' of various kinds, and by their condition (II), which stresses that an objective be framed in such a way that it 'describes what an observer . . . can *see* the learner doing' (p. 3, our emphasis). But the notion of 'seeing' people doing things is itself infected with a radical ambiguity. It is true, for example, that people in pain often show certain kinds of behaviour which in normal circumstances allow us to say that they are in pain. But to behave in those ways is not itself to *be* in pain, and in some circumstances the behaviour is uncoupled from the pain (as when an actor or malingerer feigns pain, or when a sufferer deliberately conceals his suffering). Hence a statement that I can *see* someone is in pain would not mean that I had perceived the pain, but that I had perceived certain criterial behaviour.[14] It is not clear whether the 'behaviours' described by Coltham and Fines are meant to be ends in themselves, or criteria for judging that something has been achieved. For the learning of physical skills, how to ride a bicycle or plane a piece of wood for example, strictly behavioural objectives (i.e. where the behaviour *is* the end to be achieved) may be appropriate. All manner of abilities of this sort may be required in the study of many subjects. Hence a history teacher may share Coltham and Fines' objectives 'Can operate filmstrip projector to find required frame' or 'Uses the alphabetic system to locate items speedily' (p. 17), and these fit two of their three conditions. It is noticeable, though, that objectives of this kind are seldom specific to history. In the case of specifically historical activities, it is much more difficult to make sense of a strictly 'behavioural' interpretation. An objective like 'Uses caution and admits doubt in interpreting material' (p. 21) is ambiguous in this respect: does it describe the behaviour to be achieved as an end in itself, or is such behaviour a *criterion* for what is to be achieved? It is hard to see how the first interpretation could even make sense: one cannot perceive another's doubt or caution any more than one perceives another's pain; what one perceives is behaviour criterial of doubt. On the second interpretation the problem for an objectives approach (which claims to specify more than general goals) is to show how such criterial behaviour could be further analysed into a series of specific, observable, caution-using and doubt-admitting behaviours to meet the immense variety of situations in which learners might handle historical material. And what of all the occasions when for one reason or another this disposition is not expressed in some observable behaviour? The exercise of doubt is after all a question of judgement. Indeed the authors use it as an example of 'Judgement and Evaluation'. But the complex thought processes involved in exercising judgement in such cases — in deciding on the weight to be given to a range of different considerations, cannot be represented by a list of behaviours.

In this context it is instructive to examine Coltham and Fines' own example of the way in which one of their objectives measures up to their own conditions. On p. 4 we find their example 'Uses his own experience to explain the described behaviour of a character'. In a limited way it meets their condition (I): '. . . describes . . . what a *learner* can do as a result of having learned . . .' The limitations become apparent when it is held up against condition (II): '. . . describes what an observer . . . can see the learner doing . . .' It may be that the observer can 'see' the learner trying to explain the described behaviour, and even that he can 'see' the learner using his own experience in the attempt, but this formulation will not allow him to see whether the learner has succeeded in the same way as does 'Can operate filmstrip projector to find required frame.' (Note that on p. 16 we are told that 'Each objective is framed so as to show the behaviour of the learner when mastery has been achieved.') In the latter case the behaviour is itself the end to be achieved, in the former it could only be criterial. A still more difficult obstacle is presented by condition (III): '. . . indicates what educational experience (the learner) requires if he is to achieve the objective.' To show that this condition is met Coltham and Fines assert: 'Moreover, the teacher has already stated, when framing the objective, that he is going to instruct or suggest to the pupils that they should draw on their experience when the task is to explain the character's behaviour' (p. 4). But, despite their insistence that they are concerned with learner, not teacher behaviour, this is a general description of what the *teacher* is going to do, and certainly not a specification of what educational experience the *learner* is to have, let alone what he *requires*. Are we seriously to take it that the educational experience required for the learner to achieve mastery in using his own experience to explain a character's behaviour is the voice of his teacher telling him to use it?

The fact is that if the behaviours listed in a catalogue of objectives are criteria for the achievement of some goal, and not themselves what is to be achieved, then the possibility of producing a set of precise and clear-cut objectives to do what Coltham and Fines expect of them is greatly reduced. The authors slide backwards and forwards between 'criterial' and 'behavioural' objectives, seeking to claim the operational precision of the latter without abandoning the more important historical areas which can only be accommodated by the former. This is not to say that it is not important to try to get clear about what it is we want children to learn in learning history: merely that Coltham and Fines cannot have it both ways.

This failure of the actual objectives suggested to fulfil their implicit promise of a new precision, or even to meet Coltham and Fines' own conditions, is repeated throughout the body of the pamphlet (see C8 and C9 for examples similar to the one above). The problems of trying to apply a narrow objectives approach to history are manifested in particular in the recurrent appearance of 'recalls that' or 'recalls' (see pp. 10, 11, 18 for whole lists of these) or 'knows that' (p. 12). This reflects both the ambiguity in their notion of 'behaviour', and the dichotomy between 'Abilities' on the one hand and 'Procedures' and 'Information' on the other.[15] Hence the passage from Section B, sub-section 2 ('Organizing Procedures') which consists of a long list of 'procedures' and is headed by the overall objective:

'knows that the following are the main procedures to be applied to primary and secondary source material . . .', appears to make sense only under a strictly 'behavioural' interpretation. The 'behaviour' in question is that pupils must know that these are the main procedures, *not* that they exercise them. But in the absence of their exercise, genuine *behaviour* of the kind which would meet Coltham and Fines' own conditions for an objective would be merely the ability to recite them.

Another difficulty arises in an objectives approach such as we have here, from the sheer number and range of possible objectives. Coltham and Fines insist on links between their sections, but their attempt to work inside a behavioural framework results in a series of lists of 'atomic' objectives, supposedly fully intelligible as individual items. (How else could they meet their own criteria for an objective set out above?) The relations between items inside sections are often obscure (see out Part IV) and as a result itemization may itself seem arbitrary, and the possibility of weighing objectives against one another and assessing their importance is greatly reduced. We have here a supermarket situation, in which we are offered a huge range of examples of possible objectives, but where there is no prospect of rational selection among alternatives. Thus in an otherwise admirable critical appraisal of traditional 'O' Level examinations Martin Roberts concludes with a section invoking the Coltham-Fines framework.[16] He declares that 'It makes no judgements between objectives, it simply defines, lists, and classifies them, and can be used by any history teacher, whatever his philosophy of education . . .' His paper includes an appendix listing the objectives in one column, with an adjacent column headed 'Used at Brays Grove', and next to each objective appears either 'Yes' or 'No'. 'Attending', 'Responding', and 'Imagining' *are* used. 'Organizing Procedures' are not, and neither are 'Products'! (It would be interesting to speculate upon the consequences of 'No' appearing after 'Attending and Responding'.) In other words we are being invited not merely to select our personal preferences from the examples within sections, but to leave out whole sections. The 'objectives' approach, construed in this way at least, leads not to greater clarity and precision, but to confusion and incoherence.

Finally, underlying all the problems which beset Coltham and Fines is a basic ambiguity in the nature of the task they have undertaken. This is most evident in their wrestling with Section B, the 'Nature of the Discipline'. On p. 5 they claim that '. . . Section B gives an analysis of the particular form of knowledge, history. . . .' They nowhere recognize that analysing a form of knowledge is a task very different in scope from listing behavioural objectives for teaching. Throughout the pamphlet the exigencies of analysis clash with the self-imposed restrictions of the objectives approach.

PART IV. CONTENT

In Part III we argued that the objectives framework concealed an implicit analysis of history. In Part IV we will examine some important claims and assumptions made by Coltham and Fines about history.

At the beginning of their pamphlet (Sections A3 pp. 7-9) Coltham and Fines offer an account of imagination in which it is classified as an 'attitude' and as 'conative'. They associate imagination at one level with imaging, and add that 'historical imagination requires not only this but usually something more; the words "sympathy" and "empathy" are useful here. Sympathy can be defined as "the power of entering into another's feelings or mind", and empathy as "the power of entering into another personality" and "imaginatively experiencing his experience".' A sentence later they assert 'Such behaviours are, perhaps, only a little more than a particular form of "responding". . . .'

It will be argued here that their account is both confused and misleading. Imagining is not an 'attitude'. It is only vacuously conative (see our Part II above). Because Coltham and Fines see imagination in emotional terms as an intuitive 'power', or faculty, they are unable consistently to distinguish between 'empathy', 'sympathy', 'involvement' and 'identification'. Despite the earlier definitions the examples of objectives given in this section in fact make no mention of 'empathy', or 'sympathy', but refer instead to 'involvement' and 'identification'. This is what one would expect from the unanalysed ambiguities in the notion of 'sympathy'. Hence we are offered, 'Describes an historical incident with signs of personal involvement', and 'Identifies with a character under study so as to be able to declare the viewpoint of this character.' Of course it *may* be that (empirically) identification is a stage through which children must pass before they are capable of genuine historical imagination. From a Piagetian point of view identification might be regarded as a form of centration, or at any rate as assimilation without compensating accommodation. But this is a separate question, and we cannot discover whether or not such a hypothesis is true if we confuse the concepts involved. For it is a serious mistake to confuse identification and involvement with historical imagination. The former may actually impede the latter. Identification may distort or preclude the wider view of an agent and his circumstances which is essential to historical imagination. In any case historical imagination does not *require* taking the part of a historical agent: do we really want children to *identify* with Hitler (or for that matter with Ghandi or Churchill)? Or indeed to become 'emotionally involved' with him? That this is what Coltham and Fines are thinking of is shown by their discussion of the developmental context: '. . . *intensity of emotional activity* is not a direct function of age since a high level of . . . imaginative behaviour can be looked for as much in a sixth former as in a primary school child. . . .' (p. 9, our emphasis).

The most revealing clue to what is going wrong here is the assertion in the objective quoted above that a pupil is to 'identify with a character . . . *so as to be able* to declare' that character's viewpoint (our emphasis). Historical imagination is evidently seen as a special kind of tool employed by historians to gain a special kind of knowledge — it is a 'power' (p. 7) or faculty enabling us to get inside someone else's skin. Coltham and Fines are quite right to separate 'imaging' from other aspects of historical imagination, and right to insist that more is required. However, their analysis leads them drastically to underestimate this 'more'. It is not some special kind of intuition, let alone identification, which is involved here, but something more akin to *supposing*. It does not presuppose involvement: one does not have to feel what the agent felt. One has to *know that* the agent saw the world as he did, and *that* he felt as he did. And it is seriously misleading to suggest that the activity required of children here is 'only a little more than a particular form of responding'. Coming to see a situation from someone else's point of view, and to understand his purposes and intentions, is to be done by *inference* from *evidence*; it requires a high level of thinking. 'If so and so believed this and this, and wanted to accomplish that, *then* his view of his situation would be this.' Such a schema might be called hypothetico-deductive, and in Piagetian terms would be likely to demand formal operations. At every step such reasoning is tied through its premises to the evidence, and the view which the evidence suggests itself requires further checking against evidence before any confidence can be placed in it. There are no special intuitive powers at work here: just hard thinking on the basis of the evidence available. Just how seriously Coltham and Fines' account underestimates the kind of thinking involved is shown on p. 18, where under 'Comprehension'— 'behaviour' which they say 'is the result of examination at the surface or literal level'—they list the objective, 'Uses own experience to explain described behaviour of a character'. Indeed the passage already quoted from p. 9, in which it is asserted that imagination is to be expected just 'as much in a sixth former as in a primary school child' suggests that historical imagination is regarded as essentially a low-level mental operation, open to the youngest child, which despite a presumption to the contrary, persists into adult life.

As suggested in Part II the overall division of the objectives into conative, affective and cognitive behaviours is partly responsible for this mistaken treatment. In Section C, 'Skills and Abilities', we find the sub-section 'Extrapolation' (p. 20). This is classed as a cognitive behaviour, and is much closer to a genuine characterization of historical imagination than anything specifically described as such by Coltham and Fines. Their basic division of the framework precludes the authors from seeing the contradictions and opportunities here. They discriminate between 'extrapolation' and 'fantasy' in such a way that the latter would be scarcely distinguishable from their own earlier concept of imagination; and they fail to see that some of the difficulties implicit in their notion of empathy could have been resolved if the connections between extrapolation and empathy had been properly developed.

Similar problems arise in the area of Interpretation and Explanation. There are important relationships between explanation, interpretation and imagination which elude the framework established by Coltham and Fines.[17] Explanation and interpretation are treated in places as one and the same thing (p. 14). This is at least debatable, and requires some indication of what is meant by 'interpretation'. Interpretation of evidence, of a period and of an action, for example, exhibit differences which are as important as their similarities. And for each of these, the word 'interpretation' may be understood in several ways. Far from offering a new precision, or at any rate the precision required for an 'objectives' approach, the objectives set out here serve to confuse important notions.

The tendency of the 'objectives' approach to emphasize products at the expense of processes (referred to above in Part III) is particularly evident here. On pp. 13-14, for example, 'Explanation and Interpretation' appears as a 'type of product'. This seems to us a thoroughly misleading conception. Interpretation is not to be regarded simply as a 'product' or conclusion of history, but as something which suggests ways of viewing evidence, and provides a framework for using evidence to arrive at assertions, and, where required, at a coherent narrative. Interpretations are not finished end-products, but part of the process of inquiry. (Confusion on this question is closely related to confusion on the nature of evidence which we discuss below.)

Within this category of 'products' Coltham and Fines distinguish sharply between explanation and narrative, classing the latter as 'Reproduction and Description'. In reality it is difficult to maintain this distinction in history: narrative is a form, and (*pace* examiners) to assert that a piece of history is narrative is to say nothing about its explanatory powers. A narrative is already an account organized in terms of the intentions and purposes of the agents involved, and may therefore be more, or less, explanatory. Coltham and Fines list the question 'What happened?' under 'Reproduction and Description'; but this question is often related to the question 'What was he doing?' and hence is not always easily marked off from the question 'Why did he do that?' which is listed under 'Explanation and Interpretation'.

The mistaken treatment of Interpretation as a 'product' which we have discussed above is especially important because of its effect on the authors' view of evidence. Coltham and Fines lay great stress on the importance of primary sources to the extent that secondary sources are relegated to *faute de mieux* status. Thus they write that 'strictly speaking, the information relevant to history consists only of material in this primary source form. However, no learner (and no historian) could proceed far without the use of secondary source material . . .' (p. 10). This impression is reinforced by frequent reference to primary sources throughout the paper. Secondary sources (embodying interpretation) are incorporated in the category of products: '. . . present practice stands on the shoulders of past practice and *makes use of the available products*' (page 10, our emphasis). This sounds like a recognition of the importance of secondary sources, but the idea that these are 'products' which the historian 'makes use of' gives the impression that history is really the cumulative total of fixed and finished results. Secondary sources provide the framework of history as a public form of knowledge, a framework not merely of established facts but of interpretation and selection. It is within this public form of knowledge that the questions arise which determine what is to count as knowledge.[18]

The failure to recognize this point leads to some very misleading assumptions about the nature of historical evidence. On pp. 10 and 11 Coltham and Fines give a long list of '. . . types of material which may be examined as evidence'. (They include, for example, pictures, documents and artefacts.) It may be seen as an outcome of their 'objectives' approach that they should attempt such a task, but this prevents them seeing that only in relation to particular questions can there be any criteria of what is to count as evidence. Historical evidence is not a category of objects.

Almost as noticeable in Coltham and Fines as their stress on evidence is their emphasis on the learner's 'fund of personal knowledge and experience'. In part they seem to be making an important pedagogical point with which we are in full agreement, namely that the pupil does not come to the study of history *tabula rasa*, but brings to it his own experience and preconceptions which the teacher has to recognize. However they wish to make a separate point which confuses the issue and has misleading consequences. They give as an objective 'Evaluation of source material in terms of . . . *agreement with* personal experience and knowledge of human nature and behaviour' (p. 13, our emphasis). Here they seem to regard personal knowledge and experience as a yardstick for evaluating evidence of the actions of people in the past. But the personal knowledge and experience of a contemporary pupil, or of a contemporary adult for that matter, will be too narrow to give any real understanding of the thoughts and attitudes involved in the actions of people in other times. This is not in any way to devalue pupils' personal experience, but to point out that precisely because of the difference between such experience and that of most of the historical characters pupils will meet with, the teacher must give it serious recognition. Coltham and Fines' account distorts this point and introduces a dangerously subjective notion of historical understanding.

Coltham and Fines' recommendation of local primary sources, for use with younger pupils especially, is connected with their misleading views on personal knowledge and experience. We are not criticizing the teaching of local history, but Coltham and Fines' unexamined assumptions about 'the environment'. It is taken for granted that the local environment will provide evidence of its own past which will be more rewarding to the learner, because it is closer to him. It is not clear that this is so. Evidence for local history is not necessarily easier for the pupil to understand as evidence than that for national or foreign history. Whether local history provides a greater stimulus cannot just be assumed; it may be that younger pupils' interest is aroused just as well by historical situations remote from their own experience.

The confused views expressed on pupils' personal experience and on the relationship between primary and secondary evidence leads Coltham and Fines to state that 'Overall, the only important objective is that learners shall proceed to independent operation in all sections described here (i.e. Section B: "The Nature of the Discipline") . . . so that their products are truly *their personal versions of history*' (p. 16, our emphasis). On the mistaken premise that historical skills are unitary faculties with varying levels of difficulty they imply that the pupil is doing something which is in a real sense the same as the historian does. (This is discussed above in Part II.) In doing this they disregard the character of history as a public form of knowledge. The danger is that history then becomes a subjective undertaking, a danger foreshadowed in their account of historical imagination, and brought out here in their talk of 'personal versions of history'.

We would add that nothing in this section is intended as an argument against the use of primary sources in history teaching, a very welcome development, nor as an attempt to relegate them to the status of 'illustrations'. What we do wish to point out is that work with primary sources to produce 'personal versions of history' does not necessarily mean that pupils are doing the same things as historians.

PART V. CONCLUSIONS

As we remarked in the Introduction, we have felt it necessary to examine *Educational Objectives for the Study of History* in detail because of its currency and because of the importance of the issues it raises. There is no doubt that the pamphlet has done a great deal of good. It has stimulated argument and more careful thinking among teachers. It has provided a basis for student teachers to sort out their own assumptions about history teaching. It has been another blow for a revitalized history in the schools, and against unthinking traditionalism. We have therefore thought it opportune now to attempt a detailed re-assessment, before its very success carries it into the realms of established orthodoxy—a fate we feel sure its authors did not intend.

One caveat should be made. We hope we have not been unjust in our interpretation of Coltham and Fines' views: a major difficulty of discussing their pamphlet is that their sometimes rather vague analysis results in a number of contradictions. It is possible to point to passages in which the problems here discussed seem to have been felt by the authors as tensions in their account. (See for example the way in which the sub-section 'Extrapolation', discussed above in our Part IV, comes closer to an account of historical imagination than anything offered under 'Imagination' as such.) We have tried to concentrate in this chapter on what seem to be the central assumptions involved in their account.

Educational Objectives for the Study of History has as its basic premise the assumption that it is possible and useful to produce a list of *objectives* for history teaching. We agree that history teachers need to think very hard about what they are trying to achieve, but as we have tried to show, precise objectives of the kind required by Coltham and Fines are (at least) extremely difficult to formulate in history, and indeed their value and attainability is a matter for doubt in a wide range of disciplines. Bloom's taxonomy was a child of examiners and psychologists: it is interesting to see how Coltham and Fines' framework has received particular emphasis from those concerned with examinations in history. We think that the full-fledged 'behavioural' objectives approach offers only spurious precision, and that it is likely to do more harm than good by distorting history for the purposes of assessment. This distortion is all the more serious because, as we have emphasized throughout our discussion, Coltham and Fines are presenting less a list of objectives than a partial analysis of the discipline of history. This analysis breaks down partly because it is forced into the procrustean bed of the 'objectives' approach, and partly because of its confused account of imagination, explanation, interpretation and evidence. It would be ironic if confusion here gave strength to the arguments of those who wish to deny the importance of imagination and evidence in the classroom.

Finally, while we sympathize with many of the aspirations implicit in the Coltham and Fines pamphlet, it displays several of the weaknesses present in much recent thinking about history teaching. There has been a reaction to history as received information, which, while itself encouraging and healthy, offers as an alternative a somewhat subjective account of history, manifested for instance in the assumptions made about imagination. Underlying these features of the 'new history' is the desire to teach history as a mode of knowledge: out of this has come a welter of suggestions for the use of evidence in history teaching, without any real analysis of its implications; at the same time the obvious fact that doing history is in some way connected with using evidence has been allowed to obscure the point that history also involves *understanding*. Acquaintance with materials which *may* be regarded as evidence no more guarantees understanding than did the 'handing down of the facts' by the teacher. What is required is firstly more careful analysis of what is involved in historical understanding, and secondly much more empirical work to discover what can and what cannot be expected of children in this area, and how teaching can serve to promote understanding. The danger is that, taken as it stands, *Educational Objectives for the Study of History* will give ammunition to those who wish to reverse the important developments in history teaching which have already been achieved, and may distort future progress.

NOTES

1. Coltham, J. B., and Fines, J., *Educational Objectives for the Study of History, A Suggested Framework*, Historical Association, Teaching of History Series, No. 35, 1971.

2. Ben Jones, R., 'Introduction: The New History' in R. Ben Jones (ed.), *Practical Approaches to the New History*, Hutchinson Educational, 1973. (See particularly the papers by Marilyn Palmer, Martin Roberts and H. G. Macintosh.)

3. See, for example, Roberts, M., 'Educational Objectives for the Study of History: The Relevance of Dr Coltham's and Dr Fines' *Framework* to "O" Level Courses', in *Teaching History*, Vol. II, No. 8, November 1972; Brown, R., and Daniels, C., 'Sixth Form History — An Assessment', in *Teaching History*, Vol. IV, No. 15, May 1976, p. 210; and Palmer, M., 'Educational Objectives and Source Materials: Some Practical Suggestions', in *Teaching History*, Vol. IV, No. 16, November 1976, p. 326.

4. Associated Examining Board, *Syllabuses*, 1978, Section III, p. 119.
5. Considerable reference to Coltham and Fines' pamphlet is essential to our discussion. Their framework contains three, and in places four levels of classification, and in order to avoid confusion we have therefore kept our own formal divisions to a minimum: we refer to them throughout as 'Parts', distinguished by upper-case Roman numerals. References to the pamphlet follow the authors' own system—hence any mention of sections or sub-sections, or letters, or numerals other than upper-case Roman preceded by 'Part', indicate Coltham and Fines' divisions.
6. The argument here may be broadened to link up with what Richard Peters has called the 'rational passions'. (Peters, R. S., 'Reason and Passion' in R. F. Dearden, P. H. Hirst, and R. S. Peters (eds.), *Education and the Development of Reason*, Routledge and Kegan Paul, 1972, pp. 225-7.) Clearly children must be brought to care about standards of truth, correctness and objectivity which are built into particular modes of inquiry. Part of what is *meant* by thinking historically is that some concern be shown for these standards as developed in characteristic historical procedures.
7. See our further discussion of this example on p. 29.
8. The distinction is, of course, valid: what is in question here is the crude way in which it is operated.
9. This argument appeals to a general criterion of knowledge. See the discussion in Pring, R., 'Bloom's Taxonomy: A Philosophical Critique (2)', in *The Cambridge Journal of Education*, No. 2, Easter 1971, pp. 83-91. We are particularly indebted to Richard Pring for his comments on an earlier draft of the present paper, which saved us from a number of mistakes, and enabled us to take a wider view of the problems involved in objectives. (Any mistakes which remain are, of course, entirely our own responsibility.)
10. See Chapter 1 of this book (especially pp. 4-8).
11. See Chapter 5 of this book (especially pp. 74, 80, 81).
12. Stenhouse, L., 'Some Limitations of the Use of Objectives in Curriculum Research and Planning', in *Paedagogica Europaea*, Vol. 6, 1970-1.
13. Eisner, E. W., 'Instructional and Expressive Educational Objectives: Their Formulation and Use in Curriculum' in W. J. Popham *et al.* (eds.), *Instructional Objectives*, AERA Monograph No. 3, Rand McNally, 1969.
14. There is still an ambiguity in this brief account, since behaviour may be *criterial* in (at least) two ways. Where a given behaviour *always* accompanies something for which it is a criterion, it is criterial in the sense that the latter may be simply deduced from the occurrence of the behaviour. But pain is not like this, and it should be clear that we are using *criterial* in another sense. Here criterial behaviour is the sort of behaviour which *gives application* to a concept (e.g. pain); the concept is learnt in connection with the behaviour, and if pain-behaviour did not *usually* (but only usually) accompany pain, we could not have the concept we in fact have. See Wittgenstein, L., *The Blue and Brown Books*, Basil Blackwell, 2nd edn., 1969, pp. 24-5.
15. Lists of this kind have their origin in the distinction made in Bloom's *Taxonomy of Educational Objectives* between *knowledge* and *intellectual abilities*. Bloom's 'cognitive domain' is divided into six sections, the first of which is 'knowledge', the remaining sections being described as 'skills and abilities'. (Bloom, B. S. (ed.), *The Taxonomy of Educational Objectives*, Handbook I, Longmans, 1956, p. 68.) This distinction is echoed in Coltham and Fines' separation of knowledge of information or procedures from their application. (See our Part II.) Bloom's distinction is discussed in Pring, R., op. cit.
16. Roberts, M., 'A Different Approach to "O" Level', in R. Ben Jones, op. cit., p. 126 and pp. 129-31.
17. See Chapter 5 of this book (especially pp. 80-1).
18. See Chapter 1 of this book.

3. New Views of History: From Innovation to Implementation

I. GOODSON

The distance between new definitions of history and new definitions of history *as taught* reminds me of my return to my home town after qualifying as a teacher. Revisiting my old 'local', I was confronted by an acquaintance from my misspent teenage years. Over a beer he asked: 'So what'ya doing, kid?' Jubilantly I replied: 'Teaching'. 'Teaching what?' 'Teaching history.' His face clouded: 'Teaching it! I'm bloody making it!'

The response of teachers of history to the redefinitions of theorists and philosophers has been similar — 'Redefine it! I'm teaching it.' In this respect history teachers have joined a long line of respectable civil disobedience: the elegant exhortations of curriculum reformers have all met remarkably similar fates. Before scrutinizing attempts to implement new views of history in the classroom, therefore, I want to look at the background of curriculum reform against which such moves have taken place.

THE CURRICULUM REFORM MOVEMENT

In the past decade a broad-based curriculum reform movement has gathered momentum. At the national level 'Projects' to implement curriculum reform have been sponsored by such bodies as Schools Council and the Nuffield Foundation. These centralized projects have been concerned to re-examine school subjects in the light of the changing educational system and societal climate: clearly a much-needed exercise.

A general 'model' for projects has emerged: the subject is redefined according to new theories and new visions of 'relevance', curriculum materials are prepared which illustrate these redefinitions, new classroom practices are advocated and finally the outcomes of the project are evaluated. In general the results have been disappointing: materials have often reached the schools only to be used in an idiosyncratic or ephemeral manner, and the overall pattern of classroom practice has often survived unchanged.

Initiatives at other levels have shared similar fates. Attempts to establish new areas of the curriculum such as social studies, environmental studies and humanities, with the intention of radically transforming classroom practice, have been severely compromised. The fate of social studies is particularly informative. Here, if anywhere, was a group of practitioners who themselves held an explicitly critical opinion of 'normal' classroom teaching. In this case the teachers were not inimical but actually on the side of change, acting positively to implement new views of classroom practice. One of them recently commented on the results:

> I am forced to reflect on the numerous occasions when teachers and students thoroughly conscious and critical of dominant styles of pedagogy have reflected upon video-tapes with a sense of complete incomprehension of the ways in which their lessons echoed in practice, though not intent, just that of which they are so critical. I am forced to reflect upon the capacity of pupils to reinterpret apparently radical orientations of pedagogy in terms of their conceptions of 'normal schooling' and their refusal to entertain the possibility that sir's style is anything but a new, and probably incompetent, way of telling it like it is. I am further forced to reflect upon the plight of the larger group of teachers who, accepting the critiques of prevailing approaches and the desirability in theory of proposed alternatives, see no way in which *they*—in the real world—can resist the constraints and demands of the examination system, the job market, the timetable, etc., etc. which seem to force upon them a particular approach to knowledge and pedagogy and make alternatives impossible.[1]

Radical schools have often encountered similar constraints to would-be radical subjects. Countesthorpe College in Leicestershire was a school set up to challenge traditional patterns of teaching and to encourage a greater degree of pupil involvement in curriculum activities and decisions. Particularly under attack was the 'Teachers' Curriculum' which epitomized a classroom approach where the teacher decides beforehand the whole of the package of knowledge to be transmitted. In the classroom, this package is delivered by recitation or question and answer, or even discovery methods, but ultimately the lesson's aim is that preconceived and preordained by the teacher. Thus, while the pupil can participate at certain levels, it is assumed that all basic curricular decisions must be made by the teacher. The curriculum consists of the teacher's knowledge and the pupil is passive in that at this level his knowledge is not deemed relevant.

The efforts at Countesthorpe to involve pupils in basic curricular decisions proved largely unsuccessful in the initial stages of the school. I wrote:

> At the end of this period there was profound dissatisfaction at the way our teaching had come to reflect the very teachers' curriculum we had set out to reform . . . in spite of integration and individualization there was, in practice, virtually no reform of the teachers' curriculum.[2]

It is significant that progress only began when the organization of the school was changed. Not surprisingly, attempts to reform the 'teachers' curriculum' failed whilst the organization of the timetable continued to be derived from an implicit learning model based on forty-minute sessions of teacher transmission.

Both of these statements about curriculum reform at both subject and school level seem to exemplify a sort of 'regression to the norm' syndrome, the norm being the teacher relating the 'facts' to passive students. This phenomenon has been analysed in a paper on 'The Persistence of the Recitation' by Hoetker and Ahlbrand in which they discern:

> . . . a remarkable stability of classroom verbal behaviour patterns over the past half century despite the fact that each successive generation of educational thinkers, no matter how else they differ, has condemned the rapid-fire, question-answer pattern of instruction. This opens a number of interesting avenues of inquiry. What is there about the recitation, for instance, that makes it so singularly successful in the evolutionary struggle with other, more highly recommended methods? That is, what survival needs of teachers are met uniquely by the recitation? [3]

The mention of 'survival needs', I think, focuses down close to the 'reality' of most of our classrooms. Classrooms are enormously demanding and challenging places in which the teacher has first to survive. Any suggested curriculum reform must acknowledge the pressures on teachers to survive by going on doing what they know they can do.

> All proposals for change that ignore the difficulties that the classroom environment poses for teachers will run foul of the same setting-induced constraints that have frustrated most past reforming initiatives.[4]

The pressures for history teachers are similar to those on other teachers and the 'persistence of recitation' is consequently as common. As one of Booth's teachers commented about this style of teaching: 'It's the main way of teaching anything, I should have thought. After all, it's human communication between person and person.' [5]

What is not accepted (or at least, not stated) by advocates of innovation is that this backwoods response among teachers is often the most rational response. Why should advocates of broader curricular rationality find its expression in the classroom so reprehensible? Given contemporary school timetables and organizational patterns and emergent priorities *vis-à-vis* the educational system and its resources, traditional teaching, with all its known faults, may well be the best that can rationally be attempted. In such a situation, to talk of teachers failing to innovate is to conceptualize the problem wrongly. Similarly, to say, 'if we had better teachers, then innovations would be possible' is unduly to concentrate culpability.

If an over-demanding, ill-organized and under-resourced situation is provided for somebody to work in, and if his efforts then achieve little, it does not logically follow that *he* or *she* is failing. Of course that person is the immediate, observable agency of failure, but the problems may well be elsewhere.

CURRICULUM REFORM IN HISTORY

The major initiative in recent years seeking to reform the secondary-school curriculum in history has been the *Schools Council Project: History 13-16*. A detailed discussion of the project is of particular interest because of the attempt to move from new definitions of history towards new strategies for teaching the subject.

New Definitions

The project began by reviewing practice. Such reviews often focus, quite understandably, on better practice: thus Sylvester reported that 'LEA's were invited to send us the names of schools where interesting history teaching was taking place'.[6] In spite of this initial bias the results of the review seem to have been clear. Commenting on the teaching of history 'over the past 20 years or so', the project stated, 'In the period, history teachers have not, in general, consciously aimed to improve their pupils' thinking abilities, but have concentrated rather on making history interesting and on transmitting a body of factual knowledge about the past.'[7]

The dominant pedagogy of history teachers was reflected in their syllabus designs. The project gave a content summary of a 'Typical History Syllabus 11-16'.

Age		
11-12	Ancient World History to Norman Conquest	
12-13	British, European and World History	1066-1485
13-14	British, European and World History	1485-17th, 18th, 19th Centuries
14-16	*Either* Modern British History	1815-1945
	or Modern British and European History	1789-1939
	or British Social and Economic History	1700-1945
	or Modern World History	1870-1945

The project commented that 'It is a logical pattern if it is accepted that it is based on a view of history as a subject with a chronological structure.'[8] The project was unwilling to accept such a structure, arguing that 'adherence to this structure has been the cause of many of the past ills of history teaching in schools and more than this, that in giving only a linear view of history it gave a limited one'.[9] Therefore history teachers should place less emphasis on chronology. Once this is questioned, the way is open for alternative patterns of syllabus making.[10]

Whilst the project's position was clear on this point, the advocates of chronological structure have in fact proved very resistant to such questioning. An Oxfordshire teacher's views were reported in a *Guardian* review of the Project:

> He argues that history cannot make sense to anyone who doesn't have some framework, however skeletal, of the actual sequence of events in this country from the time of the Romans to the present day. He thinks that teaching history through projects related to a theme (an

extension of primary methods into the secondary sector) leaves the proper understanding of a time scale to chance.[11]

In questioning the use of chronological structure as the basis of history and in seeking to define an 'alternative pattern' the project reported, with laudable honesty, some of the difficulties. Firstly:

Though it tried, the Project could find no adequate conceptual structure to history which would either meet with general consensus, or form a basis for the teaching of the subject. Concepts there are, such as change, continuity, revolution and reaction, challenge and response. Other more specific concepts may be particularized, such as trade, war, family and government.

The report adds with assumed conclusiveness:

The list could easily run into thousands, and consequently . . . could not do for history what Jerome Bruner originally suggested was possible for all subjects, and base the teaching on its conceptual structure.

Secondly, the project

. . . failed to isolate an adequate methodological structure for history. That historians look at evidence and then write a story of some past human experience is a general description of the historian's method which would receive fairly universal acquiescence, but it does not provide an adequate framework for the teaching of history in schools.

Thirdly, the project considered structuring a syllabus on a taxonomy of educational objectives but again concluded that:

. . . though this has relevance for the teaching of history, it is inappropriate as a basis for syllabus framework.[12]

To summarise, history is a subject which has an immense variety of content but which lacks any structure which can dictate how this content should be studied.[13]

Because of these difficulties the project decided to devise a syllabus which was 'based on the uses of the past for adolescents'. There were to be four sections in the syllabus, each of which was of specific use to adolescents in the opinion of the project.

1. Studies in modern world history because 'it helps to explain their present'.
2. Depth study of some past period because 'it helps them to understand people of a different time and place'.
3. A study in development of a topic because 'it provides material for the understanding of human development and change in time and also of the complexity of causation in human affairs'.
4. History around us because 'it contributes to leisure interests'.[14]

The definition of the project's history syllabus was therefore based as much on an understanding of adolescents' needs as on an understanding of history. Such a position has certain pedagogic implications which the project consistently pursued:

It has been contended in this book that history is not a body of knowledge structured on either chronology or any other conceptual framework. Such a negative position is not however helpful when it comes to thinking about the appropriate teaching methods to be employed. If history is not a coherent body of knowledge what is it? The suggestion here is that it might be more meaningful to see history as a heap of materials which survives from the past and which historians can use as evidence about the past. . . . History in this sense involves a perpetual act of resurrection in which pupils, teachers reconstruct the past and so make it become real and 'present' to them. . . . It implies active enquiry of pupils into the various kinds of primary and secondary sources which make up the raw material of history.[15]

The stress on adolescents' needs and 'active' pupils had been present in the first proposal to Schools Council:

many teachers would find helpful a project which provides stimulus, support and materials to help them revitalise their own practice in general and more particularly help them to encourage more pupil-participation in their study of history.[16]

The teaching methods some advocated were summarized in the *A New Look at History* booklet:

The general conclusion which emerges . . . is that since the outcomes hoped for are attitudes and abilities rather than memorization of facts, classroom methods should be favoured which create an active learning situation for the pupil rather than those which cast the teacher in the role of a transmitter of information.[17]

Implementing Strategies

The Schools Council Project then moved from a consideration of the nature of history to defining a new syllabus based mainly on considerations of students' needs and a pedagogy involving pupil participation. In arguing this way the project was very much in the 'mainstream' of curriculum reform proposals: much of the rhetoric of curriculum reform discussed earlier advocated more pupil participation, more 'active learning'. We have seen however that it has often proved difficult to move from advocacy to classroom implementation.

One of the strategies for implementing a new view of history was of course the construction of the new syllabus that has been described. The project considered that

One major problem for history teachers is the age-old one of having too much history to teach. Consequently, the difficulties of syllabus construction and selection remain, even if unacknowledged by some, as a central issue for history teachers.[18]

Alongside the syllabus the project, quite rightly, saw the need to develop a comparable examination, arguing that 'teaching and examining are different ends of the same continuous process'[19] and that

the examination is central to our work. Teachers must necessarily, for their students' sake, make the examination their priority and a History Project designated 13-16 cannot shirk this issue if it is to be realistic in its approach and to have effective results to its work.[20]

A complicated examination format was finally accepted for a GCE 'O' Level/CSE to be jointly operated by the Southern Universities Joint Board and the Southern Regional Examinations Board. There are two examination papers: Paper 1 counts for 40 per cent of the total marks and tests the student's knowledge of modern world history, one Study in Depth and one Study in Development; Paper 2 counts for 20 per cent of total marks and aims to test the exercise of historical skills through 'questions based on unseen evidence'. Course-work assessment covering a wide variety of student work accounts for the other 40 per cent of the marks.

Closer scrutiny of the examination structure leads to doubts as to how teachers would best train their pupils to perform successfully. Apart from the 20 per cent given for Paper 2 the rest of the examination could be adequately catered for, perhaps best catered for, by traditional history teachers transmitting facts or setting pupils pieces of work to complete. Paper 1 relies very much on testing the factual recall skills which traditional history papers have always tested — a good example of Lamont's lament: 'History does not repeat itself; examination papers in History do'.[21]

In the course-work assessment one is reminded of the project's intention of alleviating the history teacher's age-old problem of having 'too much history to teach'. In fact the requirements of the new assessment procedure are more formidable than those they replace! Course-work covers an individual study of a current issue, the complete assignment work in one study in modern world history, one study in depth on provided materials, one piece of work from biographical study, one piece of work involving imaginative reconstruction, and a folder of a pupil's individual study of a 'history around us site, including a record of work done on the site and an imaginative reconstruction'.

To support history teachers using the new examination syllabus, the project produced a large set of curriculum materials covering the main themes. These materials have since been marketed by Holmes McDougall, although the cost may well prove a major obstacle to widespread adoption. Initially adoption was limited to certain selected 'trial schools' in seven areas of England and one in Northern Ireland. These trial schools could form the focus for broader acceptance of the new examinations in the future. A number of national and local conferences were held to introduce trial school teachers to the new syllabus and new materials.

Clearly there are limits to what any project can attempt. By any standards *History 13-16* has a creditable record: large numbers of guides and materials have been produced and meetings and conferences held. Significant numbers of schools are now teaching the new history syllabus. In a real sense I think the project has done all that could have been expected of it.

Yet the record of other curriculum reform movements and projects show that it is very difficult indeed to achieve basic changes in classroom pedagogy. As has been noted, this is often because of a range of constraints which greatly encourage teachers to recite factual knowledge to more or less passive students. This 'transmission' style can actually cover a broader spectrum of lessons than those where the teacher stands at the front and lectures: the teacher is often relating facts to passive students in lessons which might be styled 'discussion' as well as through 'individualized worksheets'. 'Active learning situations', where the teacher ceases to be a 'transmitter of information' are certainly far more elusive than the implementing strategies, drawn up by the project, ever hint at.

The project hardly offers a coherent scheme at this level; more a mixture of *laissez faire* and hope. The former is illustrated by comments about how to deal with third-form history: 'It is a problem which teachers must work out for themselves, in the light of the differing circumstances in which they are placed'.[22] Hope is evident in a range of statements. The strategy for getting teachers to use evidence more in their history lessons was described in this way: 'The Project hopes to give teachers a rationale for making evidence central to history teaching and also give to them, by the production of materials, some of the tools for the job'.[23]

Fundamentally the project's hopes seemed to have been in a change in pedagogy *through* exhortation. This is well illustrated by the attempts to get teachers to use discussion with the 'What is History'-materials: 'If pupils can be led to see through discussion with their teachers what history has to offer them, then there is more chance they will co-operate in the process of education'.[24] The case for discussion was presented generally because of the newness of these ideas and the syllabus:

They present a new look at history in school which is unfamiliar to most teachers. If this is so, they are certainly unknown to most pupils, and one way in which pupils will be able to appreciate them is through discussion with their teachers. There are two main reasons for this. First, the ideas are difficult for pupils aged 13-16 but they may be perceived more clearly in a process of discussion with fellow pupils and with teachers who can appreciate them and articulate them more easily. Secondly, they are ideas which cannot be learned parrot-fashion. In some way they must be acquired self-consciously and for this to happen teachers will need to be willing to discuss with pupils their own reasons for teaching history and for seeing it as useful educative experience for adolescents.[25]

These strategies for achieving more discussion in history lessons via materials and exhortation illustrate the central problem in these efforts to change the history teacher's pedagogy. The history of the Humanities Curriculum Project surely illustrates the massive difficulties involved in such a change. The role of the teachers in discussion, whether parading as a neutral chairman or not, involved major problems of definition and execution. Such problems were seldom solved by exhortatory teacher guides, new materials or syllabuses, and there is little reason to believe the situation has been any different with regard to new views of history.

In seeking to change classroom pedagogy a curriculum project is approaching one of the vested traditions within teaching and one supported by a huge range of rational and irrational arguments.

Traditional teaching patterns have not and will not be changed by exhortation or by *new* materials that can readily be put to use in teaching with the *old* method. What is required is to begin a *process* of change, involving teachers themselves in questioning current practice and drawing up and supporting new definitions of practice.

Strategies for the Future

The achievement of the curriculum reform movement in general and the Schools Council History Project in particular has been to redefine subject matter. The 'new view of history' evolved by the project has revolutionary implications for the classroom practice of history. For these implications to be confronted teachers require a great deal more support and guidance than it has so far been possible to offer.

Classrooms are enormously busy and fatiguing environments; in the absence of support and guidance at the level of *classroom activities* it is an understandable, indeed sensible, reaction to resist changing history lessons. Yet such resistance fundamentally subverts a new view of history aiming to replace 'factual transmission' with 'active learning'. To implement the new history, future strategies must therefore focus on ways of assisting and analysing the history teacher's efforts to reform classroom activities.

One strategy for 'bridging the gap' between new definitions and examinations and their classroom implementation has been developed by the Associated Examining Board over the past six years. The process of development began with a pilot project in the assessment of world history at 'O' Level. World history was chosen for three reasons: firstly because 'in an increasingly interdependent world, it gives the background and perspective necessary for an understanding of current problems from a global rather than a national or continental view'; secondly because 'there is ample evidence of its increasing popularity in both schools and colleges of further education'; and finally because 'it lends itself particularly well to a study of an essentially inter-disciplinary nature'.[26] I remain somewhat unconvinced by some of the Board's claims relating to the nature of historical content, but am mainly concerned with their strategies for changing assessment and teaching methods.

The assessment procedure perfected during the pilot project is now available as a public examination, the first pupils sitting for it in June 1976.[27] The examination is based upon a written paper derived from the teaching programmes submitted by the participating centres (50 per cent of the marks).

I want to focus on the strategy the Board devised to ensure that the project was correctly taught and examined. In contrast to the exhortation strategies previously described, the AEB sought to provide clear guidelines to teachers and candidates on how to undertake an individual history project. By clearly defining *and* rewarding each stage in this historical undertaking the strategy seeks to *ensure* that work is taught and undertaken in the manner desired.

The project is envisaged as a piece of work taking the student three or four months. Project titles need to be registered with the Board in December of the year prior to the terminal written examination, and the projects must be completed by 1st May. In terms of content the main requirement is that the project should be about the twentieth century and broadly related to the world perspective. Group projects can be submitted, but 'in such cases the individual contribution of each student must be clearly stated and worked'.[28] Similar titles can be submitted for individual projects, provided the treatment is distinctive.

In the assessment of the project the Board is concerned with three aspects which make up the total of 35 per cent: (i) the plan of campaign; (11 marks; 8 written, 3 oral); (ii) the execution with particular reference to the intensity of treatment (12 marks; 8 written, 4 oral); and (iii) the use of resources (12 marks; 8 written, 4 oral).

The Board envisages that any plan of campaign will contain three broad sections:

1. 'A list of statements and questions which the student has devised for his chosen topic':[29] the aim of this list is to reveal, both intrinsically and sequentially, the nature of the argument that the student subsequently develops as he completes his plan.
2. Related to this list will be notes and references to resources which the student judges to be relevant to his enquiries and to a proper communication of his ideas.
3. An outline or plan of 'the way in which the student plans to reveal his understanding of his subject to a wider audience and to communicate his findings'.[30]

The inevitably evolutionary nature of any piece of historical research is catered for in two ways. Firstly modifications to the original plan of campaign can be submitted. Secondly one of the major functions of the oral assessment is to clarify the extent to which students modify their original plans and the reasons for such modification:

Assessment would involve a discussion of how the student planned his research, the need for modification of his plan at various stages, how the work had been presented, and the reason why it had been relatively successful or unsuccessful. The Board is as much concerned, therefore, with the emergence of the plan in relation to the question 'does it work?' as it is with the polished final version.[31]

In the assessment of the execution of the project the Board has developed the notion of 'thresholds' through which to evaluate the students' intensity of treatment. A first threshold topic might be Migration or Revolution or Ideologies. Taking Ideologies as an instance, this might be broken down into sections on Fascism, Nazism, Marxism and Communism. These might be regarded as second threshold topics which themselves admit of further sub-division. The Board suggest that 'the teacher or teachers taking the course should be teaching to second threshold topics and that projects should develop from third threshold topics'.[32]

In practice the thresholds notion offers only a broad guideline and much of the judgement on intensity of treatment is inevitably specific to each individual project. Again the oral interview offers a method for closely monitoring the way in which students handle their projects' subject matter.

The final assessment on the students' use of resources was included to promote awareness and evaluation of primary and secondary historical sources. The Board notes that 'to answer this question satisfactorily the candidate must enquire, apply appropriate criteria, select or reject, and organise; functions which seem to be the essence of any enquiry-based study in depth'.[33]

The projects are assessed initially by the teachers following the guidelines given above. The marks are filled in on a sheet which details the sections and sub-sections for which marks are awarded. This assessment, together with a taped oral with the student is then moderated by the Board.

The importance of this project-based assessment strategy in facilitating changes in pedagogy remains at this stage inevitably conjectural. That the Board hoped such change would be encouraged was made clear both in the briefing conferences of the pilot project and in subsequent literature. About the assessment of individual projects it was recorded that:

It is hoped that throughout the course there will be a series of studies in depth and not merely a single terminal project. Indeed it would be possible to build the whole course around such a series, with the students working at times altogether, at other times in small groups, and at other times again on their own.[34]

In fact the Board's strategy moves beyond such hopeful statement and seeks to *ensure* that there are changes in classroom practice. By apportioning over a third of the marks to a project completed by the individual student the Board offers clear encouragement to the teacher to move away from his traditional history lesson. It would be impossible to teach this section of the syllabus through the normal 'chalk and talk' method of factual transmission. By focusing assessment on the procedures and idiosyncrasies of individual historical investigation, the Board ensures that 'active learning' and 'pupil participation' will be fully rewarded.

As well as the 'carrot' of examination rewards the Board's coherent guidelines aid the teacher in reforming his classroom practice. The way in which the project's assessment is broken down into categories and defined can be readily understood in terms of specific classroom work: drawing up plans of campaigns, lists of resources, bibliographies and similar activities. The assessment plan can be as readily understood as a plan for teaching about individual historical research.

From the student viewpoint the assessment procedure enables greater personal participation in the history lesson. The examination is potentially emancipatory in a number of ways: firstly, the students have a more or less free choice of a subject that they are interested in; secondly, project work is viewed in a broad way and can include cassettes of interviews, sets of documents, collages of photographs; thirdly, the oral breaks down the monopoly of the written work even further and allows the student to explain and justify his project. A final factor has been reported elsewhere:

Above all project work allowed the student in a limited sense to write his 'own' history, not simply to study that written by somebody else. Students were involved in a direct primary experience; they were not reading an impersonal secondary account.[35]

In the author's judgement this direct experience

far from dissuading students from reading history written by other people, made such an exercise so much more positive. Reading other people's history now became both a rewarding and frustrating experience, for the student now had his own set of insights into the nature of historical research.[36]

As an illustration an interview with a boy after reading a textbook on Britain and world affairs is recounted:

After reflecting on the magnitude of the task facing the author and the excellent way in which he had dealt with much of the materials, he said that textbooks were apt to be too general: 'they leave out the people, so that kind of history misses out the main things I want to know about. I mean, I've just been talking to this old boy who was wounded in the trenches — he even showed me his wounds. That's what I mean by history, that's when it clicks for me.' [37]

The AEB strategy then moves beyond the definition of a new examination and prescriptions of pedagogy and seeks to provide coherent guidelines for the teacher in reforming his history lessons. The strategy is concerned not only with the 'content' and 'materials' of the history lessons, but also with the *process* of history teaching.

The concern for *process* has been further developed by the Schools Council Project, *History, Geography and Social Science 8-13*. This project's strategy has been based on two fundamental ideas. Firstly, that 'No one set of materials can fulfil the differing needs of particular *teachers* teaching particular *children* in particular *schools* in particular *environments*'. Secondly, that 'the key to effective curriculum development lies not so much in the production of materials as in the thinking and planning carried out by the teachers themselves'.[38]

The concern for *process* rather than 'materials' is later articulated fully, and could be taken to include other externally-devised packages whether in the form of new examination modes or pedagogic strategies:

The need to support teachers is fully recognized; but this is not the same as providing kits of materials. At first, kits look like the answer to a teacher's prayer, because the people who produce them have time to hunt out the sources and to make the packs, just because they do not have to rush away to take the next lesson and then stand in for someone who is off with influenza. But in fact there is no real point in handing out materials unless teachers have thought their way towards how to use them, and there is no real point in producing materials just during the lifetime of a Project if they are to become out-of-date almost at once and then to disappear into obscurity. What is really needed is to start a *process* in which teachers have the time and facilities and circumstances in which they can think out their own schemes effectively and can work with other teachers in the making of the materials that *they* need. All that a Project can do is to point the way and start the process; its own output can only be fully helpful if it is set in this perspective.[39]

By stressing the teachers' roles, their ability to 'think out their own scheme', the project places 'teacher development' or, in their term, 'extended professionalism' at the centre of the reformist strategy. In the 'revaluation of the teachers' role':

The Project will need to provide some lead and support. However, the development of in-service education and the increasing recognition that teachers, like many others, need to 're-cycle' themselves more than once during a working lifetime . . . should help to ensure that this extended professionalism can be soundly based. One outcome of this development should be that teachers will assume, and will be able to assume, responsibility for maintaining the impetus of innovation within schools and between schools.[40]

The acknowledgement of the centrality of teacher development in curriculum reform has been for long overdue. As we have seen, the Schools Council History Project followed the general models of curriculum reform practised at the time. From an understanding of history, new materials and examinations were produced, new classroom practices, stressing pupil participation, prescribed. The journey from new understandings and definitions of history at central project level to their implementation by individual teachers in particular classrooms has been seldom completed. What was often missing alongside a new understanding of history was a new understanding of history teachers.

The supreme paradox of much of the recent curriculum reform movement was that in advocating more pupil participation in lessons so little consideration was given to teacher participation in implementing such changes. There is indeed little point in offering new materials or new definitions to history teachers unless, as Blyth noted, 'they have thought their way towards how to use them'. The reform of history lessons will only follow from the widespread participation of history teachers in this process of re-thinking. Only such individual re-thinking begins the process of reforming classroom practice, constituting the vital prerequisite that has so often been missing.

Once history teachers have begun to re-think their intentions and objectives the reform of history in the classroom becomes a possibility. The complex and varied nature of classroom practice and its reform has recently been elegantly elucidated by the work of the Ford Teaching Project.[41] Following an action-research mode the project personnel sought to understand and document the work of teachers concerned to implement Inquiry/Discovery methods in their classrooms. In seeking to understand such reforming attempts the research focused on the teachers' definitions of their situation and intentions. The problems encountered by the teachers are many and varied, the project lists forty categories. Further, the conceptual confusions and varied interpretations of those teachers, all of whom are convinced of the need for change, points up the inevitably individual and idiosyncratic nature of curriculum reform in practice.

New understandings can lead to a redefinition of history in theory. Only a strategy which envisages a central role for the classroom teacher in developing and analysing his work will change history in the classroom.

NOTES

1. Whitty, C., 'Studying Society', forthcoming in G. Whitty and M. F. D. Young, *Exploration in the Politics of School Knowledge*, Nafferton, 1977.
2. Goodson, I., 'The Teachers' Curriculum and the New Reformation', *Journal of Curriculum Studies*, Vol. 7, No. 2, November 1971, pp. 167-8.
3. Hoetker, J. and Ahlbrand, W. P., 'The Persistence of the Recitation', *American Educational Research Journal*, 6, 1969, p. 163.
4. Westbury, I., 'Conventional Classrooms, "Open" Classrooms and the Technology of Teaching', *Journal of Curriculum Studies*, Vol. 5, No. 2, November 1973, p. 100.
5. Booth, M., *History Betrayed*, Longmans, 1969, pp. 53-4.
6. Sylvester, D., 'First Views from the Bridge', *Teaching History*, Vol. III, No. 10, November 1973, p. 143.
7. Sylvester, D., *et al.*, *A New Look at History*, Schools Council Project publication, Holmes McDougall, 1976, p. 10.
8. ibid., p. 26.
9. Sylvester, D., op. cit., 1973, p. 145.
10. Sylvester, D., *et al.*, op. cit., p. 26.
11. Toulson, S., 'Down with 1066 and All That', *The Guardian*, 3 February 1976, p. 15.
12. Sylvester, D., op. cit., 1973, p. 145.
13. Sylvester, D., *et al.*, op. cit., p. 18.
14. ibid., p. 18. (N.B. each of the four units corresponds to a specific use but also bears a general relation to some of the other uses.)
15. ibid., pp. 36-7.
16. ibid., p. 8.
17. ibid., pp. 47-8.
18. Sylvester, D., op. cit., 1973, p. 143.
19. Sylvester, D., *et al.*, op. cit., p. 49.
20. Sylvester, D., op. cit., 1973, p. 143.
21. Lamont, W., 'The Uses and Abuses of Examinations' in M. Ballard (ed.), *New Movements in the Study and Teaching of History*, Temple Smith, 1971, p. 192.
22. Sylvester, D., *et al.*, op. cit., p. 28.
23. Sylvester, D., op. cit., 1973, p. 144.
24. Sylvester, D., *et al.*, op. cit., p. 22.
25. ibid., p. 25.
26. AEB Circular to Trial Schools, 1970.
27. AEB Syllabus VI 058.
28. AEB Syllabus Requirements, 1976.
29. ibid.
30. ibid.
31. ibid.
32. ibid.
33. ibid.

34. ibid.
35. Goodison, I., 'The AEB World History Project: One School's Experience', *Teaching History*, May 1975, Vol. IV, No. 13, pp. 18-23. The article draws on experiences of the teaching of AEB World History from 1970 to 1975.
36. ibid. This is not to claim that he was doing just the same things as a historian, but that what he *had* done provided some insight into what would be involved in doing those things.
37. ibid.
38. Blyth, W. A. L., *Spotlights: A Summary of the Project's Approach*, Schools Council, 1973, p. 3.
39. ibid., pp. 4-5.
40. ibid., p. 38.
41. Ford Teaching Project, Centre for Applied Research in Education, 1975.

4. The 'Language of History' and the Communication of Historical Knowledge

A. D. EDWARDS

INTRODUCTION

This chapter is mainly theoretical, an adjective which often connotes that 'one knows too little about the subject to say something practical'.[1] Such a cautious opening is properly realistic. Most classroom researchers have coded rather than recorded verbal interaction, and few descriptions of teaching include much transcript material. We therefore *know* little about the language teachers and pupils normally exchange, and even less about the distinctive forms and functions associated with transmitting particular bodies of academic knowledge. Since even the theory being offered comes from socio-linguistics and sociology, and not from the relatively well-mapped areas of psycholinguistics and Piagetian psychology, any applications of it to the teaching of a single subject may be dismissed as mere speculation.

There is a strong temptation, then, to move quickly to some apparently safe ground. One obvious strategy would be to refer to the extensive evidence of social class differences in language use, and so to identify any distinctive (or distinctively onerous) demands which that subject makes on working-class pupils. For example, it might be argued that the relative 'concreteness' of their language brings special difficulties when they confront historical analysis and high-level generalizations. This is the main approach adopted by Bernbaum in discussing language in history teaching.[2] Although he is following 'normal' scientific procedure in making specific applications of general theory, I believe the approach to be misleading in this context. By appearing to build on 'fact' it presents an unjustifiably firm diagnosis of what the 'problems' are; yet the evidence for pervasive and *cognitively significant* social class differences in language is open to such serious objections and conflicts of interpretation as to demand the greatest caution in arguing from what research has 'shown'.[3] Caution about its results should not detract, however, from the important questions that some of this research has raised, especially about the functions of language in certain typical (and 'critical') contexts of use and about the relationship between its forms and what it is being used to *do*.[4] In this chapter, I hope to show the value of such questions in considering what distinctive uses of language may be involved in the construction and communication of historical knowledge.

There is a frequently occurring paradox in discussions of the problems of teaching history. The subject is commonly described as lacking an extensive 'technical' language and so as perhaps the 'least mysterious' of disciplines, 'the least removed from common human experience'.[5] It might therefore seem to be unusually accessible to pupils who can apply their common-sense knowledge to the study of the past. Yet it is also commonly described as presenting unusual linguistic *difficulties*. In trying to resolve this paradox, I begin with the concept of 'register' and its applicability to subject-specific language. The more comprehensive notion of a 'special language' then directs attention to the dependence of form on function, and to the relationship between the heavy burden of abstractions supposedly facing the student of history and the peculiar nature of historical narrative. Such narrative depends not only on the *forms* of 'ordinary language', but on a back-cloth of everyday meanings that the historian (or history teacher) so takes for granted that they may not be mentioned at all. There is an obvious risk of confusion between the 'common sense' of then and now. This problem seems to raise critical questions about how pupils can proceed from a passive reception of 'historical knowledge' to an active participation in its construction.

1. SUBJECT-REGISTER: THE 'LANGUAGE OF' HISTORY

The term 'register' describes a set of linguistic features regularly associated with some situation or activity. It refers to 'style' *as explained by* the participants' sense of what constitutes appropriate usage in a particular context. Unfortunately, it is extremely difficult to identify the precise linguistic relevance of whatever social categories are included in the explanation, and so to mark the boundaries of a distinguishable stylistic entity by showing what features of linguistic choice can be seen as socially determined. References to the register of (for example) Parliamentary debate or sports' journalism may seem persuasive when supported by suitable examples, but such exampling often exaggerates the extent of their peculiarities. A thorough description of any register requires extensive sampling of typical usage, and the whole area of study is one in which 'theory would do well to wait for practical analysis to catch up'.[6]

Discussion of academic 'subject-registers' certainly lacks much foundation in 'practical analysis'. Studies of textbook usage have sometimes revealed unusual grammatical constructions or unusual frequencies of certain structures, but even in written exposition the main source of subject-differentiation is the proliferation of 'technical' terms in areas of special interest.[7] Such terms are likely to be reduced, 'diluted' or elaborated in spoken exposition. But we know very little about the verbal adjustments teachers make with pupils of different ages and levels of ability — for example, about the extent to which the 'language of' physics teachers is a modified or colloquialized version of the 'language of' physicists, or the extent to which they expect pupils to match or approach their own subject-specific usage. There is certain to be *some* specific usage. But intermittent lexical 'landmarks' may create an impression of pervasively esoteric language which systematic stylistic analysis would not justify.

To refer to the 'language of' an academic subject is therefore to use a metaphor with possibly misleading implications of purely *linguistic* distinctiveness. Nevertheless, even a thin topsoil of technical terms may have great importance from a wider perspective. Any 'special language' — criminal argot, schoolboy slang, occupational jargon — serves two main functions. It facilitates common action by providing words which have precise meanings for fellow-specialists, and it reinforces group feeling and group loyalty. This double function is apparent in the use of academic special languages. Some of the distinctive terms associated with a discipline can be seen as essential tools of the intellectual trade, discriminating between and classifying phenomena in ways which are not available (because they are not needed) in everyday or other academic language. But other terms may be seen as merely conventional usage — as verbal habits which do nothing to organize the world in new ways though they may well add a sense of mystery. Examples can be found in any discipline in which a conceptual nakedness is being covered with 'verbal substitutions masquerading as knowledge'.[8] Jargon may be defined as 'technical' language which is not strictly necessary.[9] Unfortunately, however, the smokescreen of jargon is more easily seen than penetrated because one man's unnecessary verbal 'substitution' is another man's necessary clarification. Nor is the apparently 'conventional' usage just intellectual lumber that the student picks up on his way. As he comes to employ it 'properly' — that is, in ways which his fellow-specialists can recognize and accept — so he reinforces his sense of belonging to that field of knowledge. If teachers' preoccupation with terminology often goes far beyond what is 'intellectually' necessary, it is because the common classroom game of 'hunt the label' is a potent way of marking boundaries between academic territories, and between school and everyday knowledge. By insisting on the 'right' word, the teacher is effectively saying, 'This is part of the reality we call (e.g. chemistry), and this is how we talk about it. For the next forty minutes, other forms of reality don't matter, and you must see things, and try to talk about them, in the appropriate way.'

This lengthy preamble provides a context for considering more closely history's supposed lack of a 'language' of its own, and the associated blurring of boundaries between 'historical' and other forms of knowledge. The 'intellectual' function of a subject-register is to provide the specialist with some distinctive forms of perception and categorization. Adapting Sapir's definition, its vocabulary represents 'a complex inventory of all the ideas, interests and occupations that take up the attention of the (academic) community'.[10] Now the historian cannot be denied 'interests and occupations' of his own. In discussing his lack of a special 'language' for expounding them, a clear distinction must be made between a vocabulary of names and a vocabulary of concepts, and between 'technical' and 'semi-technical' usage. His concern with the particularity of past events leads him to use a large vocabulary of proper names for that huge cast of characters and panorama of scenes which he must identify and label. A great deal of history teaching deals *in detail* with 'explaining what' and 'explaining who', and many of these explanations will be of *particular* persons, objects and events. Will not the relevant labels share one of the main advantages of 'technical' terminology in having relatively fixed and determinate meanings? There was, after all, only one explorer called Columbus, only one gadget called a flying shuttle, and only one Battle of Marston Moor, and there are reasonably well-established facts about each. But there is a *plurality* of facts about each. The apparently specific names are often condensations of many 'smaller' events, and when used at a certain point in a historical narrative they may 'index' very different details to those who encounter them. Thus a brief reference to Marston Moor may be intended to exemplify the new discipline of the Parliamentary army, while the listener remembers only the confusion of the battle's early stages. Of course, all technical terms involve abstractions which may on occasion be referred back to very different phenomena. But even the proper names in historical narrative tend to have a wide range of potential denotation; in the more dramatic episodes, they have powerful and diverse connotations too (the Black Death, the Peterloo Massacre, the Night of the Long Knives). Names may therefore summon up very different facts and images, and give a misleading impression of 'hardness'. This is especially so when, as with the Reichstag Fire, they index deep disagreements as to what is 'really' being referred to. Despite the historian's frequently alleged preoccupation with the unique, many of his names are overtly categorical. They draw together a number of narrative or biographical instances—the Scramble for Africa, the Little Englanders—and their frequent capital letters indicate their status as temporally limited generalizations. It is common, then, to make sense of individual events by treating them as examples of some underlying pattern.[11] The resulting labels may be very loosely and controversially related to their referents (the Renaissance, the Enlightenment and the New Imperialism are obvious examples), and so be subjected to frequent redefinition. Sometimes this looseness can be an advantage, in that a term like 'the American Revolution' may be used 'without committing oneself to a precise determination of what constitutes that event'.[12] Indeed, too much precision may bring the danger of reifying the label as a 'fact', and so excluding alternative interpretations.

These matters may seem to be of concern mainly to the professional historian. In fact, they touch on the 'indexicality' of historical terms in ways which will be the main theme of the rest of this chapter, where 'historian' will usually refer to both the writer *and* the teacher. For the moment, I want to consider some of the communicative problems which arise from the frequent indeterminacy of these terms—problems which are highlighted (and perhaps exaggerated) by comparison with the natural sciences. Such scientific labels as crustaceans, alkalis, or digestion and assimilation, are also abstractions from a range of phenomena, but they are likely to be defined with sufficient care to provide the student with a clearly delimited set of meanings to which the label will consistently refer. The teacher may well continue to check that the 'common' meanings appropriate to that stage in his students' development are being maintained. Now the history teacher too may ask questions like—'Who can tell me something about Magellan?'—without causing bewilderment at the sheer diversity of possible replies. He can do so if the 'relevant' facts have already been provided so as to constitute a very narrow frame of reference. At a higher level of generality, he is unlikely not to have clarified what he 'means by' the Eastern Question or the 'new unions'. But many of the apparently specific names he uses will have that wide range of denotation and connotation which make it far more likely than in the teaching of chemistry that he and his pupils will not be talking about the 'same things' at all. The large vocabulary of names required to identify and group 'past facts' is no guarantee, therefore, of a base-line of shared meanings.

This lengthy discussion of *names* is a variation on a much more common theme—that the historian lacks specifically 'historical' concepts with which to organize and explain his facts. Many of the concepts he does use are drawn from, or shared with, other disciplines. Many more are drawn from 'common sense'.[13] The following extract illustrates the point so nicely that it might have been constructed for the purpose (which it was not).

Teacher: What would you say a man like Turnip Townsend did to make sure that food was going to be on a much more productive level?
Pupil: He got rid of the fallow field.
T: He did, he eliminated—we use a rather posher word, Jane—he eliminated the fallow field. I get rid of people, I don't eliminate them, but he eliminated the fallow field. And in its place what did he think of? Sandra?
P: Clover.
T: Yes, how funny that you thought of that before the other one—
P: —and turnips.
T: Right, turnips—that was his *real* discovery. And why was that discovery so important?
P: Put goodness back into the soil.
T: It did, yes. And when you said that something like a turnip gives

goodness back into the soil — I mean, to some people goodness is cornflakes, to some people goodness is whisky. What sort of goodness? Ann?

P: Nitrogen.

T: Nitrogen, right. Nourishment in the form of nitrogen, so we said at the end of that particular year the soil was even better and ready to respond to a crop that might be taking nourishment out of it.[14]

Only the name of the agricultural innovator could be seen as specific to the teaching of history, and the main 'organizing concept' is clearly borrowed. The frequent abstractions in this teacher's exposition also illustrate another frequently identified communicative problem, one of several levels of linguistic difficulty which the subject is said to present.[15] Firstly, most of the key terms in historical narrative are not esoteric but are part of 'normal educated usage'. Despite the basic problems of comprehension which some pupils may experience, they are much less likely to be *taught* than are similarly salient terms in other subjects. Pupils are therefore unusually dependent on the language they 'bring with them'. Secondly, the prevalence of abstractions like 'trade', 'transport', 'revolution' and so on raise not only general linguistic difficulties but the danger that they are so detached from any context in 'real' (past) life that pupils may read in their own everyday meanings in ways which destroy their *historical* understanding. Finally, even where pupils are prepared for some changes in meaning, they may be insufficiently instructed in the *particular* significance of a word like 'reform' in the period they are currently studying. The historian's use of such terms can be described as 'semi-technical' in that their 'standard' meanings are overlaid, or even replaced, by something more specific.

The professional historian is likely to be highly sensitive to the embedding of meaning in the contexts in which words are used. He is accustomed to treat his documentary sources as coded messages, accessible to the extent that he can identify at least part of what his 'coder' took for granted. Indeed, he may treat items of conventional usage in his period as evidence of group loyalties and affiliations, and 'locate' an individual politically or in other ways 'by ascertaining what words his functioning vocabulary contains, and what nuances of meaning and value they embody'.[16] The variability of meanings is recognized by the history teacher who makes explicit what a 'factory' was in the territories of the East India Company, or why 'enthusiast' was a term of rebuke in eighteenth-century religious argument. But he will not always be sensitive to the peculiar ways in which he uses words like 'land' (the church 'lands' confiscated by Henry VIII) and 'field' (the three-field system), or to the anachronistic associations the word 'king' may have for many of his pupils when he is describing George III, or to the frequently changing content of words like 'liberal', 'progress' and 'imperialism'. It is terms like these which cause the greatest problems, either because they are assumed to be part of pupils' general knowledge (and so to need no teaching at all) or because the teacher acts as though their context-specific meaning will simply be picked up as he goes along.

There is a further, more fundamental source of possible confusion, touched on in the earlier reference to the historian's reliance on common-sense knowledge. However exotic the characters and incidents in his story, he usually *connects* his facts in familiar ways, trading on what his listeners or readers know 'about life'. His standards of intelligibility are largely those of everyday life. Before considering in some detail the 'ordinariness' of historical knowledge, I want to approach its lack of 'mystery' from another direction. Perhaps the main linguistic difficulty associated with history as a school subject is its supposedly heavy burden of abstractions.[17] Even the 'outside' of historical events is not open to direct inspection, their tangible remains are largely aids to the sluggish imagination, and historical exposition is an attempt to summon into existence with words some image of past conditions and actions. It is because of the subject's 'literary' character that Bernbaum sees a particular relevance for history in research into social class differences in language, research which has tended to typify lower working-class children as unable, or at least unaccustomed, to cope with matters far removed from their immediate experience.[18] One of Jane Austen's characters expressed her surprise at the dullness of history 'when so much of it must be invention'. Is the assumption of abstractness surprising when so much of it is 'story'? This question will be approached from the functional perspective mentioned earlier. If language is as it is because of what it is used to do, discussion of the forms of historical narrative requires some brief discussion of its functions.

2. THE 'ABSTRACTNESS' OF HISTORICAL NARRATIVE

Critics of the 'myth' of verbal deprivation deny that the use of non-standard language has any dire cognitive consequences, or that differences in form can be equated with different modes (or levels) of thought. They see the 'abstractness' and 'formality' of so much classroom language as merely stylistic, and the exclusion of less 'standard' and personalized forms of expression as erecting unnecessary barriers between lower-class pupils and classroom knowledge.[19]

The argument has some points in common with recent attacks on 'history from above', in which most historical accounts are seen as being constructed from the vantage point of those who run the lives of others. An emphasis on social history is not an easy remedy because here too things may be seen from 'head office'. 'The magistrate's clerk, or the police officer, guides the researcher on his journey into crime, the senior partner leads him by the arm when he looks at business, the temperance advocate leads him in and out of the pubs.'[20] Where the researcher has gone, textbook writer and teacher follow. Much of the content of history is thereby removed from 'the central concerns of people's lives', and it is transmitted in a form alien to those 'outside the quarantine of formal education'.[21]

Applied either to the writing or the teaching of history, there are several strands in this argument which must be disentangled. Where eye-witness accounts are used to heighten a sense of the reality of the past, those most readily available are often of the great scenes and by the star players. The forms of expression are then the forms appropriate to public (even 'heroic') occasions; avoiding the colloquialisms of more intimate interaction, they represent talk 'as performance'. The silent majority rarely find a voice at all and so the narrative 'proceeds on two levels: out in front, the great scenes; behind, the vast anonymity of all the rest of the living and acting and dying'.[22] The recent prominence of oral history is partly explained by a determination to 'recover the experience of the oppressed' *in their own words*, in ways often impossible with the written sources of earlier periods, and so make this experience more accessible to those outside the educational 'quarantine'. But these accounts are still the raw material of history. While the historian may wish to present whatever 'humble' witnesses he can find, he rarely leaves their words, plain and unedited, to 'tell their own story'. He will comment, interpret and sometimes 'correct' what they say, and he will certainly *select* extracts which fit his narrative purpose. The kind of language in which he presents his narrative depends very little on what it is about, or on the rarified nature of the sources; it depends very much on what he is *doing* in the course of it.

Historical accounts are attempts to provide a 'significant' or 'followable' narrative rather than a mere chronicle of events.[23] At their best, they convey some sense of what it was like to be 'there', they elicit some sympathy with the characters, and like any story they create and maintain a wish to know what happened next. These are surely the aims of the history teacher. He will wish to produce some awareness 'that there was once a time when it was not history. It was experience shared by living people. . . Upon these happenings the historians write their gloss, but the first thing is that they happened, and for us the first thing is that they happen again, in our imaginations. Before we interpret, we experience. . . .'[24] If, in his 'stories', the teacher conveys this sense of the reality of the past, he will escape Harold Rosen's strictures on the aridity of most textbook language (and, by implication, much classroom language), which is described as 'language at the apex of a pyramid of experience'. In all its pale abstractions, the flesh and blood of human experience is likely to have drained away.[25] If the history teacher wishes his pupils to 'see' past events in their mind's eye, he must allow them sometimes to descend to the lower levels of the pyramid. He will want them to have some sense of those events 'as lived at life-rate' — that is, as occurring in situations where the outcomes still seem uncertain and decisions have to be made.[26] If the 'story' disappears too soon or too completely into analysis of factors and causes, then a position towards the apex of the pyramid will be realized in an appropriately abstract style.

The preceding paragraph may imply a distinction between 'stories' and other kinds of historical account which is altogether too sharp. Some form of narrative is undoubtedly the staple diet in school history. But there are many varieties of 'story', none of which simply tells a tale. To identify ascending levels of abstraction from narrative through explanation to generalization would be to distort what historical exposition normally does. For the historian does not set out the 'facts' and then explain them. Those facts he considers relevant are selected, presented and grouped together in ways inseparable from his interpretation of them. He is not 're-presenting' past events, but mediating betwen them and his audience, shaping them in some way.[27] As Passmore observes, he defines 'explanation' almost as liberally as the man-in-the-street.[28] He undoubtedly explains *why* (for example) the Saxons lost at Hastings. He also explains *how* Rome was supplied with water, *that* French peasants were subject to the corvée, and *what* the Schlieffen Plan was. His explicit explanations 'why' often occur at points in a narrative where confusion is likely, and they 'get us moving again' towards the climax of the story.[29] My examples of other forms of 'explanation' are of particular facts, and suggest 'concreteness' rather than 'abstraction'. It may indeed be true that 'historians are men for whom a mass of apparently unique facts still offers certain undeniable delights'.[30] But as was argued earlier, he is often engaged in categorization, describing particular events in detail in order to show what was generally true at the time. Guides to the practice of history teaching often emphasize the need to 'build up to' such generalizations from concrete instances. The advice is important because of the besetting danger that the abstractions float away entirely from any grounding in what real people said and did. But generalizations are rarely the explicit goal of historical exposition. They are often there 'by default', when there is no time for detail or where the instance we *do* know something about is used to highlight the larger story or to 'stand for' evidence not yet available.[31] Historical narratives often contain a great deal of generalized description 'grounded' on single or scattered concrete instances, and they often swing to and fro between the general and the particular. The following textbook example itself 'instances' a common tendency:

> Cuba was among the last relics of Spain's great colonial empire. Spanish rule in the islands was oppressive, and there had been revolts before the serious outbreak of 1895. American sympathy for the Cubans was heightened by vivid press reports of atrocities inflicted on them, and by heavy American investment in the island's sugar industry. Republican leaders in 1896 proclaimed their 'deep and abiding interest in the heroic battles of the Cuban patriots against the cruelty and oppression', and called for American intervention. In 1898, the American battleship *Maine* was mysteriously blown up in Havana harbour, and Spanish apologies and concessions broke in vain against a growing war fever. In a 'splendid little war', marred only by the incompetent organizing of supplies for the American forces, two Spanish fleets were destroyed in battles in the Philippines and in Cuban waters. . . .[32]

I suggest, then, that most historical narrative, whether spoken or written, will be quite high on Moffett's 'scale of abstraction', a scale which runs from 'recording' at one end to 'theorizing' at the other.[33] A 'record' is a running-commentary on events as they happen. The historian's witnesses are likely to be people who *'saw* it happen', and who have had time since to organize their recollections *and* to offer their interpretations. This is what Moffett calls 'reporting'. His third level is that of 'generalizing' about classes of object, person or event. I have argued that it may be particularly difficult in history to separate the 'report' from the 'generalization'. I want to return now to one aspect of the inseparability of narrative from explanation — the historian's reliance on what might be called common-sense theorizing.

In telling the best story he can, the historian will be making connections between events which inevitably carry some explanation of them. An intelligible account is one that relies on explicit or on *implicit* and *familiar* connections, and deep philosophical pitfalls lie beneath 'the deceptive smoothness of historical prose'.[34] Stuart Hughes argues that this smoothness is deceptive when it is a 'literary' achievement rather than a demonstration of 'real' connections — when the story seems to 'flow' because the gaps in it are concealed. His point can be restated in a form outlined earlier. Historical narrative is so reliant on 'ordinary' language that it can often create the illusion of coherence and intelligibility because so much about the intentions of the actors and the 'meaning' of their actions is simply taken for granted. 'It is the language of ordinary experience that the historian speaks, and this is the language of continua.'[35] Continuity is often provided by implicit reference to common-sense knowledge of what the world and human behaviour are like.[36] But since the historian is concerned with 'ordinary then', how is he to guard against the intrusion of 'ordinary *now*'?

3. 'HISTORICAL' AND 'EVERYDAY' KNOWLEDGE

The technical vocabulary of a discipline often throws a convenient cloak of mystery over its activities, but its 'intellectual' function is to establish distinctive forms of perception and categorization. The specialist acquires 'a set of coloured spectacles' through which he sees 'a world of objects that are technically tinted and patternized'.[37] Lacking more than the fragments of a special conceptual language, what does the historian see that differentiates his perceptions from those of the layman? Carl Becker's famous answer to that question was that he saw very little since Everyman was himself a historian, frequently involved in offering narratives of past actions and accounting for the intentions of the actors.[38] The logic of this position is that little can be said about historical explanations that cannot be said about explanations in everyday life; they are 'common-sense applied to the study of past human actions'.[39] The linguistic implication of this position is that since ordinary language provides 'a marvellous and efficient rhetoric entirely adequate for historical discourse', then the historian has no need of a 'special language' of his own and is not entitled to take refuge in one.[40]

Though I have indicated some of the communicative problems that arise from it, I have considerable sympathy with this blurring of knowledge boundaries. But as Hexter clearly recognizes, matters are greatly complicated by wide variations in that 'common human experience' on which he bases his subject. The maxims of common-sense psychology could only be consistently applied to the past if it were true, as Hume suggested, that 'in all nations and ages . . . human nature still remains the same' and that 'the same motives always produce the same actions'.[41] Since this is not true by any useful definition of 'sameness', historical knowledge may not replace common sense but it must often transcend (or extend) the common sense of here-and-now. I want to consider this 'transcendence' more closely because of its implications for teaching history in other ways than by direct exposition of the past.

Social scientists sometimes lament (and sometimes rejoice in) their lack of a 'neutral data-language', a means of 'pure' description uncontaminated by 'metaphysical commitments and non-empirical imputations'.[42] The historian confronts this 'problem' in intensified form because his dependence on ordinary language will fill his accounts with the categorizations and value-judgements of his own time. Now his aim is to be 'true' to the past without becoming its 'accomplice', to 'penetrate' and yet 'rise above' it.[43] Thus he records 'explanations' of events in terms of witchcraft or divine intervention if that is how people saw things at the time, and then goes on to provide alternative explanations more intelligible to his contemporaries. This is an easy example. Yet it is often difficult to combine insight and detachment. 'Unconscious localisms' may impede the historian's understanding. For example, he may find it difficult to take seriously public justifications for past actions which, however much part of the 'motivational currency' of that time, he would dismiss in his own life as hypocrisy or rationalization; and he may find it hard to maintain consistently as a key element in his analysis a 'world-view' with which he is totally out of sympathy.[44] Hexter describes the historian's own view of life as a 'second record' on which to draw, a store of knowledge less systematic than that which he gathers from his sources but still invaluable as a source of *insights* — that is, as suggesting possible lines of enquiry and as sensitizing him to how his actors *might* have seen their situation. But he cannot *validate* his conclusions by referring to what he understands people to be like or to some mysterious empathy. If he often has recourse to his imagination to fill in some of the gaps in what his authorities tell him, it is his *historical* imagination which must be brought into play — his awareness of what things were like at *that* time. Indeed, Hexter defines as the humanizing function of history that it should 'liberate Everyman from the constricting limits of the common-sense of here-and-now'.[45]

This discussion may again seem relevant mainly to the task of the professional historian. Yet it raises in more general form a problem touched on earlier — that history's unusual reliance on ordinary language leaves pupils unusually dependent on the language they bring with them. This *may* be a source of social class differences in the difficulty of the subject if some version of 'deficit theory' is accepted—especially, for purposes of the present argument, if working-class children are typified as relatively less able to take the role of others in contexts far removed from their own experience. However, it is the general problem that concerns me here. Hexter's high regard for the 'second record' might imply that the more varied has been the historian's own life, the 'better' (more sensitive, insightful) his work will be. This would greatly exaggerate the importance of *direct* experience of what he describes, and underestimate the obvious possibility of extending appreciation of human diversity vicariously—through literature, for example, or through reading more history. But it could be argued that it takes time, and a certain stage of cognitive development, before children acquire a wide appreciation of beliefs and behaviour very different from those encountered in their daily life. Thus they may find it much harder to enter imaginatively into the position of a slave-owner than into that of a slave because to do the former requires 'a much longer experience of human nature and its motivational forces'.[46] Children will have had considerable experience of submission to authority, but very little of being *in* authority. They will presumably not find it easy to appreciate a view of human life as readily expendable in the pursuit of profit. However 'democratic' his approach to problems more accessible to their common sense, the teacher may feel it necessary on this occasion to 'talk' his pupils into some understanding of a frame of reference only faintly related to their own.

The potential gulf between the meanings of 'then' and 'now' is vividly illustrated in a recent account of using improvised drama in history teaching. One of the improvisations involved a deputation of early nineteenth-century farm labourers to the 'big house'. The 'labourers' displayed a truculence so thoroughly modern that several lessons were devoted to extending pupils' notions of 'deference' and 'authority' so that a more *historically-situated* performance became possible.[47] It is certainly important to give children time to collect the 'resources' they bring to such acting out of past situations—resources which include 'some facts, some feelings, some gestures, some objects'. But the sheer pace of the improvisation, requiring instant recognition of (and response to) the actions of others, makes it likely that pupils will often 'fill-in' the meanings of those actions from their everyday knowledge. If the teacher's concern is with history as well as drama, he will need to 'ground' the action in some facts about what *that* situation would have been like. Too many facts will stifle the drama; too few, and the *historical* imagination will collapse from ignorance. As in more conventional lessons, he will often have to indicate that 'they didn't have those things (or know that, or behave like that) in those days'.

I have argued that any historical narrative trades on connections between events which are not explicitly supplied but which the reader or listener 'fills in'. The danger that he will do so inappropriately is reduced by providing sufficient detail for him to 'reconstruct' the salient ingredients of the situation and so recognize its particular 'logic'. Perhaps the main problem in communicating historical knowledge in schools is that the frequent lack of detail drives pupils to combine the few historical facts they have been offered with their much larger store of a historical common sense. It is not the combination as such which is dangerous — I have no wish to revive that sharp separation of historical from everyday knowledge which was rejected earlier — but the possible imbalance between them. I want to conclude this paper by elaborating the point with reference to two highly influential orientations in recent sociology.

Garfinkel uses the term 'documentary method' to describe how participants in everyday conversation regard what is actually said as the 'document' of some underlying pattern of meaning. What is said is therefore 'only a sketchy, partial, incomplete, masked, elliptical, concealed, ambiguous or misleading' version of what is 'really' being talked about.[48] Historical documents can also be regarded in this way. The more steeped in his period the historian is, the more easily he will recognize those background meanings which are not put into words because they are simply taken for granted. But when he constructs his own narrative, he must 'bring out' and make explicit much of that 'masked, elliptical' background if his audience is to understand what he is 'talking about'. This notion of a 'back-cloth of shared meanings' is fundamental to Bernstein's distinction between elaborated and restricted codes. Because what is said is *always* an incomplete version of what is being talked about, the codes refer to a continuum and not to a dichotomy, and what Bernstein has done is to examine the *extent* to which speakers rely on their listeners filling in appropriately what is left unsaid. Elaborated codes regulate speech which is relatively explicit because the speaker recognizes some gulf between himself and his listeners which he must 'cross' with words.[49]

In history lessons, this gulf appears when the everyday knowledge on which the subject so largely depends has to be 'transcended' so as to clarify *differences* between 'then' and 'now'. This seems to me to call for some redefinition of the three broad categories of teacher-questions so suggestively outlined by Barnes, and especially of the 'openness' of historical knowledge.[50] In what he calls the 'instructional' context, Bernstein associates elaborated codes with an active, exploratory mode of enquiry in which the learner 'makes' his own meanings. Now history may be taught in this way. It may also be taught as so many facts to be learned, as a firm record of events which happened 'like that' and for reasons in which the teacher has (or pretends) confidence, and there will then be a predominance of 'closed' questions which simply invite the recall of information already provided. The answers to such questions will tend to be brief. The pupil need only indicate his awareness of the 'relevant' information for the teacher to assume his possession of the rest. In Garfinkel's terms, his answer is taken as a 'document' of an underlying body of knowledge. In Bernstein's terms, the pupil's contribution is in a restricted code in so far as the teacher assumes a backcloth of shared meanings to which implicit reference is being made. 'To ask children to tell each other or the teacher things which they know about already simply invites inadequate accounts because detailed and explicit ones are not necessary, and the children know they are not.'[51] In history lessons, the accounts will be especially inadequate if the intrusion of present-day meanings into past events is not brought into the open. In short, the teacher cannot 'talk' pupils into an understanding of past events without giving them many opportunities to talk back and so reveal that possible gulf between the everyday knowledge of then and now. 'Pseudo-open' questions are no help either. These occur when the apparent openings for alternative responses are quickly closed off by the teacher's unwillingness to accept those that deviate from a predetermined answer ('Yes, but that's not what I had in mind'). They are like 'closed' questions in generating triadic sequences of teacher-pupil-teacher, in which the teacher comments on, expands or evaluates each response as his pupils proceed through some tightly-structured content. They also make it unlikely that the teacher will 'hear' the intrusion of present-day meanings because he is so intent on selecting out whatever part of an answer he can use.[52]

History might seem to offer unusual scope for that third category of 'open' questions. It is, after all, 'a damn dim candle over a damn dark abyss'.[53] There are innumerable questions to which it is impossible to give authoritative answers, or on which contradictory evidence can readily be provided. The teacher then becomes an expert in the process of enquiry rather than a source of right answers.[54] His questions allow pupils much more control over how the problem confronting them is to be defined, and over what are to count as revelant contributions to its solution. This is the theme of Barnes' recent work on classroom communication, in which he argues the need for children to 'recode' new knowledge by talking (or writing) it into some meaningful relationship with what they know already. In a persuasive illustration of the dependence of form on function, Barnes suggests that the resulting 'exploratory' talk is likely to be more complex, tentative *and* explicit than when pupils make a public 'presentation' of remembered 'facts'. Nothing in his analysis would support the idea of 'leaving pupils to it'. What he is arguing is an integration of 'school knowledge' and 'action' (or everyday) knowledge so that pupils 'grasp the pattern of events which they are witnessing by interpreting them through analogous patterns which they are familiar with'.[55] While accepting the argument in principle, I would only emphasize again that the analogies must 'fit'. Identifying what was the thing to do, or what was 'on', in some past situation, may require detailed information about the particular circumstances if pupils are not be be baffled either by the apparent *range* of possibilities or by the meaninglessness of *any* of them. As Lee suggests, the minimal descriptions so often offered in history lessons make too many assumptions about children's *general* knowledge about how people behave.[56] They also make it likely that pupils will fail to appreciate the lack of 'fit' between that knowledge and the situation to which it is applied. Studying fewer past events in greater detail is therefore a necessary condition for 'explorations' which build on the 'ordinariness' of historical accounts without simply reading the present backwards. Such explorations may also bring out for conscious inspection some of that taken-for-granted knowledge on which present-day life is based. In Gallie's phrase,[57] to tackle a problem historically is to 'receive a lesson in liberation from provincial brashness'. The common sense of here-and-now is 'transcended' but not replaced.

NOTES

1. Dell Hymes, 'On Communicative Competence' in J. Pride and J. Holmes (eds.), *Sociolinguistics*, Penguin 1972, p. 269. Whatever clarity my own chapter may have as 'theory' owes much to the criticisms of those who read one of its several drafts. I am grateful to David Aspin, Keith Drake, Viv Furlong, David Hargreaves, Christopher Portal, and especially Peter Lee.

2. Bernbaum, G., 'Language and History Teaching' in W. Burston and C. Green (eds.), *Handbook for History Teachers*, Methuen, 2nd Edition, 1972. Bernbaum's main references are to American research on 'verbal deprivation', and to the work of Bernstein and his associates which he describes (p. 43) as having 'confirmed the existence of the distinctive (linguistic) codes and their association with social class'.

3. For a review of the evidence and of the controversies surrounding it, see Edwards, A., *Language in Culture and Class*, Heinemann, 1976, chapters 3 and 4: also Cazden, C., *Child Language and Education*, Holt, Rinehart & Winston, 1972; and Trudgill, P., *Accent, Dialect and the School*, Arnold, 1975.

4. The implicit reference here is to Bernstein's theory of socio-linguistic codes. For an elaboration of the argument (closely related to Bernstein's) that 'language is as it is because of what it is used to do', see Halliday, M., *Explorations in the Functions of Language*, Arnold, 1973.

5. Hexter, J., *The History Primer*, Basic Books, 1971, p. 77. The same point is made, in similar form, in Swabey, M., *The Judgment of History*, The Philosophical Library, New York, 1954, p. 33. There is a more general discussion of the 'ordinariness' of historical discourse in Demos, R., 'The Language of History' in R. Nash (ed.), *Ideas of History*, Vol. 2, Dutton, 1969, pp. 279-98.

6. Crystal, D. and Davy, D., *Investigating English Style*, Longmans, 1969, p. 62. The 'slipperiness' of register as an area of enquiry is emphasized by Davies, A., 'Some Problems in the Use of Language Varieties in Teaching', *Educational Review*, 20, 1968, pp. 107-122.

7. Barber, B., 'Some Measurable Characteristics of Modern Scientific Prose' in F. Behre (ed.), *Contributions to English Syntax and Phonology*, Gothenburg University Press, 1962; Davies, A., 'The Notion of Register', *Educational Review*, 22, 1969, pp. 64-77.

8. Andreski, S., *Social Science as Sorcery*, Penguin, 1974, p. 58. J. K. Galbraith offers a cautious justification for the 'language of economics' in Chapter 2 of his essays *Economics, Peace and Laughter*, Penguin, 1975. There is an extended discussion of the distinction between 'linguistic-intellectual' and 'linguistic-conventional' subject-usage in Barnes, D. *et al.*, *Language, the Learner and the School*, Penguin, 1969, pp. 46-76.

9. There is a vivid example of this distinction in Robert Merton's defence of his newly-minted terms 'manifest' and 'latent' functions. If these did not help the sociologist towards more systematic observation and analysis of cultural items, they would rightly be rejected as 'an offence against common intelligibility' — Merton, R., *Social Theory and Social Structure*, Free Press, 1957, p. 61.

10. Mandelbaum, D. (ed.), *Selected Writings of Edward Sapir in Language, Culture and Personality*, University of California Press, 1949, pp. 91-2.

11. Dray regards this as a frequent and entirely respectable form of historical explanation — Dray, W., '"Explaining what" in History' in P. Gardiner (ed.), *Theories of History*, Free Press, 1959, pp. 403-08. See also Joynt, C., and Rescher, N., 'The Problem of Uniqueness in History', *History and Theory*, 1, 1961, pp. 150-62.

12. Stolnaker, R., 'Events, Periods and Institutions in Historians' Language', *History and Theory*, 6, 1967, pp. 159-178.

13. White, M., 'Historical Explanation' in P. Gardiner, op. cit., pp. 357-73. See also Paluch, S., 'The Specificity of Historical Language', *History and Theory*, 7, 1968, pp. 76-82.

14. I am grateful to Mrs Sheila Taylor for this transcript.

15. Bernbaum, G., 'Language and History Teaching', op. cit.; the approach is even more prominent in Bernbaum's contribution, under the same title, to the first (1962) edition of the *Handbook for History Teachers*. See also Burston, W., *Principles of History Teaching*, Methuen, 1963, pp. 58-9.

16. Wright Mills, C., 'Language, Logic and Culture', *American Sociological Review*, 4, 1939, pp. 670-80; reprinted in his collected essays, *Power, Politics and People,* Oxford University Press, 1963. There is an interesting use of self-labels as evidence of the spread of revolutionary feeling among the American colonists in Merritt, R., 'The Emergence of American Nationalism: A Quantitative Approach' in S. Lipset and R. Hofstadter (eds.), *Sociology and History: Methods*, Basic Books, 1968. See also Berkhofer, R., *A Behavioural Approach to Historical Analysis*, Free Press, 1969, pp. 146-54; and Vansima, J., *Oral Tradition: A Study in Historical Methodology*, trans. H. M. Wright, Routledge and Kegan Paul, 1965.

17. Gosden, P. and Sylvester, D., *History for the Average Child*, Blackwell, 1968, advise teachers to concentrate on particular issues and specific examples and to avoid generalities (pp. 45-7). The 'burden' of abstractions is emphasized by Burston, W., op. cit., pp. 57-8 and by Coltham, J., *The Development of Thinking and the Learning of History*, Historical Association, 1971.

18. Bernbaum, G., op. cit., pp. 41-3. For examples of the evidence to which he refers, see Deutsch, M., 'The Role of Social Class in Language Development and Cognition', *American Journal of Orthopsychiatry*, 35, 1965, pp. 78-88; and Hess, R. and Shipman, V., 'Early Experience and the Socialisation of Cognitive Modes in Children', *Child Development*, 36, 1965, pp. 869-86. Though his argument is more subtle than this, such typifications are prominent in Bernstein's early papers, and in Lawton, D., *Social Class, Language and Education*, Routledge and Kegan Paul, 1968.

19. See especially Houston, S., 'A Re-Examination of Some Assumptions about the Language of Disadvantaged Children', *Child Development*, 41, 1970, pp. 947-63. The defence of *non*-standard language is well represented in Williams, F. (ed.), *Language and Poverty*, Markham, 1971.

20. Samuel, R. (ed.), *Village Life and Labour*, History Workshop Series, Routledge and Kegan Paul, 1975, p. xv.

21. The 'editorial collective's' introduction to *History Workshop: A Journal of Socialist Historians,* Issue 1, Spring 1976.

22. Stuart Hughes, H., *History as Art and as Science*, Harper and Row, 1964, pp. 62-3.

23. The first adjective is used and elaborated by Walsh, W., *An Introduction to Philosophy of History*, Hutchinson, 1951, pp. 17 and 31-3. The second is used by Gallie, W., *Philosophy and the Historical Understanding*, Chatto and Windus, 1964, Chapters 2-4.

24. Hales, E., 'Foreword' to W. Hassall (ed.), *They Saw it Happen: An Anthology of Eye-witnesses' Accounts of Events in British History 55 B.C.-A.D. 1485*, Blackwell, 1957.

25. Rosen, H., 'The Language of Text-books' in J. Britton, *Talking and Writing*, Methuen, 1967.

26. Fines, J., 'The Narrative Approach', *Teaching History*, 4, 14, 1975, pp. 97-104. Dilthey argued that history, like literature, made possible the experience of 'reliving' events in the order in which they occurred — Dilthey, W., 'The Understanding of Other Persons and their Life-Expressions' in P. Gardiner (ed.), op. cit., pp. 220-1.

27. Hernadi, P., 'Re-Presenting the Past: A Note on Narrative Historiography and Historical Drama', *History and Theory*, 15, 1976, pp. 45-51. The literary qualities of historical narrative are emphasized by Peter Gay, *Style in History*, Cape, 1975. That narrative is *already* explanation is argued by (for example) Gallie, W., op. cit., Chapter 4; Danto, A., *Analytical Philosophy of History*, Cambridge University Press, 1965, especially Chapters 7-8 and 11; Louch, A., 'History as Narrative', *History and Theory*, 8, 1969, pp. 54-70.

28. Passmore, J., 'Explanation in Everyday Life, in Science and in History', *History and Theory*, 2, 1962, pp. 105-23.

29. Passmore, J., op. cit., p. 108. The 'ancillary' function of *explicit* explanations in clearing up confusions in the narrative is argued by W. Gallie, op. cit., pp. 105-7.

30. Hofstadter, R., 'History and Sociology in the United States' in S. Lipset and R. Hofstadter (eds.), op. cit., p. 12.

31. This is what Gallie (op. cit., p. 80) describes as using a 'dummy variable' to indicate something that cannot yet be specified. The use of single incidents to 'illustrate' some larger development can suggest 'hard' evidence in the way Glaser and Strauss call 'exampling' — that is, the researcher has an 'idea', finds or selects examples for their confirming power, and so gives 'the image of a proof': Glaser, B. and Strauss, A., *The Discovery of Grounded Theory*, Aldine Press, 1967, p. 5.

32. Edwards, A. and Bearman, G., *Britain, Europe and the World 1848-1918*, Cambridge University Press, 1971; repub. Heinemann, 1975, pp. 280-1.

33. Moffett, J., *Teaching the Universe of Discourse*, Houghton-Mifflin, 1968.

34. Stuart Hughes, H., op. cit., p. 5.

35. Louch, A., 'History as Narrative', *History and Theory*, 8, 1969, p. 60.

36. Peter Gay (op. cit.) suggests that while the historian does not 'produce' general laws, he regularly 'consumes' them, and that the most valuable source of such laws is psychology. For an extension of this view see Berkhofer, R., *A Behavioral Approach to Historical Analysis*, op. cit., especially Chapters 2-3. The borrowing is rarely as systematic as this approach suggests, the 'maxims of commonsense psychology' being the main source of general explanations.

37. Wright Mills, C., 'Language, Logic and Culture', op. cit., p. 459.

38. Becker, C., 'Everyman His Own Historian' in *American Historical Review*, 37, 1932, pp. 221-36; also in R. Winks (ed.), *The Historian as Detective: Essays on Evidence*, Harper and Row, 1968.

39. Paluch, S., 'The Specificity of Historical Language', *History and Theory*, 7, 1968, p. 82. See also Passmore, J., op. cit.

40. Hexter, J., *The History Primer*, op. cit., p. 55.

41. Quoted in Swabey, M., *The Judgment of History*, op. cit., p. 8.

42. Llewelyn Gross (ed.), *Symposium on Sociological Theory*, Harper and Row, 1967, pp. 51-2. See also Dixon, K., *Sociological Theory: Pretence and Possibility*, Routledge and Kegan Paul, 1973, pp. 1-16. For a useful discussion of the inevitability of 'Moral Judgments in History and History Teaching', see the chapter by Low-Beer, A. in W. Burston and D. Thompson (eds.), *Studies in the Nature and Teaching of History*, Routledge and Kegan Paul, 1967.

43. Gay, P., op. cit., p. 215; Swabey, M., op. cit., p. 15.

44. There is a penetrating analysis of 'motivational currency' in Wright Mills, C., 'Vocabularies of Motive', in *Power, Politics and People*, op. cit. These 'vocabularies' are the moral categories by means of which actions are 'normally' described, elicited and

justified. Mills comments on the predominance of pecuniary and sexual motives in twentieth-century America, and the consequent difficulty of taking (e.g.) religious motives seriously. Some historians have found similar difficulty with the religious motives of combatants in the Civil War. I would agree with Peter Lee, 'Explanation and Understanding in History' (in this volume) that the problem is not one of empathy, but of keeping unfamiliar (and possibly antipathetic) 'suppositions' consistently in view.

45. Hexter, J., op. cit., p. 265. Collingwood emphasized that the 'historical conditions' of human life varied too much for argument by analogy to hold — Collingwood, R., *The Idea of History*, Oxford University Press, 1946, p. 239.

46. Coltham, J. and Fines, J, *Educational Objectives for the Study of History*, Historical Association, 1971, p. 9. Emphasizing children's immaturity of judgement, Peel finds it 'fortunate' that historical events can be described without reference to intentions; but in narrative, rather than 'mere' chronic, it is very doubtful if they can. See Peel, E., 'Some Problems in the Psychology of History Teaching' in W. Burston and D. Thompson (eds.), op. cit.

47. Fines, J. and Verrier, R., *The Drama of History*, New University Education, 1974.

48. Garfinkel, H., 'Remarks on Ethnomethodology' in J. Gumperz and D. Hymes (eds.), *Directions in Sociolinguistics*, Holt, Rinehart and Winston, 1972.

49. Bernstein, B., 'Elaborated and Restricted Codes: Their Social Origins and Some Consequences', *American Anthropologist*, 66, 6 (part 2), 1964, p. 60. The evolution of Bernstein's theory can be followed in his *Class, Codes and Control*, Volume 1, Routledge and Kegan Paul, 1971.

50. Barnes, D., *Language, the Learner and the School*, op. cit.

51. Gahagan, D. and G., *Talk Reform*, Routledge and Kegan Paul, 1970, p. 30. This book is an account of the experimental language programme derived from Bernstein's theory of language codes, a programme including many communicative tasks which were intended to 'push' children towards more elaborated uses of language.

52. The predominance of 'closed' questions and the very limited communicative moves open to pupils are documented (from a variety of research perspectives) in (e.g.) Bellack, A. et al., *Language in the Classroom*, Teachers' College Press, 1966; Adams, R. and Biddle, B., *Realities of Teaching*, Holt, Rinehart and Winston, 1970; and Sinclair, J. and Coulthard, R., *Towards an Analysis of Discourse*, Oxford University Press, 1975. For reviews of classroom research, see Edwards, A., *Language in Culture and Class*, op. cit., Chapter 5, and Stubbs, M., *Language, Schools and Classrooms*, Methuen, 1976.

53. The American historian Stull Holt, quoted by Winks, R., in *The Historian as Detective*, op. cit. p. 232.

54. There are lengthy transcript examples of such a change of role in Massialas, B. and Zevin, J., *Creative Encounters in the Classroom*, Wiley, 1967. See also Portal, C., 'The Place of Open Learning in Secondary School History', *Journal of Curriculum Studies*, 8, 1976, pp. 35-44.

55. Barnes, D., *From Communication to Curriculum*, Penguin, 1976, p. 22.

56. Lee, P., 'Explanation and Understanding in History' (in this volume). See also Lowe, R., 'Historical Thinking in Schools', *Educational Review*, 28, 1976, pp. 94-101; though he makes undue reference to 'empathy', Lowe does emphasize the importance of pupils' awareness of the 'structural constraints' on the actors.

57. Gallie, W., op. cit., p. 73.

5. Explanation and Understanding in History

P. J. LEE

INTRODUCTION

In history teaching one is sometimes struck by the readiness of adolescents to write off historical figures as obvious fools. Chamberlain at Munich, Louis XVI in 1789 and Trotsky at Brest-Litovsk — these are just some of the more obvious victims of pupils' condescension. No doubt many historians would regard Neville Chamberlain as having made important mistakes. But the judgement of disgusted pupils is only superficially similar to the criticism of historians. What they are getting at is more fundamental: Chamberlain was a fool because he lacked all rationality, because he failed to do what was quite obviously open to him to do — what anyone with any sense would have done in the circumstances. Even a little probing reveals that it is not just a question of a few pupils at a notoriously arrogant age being too ready to pass judgement. Given the opportunity to ask, children soon show that they are in various stages of puzzlement over why the agent in question did not take some 'obvious' course of action, even if they are less ready to write him off as a result. More important, although this kind of reaction is more noticeable where an agent seems to fail (or really does fail) to achieve his goals, even chains of 'successful' action can still appear in pupils' eyes to be arbitrary selections from more economical, effective, or obvious possibilities.

What exactly is going on here? Underlying this kind of reaction is a matter of central importance for children's understanding of history, and for research into children's thinking in history. As E. A. Peel has pointed out, in history the area of explanation has 'not generally been discussed at all systematically'.[1] This is certainly true of publications by psychologists and historians, although in the narrower context of philosophy important work has been done.[2] In what follows a preliminary attempt is made to sketch out a theoretical basis for work on children's understanding of (given) explanations in history, and on children's ability to suggest and test their own explanations. The chapter falls into two sections. Part I examines some aspects of explanation in history (and makes some connections with the related notions of interpretation and imagination). Taking the tentative framework of Part I as a guide, Part II seeks to provide a schematic outline of possible levels and kinds of understanding and misunderstanding in this area of historical explanation.

PART I

There has been a long tradition of argument between two broadly opposed views of historical explanation. On the one hand there is the account (most fully developed by Hempel) which assimilates explanation in history to a scientific model: the event to be explained is deduced from a general law (whether specifically 'historical', or imported from some branch of science), and a set of initial conditions.[3] In the absence of an adequately precise or sufficiently well validated law, what the historian achieves according to this account is typically an 'explanation sketch'. It is difficult to find an entirely suitable label for this model: for lack of anything better we will adopt the terminology employed by Dray, and refer throughout to the 'covering-law' model.[4]

On the other hand this view has been resolutely opposed by those who regard history as above all an account of past human *action*. The way in which this difference between history and the natural sciences is exploited varies considerably, and while it is easy to see a common emphasis on the importance of mind in historical explanation, the differences between the different accounts which share this emphasis make it impossible to talk of a homogeneous 'position' here.[5]

The present chapter makes no attempt to discuss this controversy (let alone to settle it), but more modestly to set out in a more or less dogmatic way a particular account of historical explanation which seems to bear some relation to the realities of history, in order to trace some of its consequences for historical thinking and the learning of history. Accordingly references to covering-law analysis in what follows are deliberately restricted and simplified: the covering-law model is used merely to elucidate an alternative account by comparison and contrast. Since historical explanation covers such a range of phenomena, it would be foolish to assume that it can be explicated with the articulation of a single model. Clearly in historical accounts it is sometimes necessary to spell out the workings of natural phenomena: climatic changes, crop diseases, the impact of grazing habits on vegetation and so on. Equally, the functioning of certain mechanical and technological devices must sometimes be explained. It seems reasonable to concede that the covering-law model is satisfactory in such cases, even if the regularities involved may remain very much implicit in a narrative. One might go further and argue that historical explanations of some economic and social phenomena will in certain circumstances also conform to the covering-law model. Nevertheless the assumption of this chapter is that, even with concessions of this kind, the usefulness of the model is limited, and that for a wide range of explanations in history an alternative account is required. Throughout the chapter a debt to the whole tradition of opposition to the covering-law model will be readily apparent; in particular the work of Dray and above all of G. H. von Wright is central to even the sketchiest discussion of these issues.[6]

Whatever else it encompasses, history typically involves human action, and historical explanation is frequently couched in terms of an agent's intentions and his reasons for performing a particular action. Such intentions and reasons are not always readily ascertainable, but it is the historian's task to seek out whatever evidence exists in order to arrive at an explanation. This is not a matter of intuitive leaps, or empathy (understood as subjective and intuitive), but a matter of public evidence. Evidence that a man had such and such reasons can sometimes be very strong: private papers, for example, or secret orders, may exist explicitly setting out his reasons for some course of action. At the other end of the scale, where certain presuppositions are shared in some common form of life, it is fairly safe to 'read off' men's intentions from the situation: when historians report a *battle*, they are already describing something of the intentions of those taking part. But the evidence of private papers is not a foundation for incorrigible judgements, and *some* men in *some* battles may have had no intention of killing or maiming their opponents.[7]

Clearly, the more a historian has immersed himself in a period, the more safely will he make judgements where evidence of a direct kind is slender. A man who is steeped in the literature, art and philosophy of a period, and who has a detailed knowledge of its institutions, a man who has explored what remains of the towns and villages in which people lived, and has operated or inspected their surviving equipment and artefacts, such a man will be able, in part, to see this segment of the past in its own terms, through its own conceptual schemes. He may go some way to taking account of what Collingwood called the 'absolute presuppositions' of a period.[8] And it is this, of course, which is behind the difficulty pointed out by Collingwood of understanding a period for which one has no sympathy. It is difficult, perhaps impossible, for a historian with (say) socialist leanings, to accept in a consistent way the moral tenets of the Third Reich, even on the hypothetical basis which is all that is required. And this is not a failure of 'empathy' (understood as a kind of mysterious intuition or fellow feeling) but the difficulty of consistently maintaining a complex of suppositions ('Suppose I believed such and such, and wanted so and so . . .') in the face of a view of the world totally antipathetic to it.[9]

If an important part of explanation in history is of the general character outlined so far, how does such explanation actually work? In order to answer this question, it is helpful first to distinguish different levels at which such explanations might operate.

At its simplest, we have the explanation of an action performed by one agent, the explanation proceeding by means of the construction of a practical inference for that agent. Suppose we have to explain why Chamberlain signed the Munich agreement in 1938.[10] We have first to establish how he saw the situation (whether he now seems to have been correct or not). This would include both long and short-term beliefs: for example that Versailles had been unjust and that stability in Europe could be ensured only by making concessions to Germany ('moral appeasement'); that Hitler would become more reasonable once the Czech question was settled; that Britain and France were not prepared (in terms of armaments or morale) for a general European war; that no direct assistance could in any case be given to Czechoslovakia. (This list, of course, is merely schematic, and could be filled out in a variety of ways.) But the agent's view of the situation is only one element in a practical inference: we need also to know what he was trying to achieve. Here we might include Chamberlain's intention to rectify the Versailles settlement, to achieve some 'reasonable' understanding with Germany, and to avoid war over Czechoslovakia at almost any cost. Putting together his intentions and his view of the situation, we are able to reconstruct his reasons for doing what he did. (In Dray's terms, we can construct a 'rationale' showing that Chamberlain's action at Munich was 'the thing to have done' in the circumstances—i.e. given the agent's intentions, and his view of the situation.)

Such a bald account of explanation by practical inference no doubt seems far too simple for history: some possible objections will be examined below. But before objections can be properly considered, it is important to see what is going on in an explanation of this sort. This involves a short excursion into slightly more formal analysis, even at the risk of appearing to depart from history.

What is the logic of explanation by practical inference? Von Wright has set out a piece of vicarious practical reasoning in tenseless form.[11]

From now on A intends to bring about p at time t.

From now on A considers that, unless he does a no later than at time t', he cannot bring about p at time t.

Therefore, no later than when he thinks time t' has arrived, A sets himself to do a, unless he forgets about the time, or is prevented.

Transposed into the past, this schema will serve for historical cases, and indeed, the qualifications made in the conclusion can be dropped once the action has occurred. In the historical case the schema acquires a logical 'tightness' which it does not have in the present tense: 'It is only when action is already there and a practical argument is constructed to explain or justify it that we have a logically conclusive argument. The necessity of the practical inference schema is, one could say, a necessity conceived *ex post actu*'.[12] In what sense exactly a practical inference schema provides a logically conclusive argument is open to question, for although practical judgements can follow from each other and be inferred or drawn as conclusions of arguments, actions cannot.[13] (How could an *action* be the conclusion of an *inference*?) Edgley has suggested that there is, nevertheless, a logical connection between practical reasoning and actions, since the premises of practical arguments '. . . in being reasons for accepting (practical) judgements, would necessarily also be reasons for acting consistently with those judgements'.[14] Put crudely, if I take p to be a reason for accepting the practical judgement q (that I ought to do x), then p is a reason for my doing x. And if I do x, and p is my reason for doing it, then I have done x *because* I think that p. Hence the reconstruction of my reasons for doing x can be the explanation of why I did x.

For the purposes of this chapter it is unnecessary to go further into the logic of practical inference: what is important is that the practical inference schema discussed above is a logical model to which explanations in terms of reasons, when successful, conform. It is *not* asserted that historical agents work through such schemas in a conscious way; still less that historical agents have always behaved rationally. Nor is it claimed that historians produce such schemas in full formal rigour. The point is that it is possible to construct a practical inference (or 'rationale') for an action, and to construct it on the basis of public evidence. In so far as such a construction achieves what it sets out to do (i.e. to give the *agent's* reasons for his action) it is a 'reconstruction', but not in the sense that the agent worked through it in formal terms. As Dray has argued, it is like the calculation which the agent might himself construct after the event in order to understand his own actions, or one which, if he had found time, he might have gone through before he acted.[15] Of course such a calculation by the agent may be a mere rationalization, and the construction of a practical inference by the historian might equally be mistaken. Just as the covering-law model provides a logical basis for explanation in the natural sciences, despite the fact that the laws on which a particular explanation is based may prove to be ill-founded, so practical inference schemas provide the logical basis for explaining human actions, even though any particular reconstruction may prove to be false.[16]

What of the agent who acts for no reason, or irrationally? Is not this account in danger of over-estimating human rationality? Three important points arise here. First, the practical inference schema is not concerned with the situation as the historian now believes it to have been, but with the situation from the point of view of the agent. It explains by showing that, given the *circumstances as the agent saw them*, and given the agent's intentions, what was done was the thing to have done (what was 'appropriate' in Dray's terms).[17] The sense in which an action is held to have been the thing to do is, then, a restricted one. Of course *further* questions can arise about how the agent came to see the situation in the way he did. These will be answered in a variety of ways, but very often they will show *how it came about* that the agent received false information, or was led into misjudging the value of some possession, or failed to appreciate the importance of some development. Hence, in the example of Chamberlain at Munich, questions may arise as to how he could imagine that Hitler's demands would cease after the dismemberment of Czechoslovakia, or how anyone could feel a *moral* requirement to reach an understanding with Nazi Germany. Characteristically answers to questions of this sort will be stories which set out a series of events in a followable narrative, itself employing further practical inference schemas for other agents.[18] Often such narratives may be regarded as, in part, temporally expanded accounts of the agents' situation, showing for example how appeasement developed in the interwar years, with British hostility to the prospect of war in the Chanak crisis, the Ruhr and Palatinate crises of 1923-4, the Dawes plan, and Locarno. Chamberlain's espousal of appeasement itself becomes explicable as 'the thing to do', bearing in mind his view of the situation and his intentions. It would appear that a great deal of seemingly irrational behaviour turns out to be open to this kind of explanation once the agent's point of view is taken into account. As Gallie says: 'It is quite a common situation in history for a succession of events to be followable only as a succession of misunderstandings or errors — things which we have no difficulty in following since we are all of us only too well acquainted with them'.[19] But errors and misunderstandings are not necessarily indications of irrationality.[20]

Interestingly enough, and this is the second point in this connection, there is some support from psychology, philosophy and history for the claim that error and irrationality must be clearly distinguished, and that the latter is not so common as might be thought. There is a long tradition of regarding errors in reasoning as more a question of slipping in false premises than of disregarding the laws of inference outright.[21] J. S. Mill, in the 'System of Logic', argued that since

> the premises are seldom formally set out, . . . it is almost always to a certain degree optional in what manner the suppressed link shall be filled up. . . . [A person] has it almost always in his power to make his syllogism good by introducing a false premise; and hence it is scarcely ever possible decidedly to affirm that any argument involves a bad syllogism.[22]

There is some suggestive, if far from conclusive, experimental evidence to support this view.[23] In history too there are strong indications that actions must not be too easily dismissed as irrational. Apparent cases of irrationality are constantly being eroded by historians. A particularly clear example of this is discussed by J. N. Watkins.[24] The collision of HMS *Camperdown* and HMS *Victoria* in the Mediterranean Sea on 22 June 1893 was the consequence of an apparently absurd order from Vice Admiral Tryon, in the execution of which *Camperdown* and *Victoria* turned in upon one another, and *Victoria* was rammed and sunk. Tryon went down with his ship, allegedly declaring, 'It is all my fault'. Since rational explanation of Tryon's order seemed impossible, attempts to explain the disaster took the form of unsupported guesses that he was drunk or smitten by fever. In a historical reappraisal of the incident, Richard Hough, following a suggestion by Sir William Laird Clowes soon after the event, demonstrates that Tryon's manoeuvre was in fact perfectly rational if taken in the way it was (probably) intended.[25] It is possible even in this difficult case to construct a practical inference for the order.[26]

The third point follows naturally from this example. Historians are not content to give up when confronted with an action which resists the construction of any rationale. It is a kind of standing presupposition of history that (unless there is evidence to the contrary) people act for reasons which, from their own point of view at the moment of setting themselves to perform the action, are good reasons.[27] Sometimes this presupposition fails, and then the alternative explanation may well best be analysed according to the covering-law model—but even then the matter can be re-opened at any time. (It is worth noticing that this presupposition of minimal rationality is one of the criteria by which historical works are judged for objectivity: if a historian has made no effort to distinguish the agent's view of the situation from what is now thought to have been the case, his story is likely to be highly misleading.) None of this, of course, rules out the possibility of criticism of an agent's actions. Perhaps Chamberlain *ought* to have known better than to think Hitler would ever be 'appeased'. He *could* have listened more attentively to Vansittart, Duff Cooper, and others who were warning him of where his policy led. But given that he did not, his actions made sense.

Actions, of course, may fall under different descriptions, and what is intentional under one description is not necessarily so under another. People often do more or less than they intend or even know. How can a rationale be constructed in such cases? This issue takes us from the 'simple' level of individual actions performed by a single agent up to the level of more complex interactions between agents. Before we leave the present level there are, however, one or two things to say which have some bearing on the question. If someone decides that in order to achieve an end it is necessary to perform a particular action, the connection between the action and the end (while itself teleogical) may depend on some causal relation (to be elucidated by the covering-law model) known to him.[28] For instance, if a naval commander wishes to avoid enemy torpedoes, he may turn his ship towards or away from them, in order to present a smaller target. This manoeuvre rests on knowledge of laws (no doubt beyond the capacities of the commander to quantify) of the probability of projectiles striking objects of various sizes in certain conditions. (These would be what Hempel calls 'probabilistic' laws.)[29] But sometimes an action, besides (or instead of) enabling A to achieve his goal, has causal side effects unintended by him. (Turning away, our commander runs his fleet into a minefield.) Such effects may attach only incidentally to the action (as in the minefield example), or may be necessary but unforeseen consequences inherent in the action. (Fighting naval battles at longer ranges in the First World War—a development favoured by Fisher at the Admiralty as a means by which the British could exploit their heavier armament—also meant that enemy shells fell on British ships with a more plunging trajectory, and so encountered relatively lightly armoured decks, instead of well protected vertical surfaces.) Unforeseen consequences of this kind take care of *some* of the cases where action is not, under at least one description, intentional. It is worth stressing that all sorts of regularities are implicit in the construction of practical inferences; and where actions achieve more or less than the agent intended, the ensuing explanation can sometimes be of the kind described by the covering-law model, and may make those regularities explicit.

We can now move to the next level, where an agent's action under one description or another can have consequences for other agents. It is precisely this feature of action which enables historians to explain a complex series of actions by employing the same basic logical model as at the previous level. What is done by one agent can give a second agent reason, or opportunity, to act. His action can be said to have been brought about by the action of the first, so that the first action, redescribed in such a way that the first agent cannot be said to have intended it under that description, becomes exactly the wider, more complex action that seemed to pose difficulties for our earlier account. Hence Scheer steamed into the broadsides of the entire Grand Fleet at the battle of Jutland, or Jellicoe allowed the Germans to escape. In this way Lloyd George destroyed the Liberal Party, and Princip started the First World War.[30]

Implicit in such examples is one of the most important logical types of historical explanation: what G. H. von Wright has called 'quasi-causal explanation'.[31] When one agent (A) acts in a certain way he creates a new situation for a second agent (B). It may be that B sees his circumstances as being such that he must now act in a certain way in order to achieve (or preserve) some state of affairs. Or it may be that he is presented with an opportunity which previously did not exist: he can now act with an intention which was, before A's action, inconceivable. Hence A's action can either necessitate B's by forcing him to re-assess his situation, or it can make possible an action by opening up an opportunity for B to reshape his intentions. B's action can have the same results for C and C's for D. Such chains of practical inferences are typically found in their clearest form in diplomatic and political history; von Wright's schematic discussion of the outbreak of the First World War uncannily fits a typical teaching diagram to explain the entry of the Great Powers into the struggle. Of course, in the teaching diagram the practical inferences are not normally set out in full, or in logical form, but it is clear how one agent's action provides reasons for another's.

5.   *Britain* allied to Belgium, unwilling to stand aside while Germany defeats France: declares war on Germany.

4   *Germany* must defeat France quickly if Schlieffen Plan is to be operated (Russian mobilization already begun): invades *France* through Belgium.

3   *Russia* feels bound to help fellow Slavs this time (has backed down twice in recent years): mobilizes armies as warning.

2   *Austria* sees an opportunity to crush Serbia: issues ultimatum.

1   Princip assassinates the Archduke Franz Ferdinand.

In most cases chains of practical inferences tie in with each other in very complex ways: it is often impossible even for teaching purposes to produce a simplified scheme of the kind used above. In such cases we have a detailed narrative consisting in part of interlocking quasi-causal explanations. It is not difficult to see why the demand for further explanation in history is typically met, not by recourse to general laws, but by more detailed narrative.

The outbreak of the First World War exemplifies another aspect of historical explanation. Where the events to be explained are 'large-scale' events, in which considerable numbers of people may be involved, rationales are constructed for groups rather than for individuals: for the Austrian Government, the German High Command, and so on.[32] This accounts for a common feature of historical argument — debates over the possibility of treating particular groups as homogeneous — and again the only recourse of a historian faced with a challenge on these grounds is to produce further evidence showing in detail just what *were* the intentions of individuals in the group.

At this point problems of explanation are closely related to matters of interpretation. Where groups of people are concerned, it is not simply a matter of constructing practical inferences, but of showing what collective actions meant to those involved in them. An individual may have had certain intentions in joining a rioting crowd which had no bearing on what the activity in question was understood as being — namely, a bread riot. (He wanted to escape his wife, prove his courage, etc.) A practical inference constructed to explain his taking part might therefore shed no light on *what sort of event* was happening. But research enabling the historian to construct rationales for a large section of the crowd might show that the event had been misinterpreted: what was taken to be a bread riot might turn out to have had a very different meaning to the participants (the beginning of a revolution, a diversion to cover a prison escape, a religious protest, etc.). In other words, questions of interpretation (*what* was this event?) and questions of explanation (*why* did it happen?) are, as Collingwood pointed out, thoroughly intertwined.[33] Much historical debate turns on the problem of interpretation in this sense, and develops through a process of explanation by rationale, re-interpretation, and further research in order to review existing explanations in the light of new interpretations. The construction of detailed rationales both throws up interpretations, and provides a means of checking them.[34]

The notions of explanation and interpretation in history are closely connected with a third concept: that of imagination. Psychologists and educationists are prone to stress those aspects of the imagination which are usually labelled 'creative', and in particular to concentrate on imaging (conjuring up images or pictures in the mind's eye) and association.[35] But in history these features of imagination are subordinate to 'supposing', and the supposing in question takes the form of hypotheticals (if so and so were the case, then . . .). One place for this kind of imagination is in connection with people's view of their situation, and their intentions. Suppose *A* believed himself to be in situation S, and given that he wanted *p*, what would he be likely to do? Given that *A* did *x*, and supposing that he wanted *p*, how must he have seen his situation? Given that *A* did *x*, and supposing he saw his situation as being S, what was he after? In history this kind of imagination cannot remain detached and free floating: ultimately it has to be tied down firmly to evidence. Indeed part of the *point* of it is that it suggests where to look for evidence, and what sort of evidence to look for.

Imaging may also be part of historical imagination, but the imaging must rest on evidence, and when some object or location is imaged in this way, it is often as a step to further suppositions which in turn must be evaluated against further evidence. The injunction: 'Imagine what it must have been like to . . .' is often asking for a very sophisticated mixture of imaging, supposing and then more imaging, the latter often accompanied by a controlled flow of associations, and the whole performance tied down to whatever evidence is available.[36] This has important consequences both for teaching and for research into children's thinking in history.

The analytical part of this paper has largely been concerned with one aspect of historical explanation. Explanations in history are, as Dray pointed out, a 'logically miscellaneous lot'. Nevertheless, while the covering-law model is applicable in explanations of natural phenomena, is implicit in connections between means and ends seen by historical agents, and is sometimes relevant where actions achieve results different from what was anticipated by those who initiated them, the most important part of historical explanation is to be analysed in a very different way. It should be clear even from this sketchy discussion that in history explanation, interpretation, imagination and narrative have important links with each other. Explanation by the construction of practical inferences, whether for individual action, chains of actions or whole complexes of actions in which numerous agents are involved, all rest on the notion of having reasons for doing things.[37] But actions may be described and redescribed at different levels: Bismarck's action in editing the Ems telegram could also be described as stirring up German feeling against France, or perhaps as laying the foundations of Imperial Germany. It might even be characterized as the inauguration of a bloody tradition which was to culminate in a Berlin bunker in 1945. Two of these descriptions could be explanatory, if evidence supported them. The last could not be said to explain the first, but like the previous two, answers the question 'What was Bismarck doing?' Crucial for distinguishing between explanation and interpretation here is the concept of 'point of view'.[38]All four descriptions could fit into a narrative as they stand.

PART II

The account given in Part I provides, for the important class of historical explanations which rest on the construction of practical inferences, a framework in terms of which to set out what is necessary if a child is to be said to have *explained* something in history, and what is involved in his understanding an explanation when it has been given.[39] Given such a framework, we can sort out a number of levels of understanding, and some important kinds of misunderstanding, in this area of historical explanation. A systematic organization of such levels and kinds of understanding and misunderstanding would go some way to providing criteria for the establishment of categories relevant to historical thinking in a way in which classical Piagetian categories — except in a very general way — are not.

A detailed or systematic articulation of the whole range of possibilities will not be attempted here, but it is worth trying to sketch out how such an analysis might be developed. What main kinds of misunderstandings of a 'simple' practical inference might be expected, where the inference is encountered in a given historical explanation?[40] Let us take the case in which an agent (A) does x in order to achieve p, seeing his situation (S) in a certain way. The agent's view of the situation (S^a) should be distinguished from the view which the historian may take of it (S^h).

First, children can fail to see what S^a actually was, either because it is simply not filled out by the teacher (historian, researcher etc.), or because the child positively mistakes it as something else (very often as S^h) and so thinks some other action x' or x'' more likely than x to have achieved p. This belief is particularly likely where x did not in fact lead to p in the events under consideration, or where there are good grounds for thinking x' or x'' more likely to achieve p in S^h. Another kind of misunderstanding arising from a failure to grasp S^a involves *qualifications* which the agent may have had in mind in trying to achieve p. These may have been in terms of ends or means (e.g. A may have wanted to achieve p but not p and q together; or alternatively he may have wanted to achieve p at least cost, or without loss of life or simply 'with flair'). Such qualifications are likely to be important where A sees x not as a necessary condition of p, but as one among a number of sufficient conditions.

This account, however, is too easy. A man's own view of his situation can never fully be spelt out (even so far as it is known) in a teaching situation (or in a research passage) so that all possible misconceptions can be ruled out. In teaching, what is needed is a chance for children to give vent to their misapprehensions, so that each one can be cleared up as it arises. This means using every available means to 're-create' the situation, and talking through the agent's 'problem' with pupils, both in considerable detail. S^a is, in other words, from the teaching point of view, almost inevitably incomplete. How then can we ever hope to arrive at a practical inference? Part of the answer is that if those elements of the situation which evidence suggests became the agent's reasons are included, we have made it possible to follow the practical inference. But, more than this, S^a can be described in a way which forecloses further characterization: A's view of his situation was such that he thought it a situation in which x was the only (best) way to achieve p in the circumstances — a situation in which x was the thing to do (S^x). Why not simply characterize A's situation as S^x to start with? Of course in history books and history teaching this is frequently done. Even for those acquainted with the historical background, such shorthand can cause problems, but for pupils the difficulties are of a different order.[41] As already pointed out, too brief a characterization of the agent's situation leaves pupils in a very confused state, in which x sometimes appears quite arbitrary because a whole range of possible alternatives suggest themselves as more sensible. With younger children and more extreme cases x can appear to fit so badly with the intentions ascribed to A that pupils are simply unable to see what A is doing, and are left in a state of complete bewilderment. They need not have positive alternative suggestions to replace x: the vagueness or incompleteness of the situation-description itself can be at the root of the trouble. Typically the situations encountered even in school history are extremely complex, and frequently the minimal descriptions offered make a wide range of assumptions about children's knowledge of how agents in particular times and places might see things.

A second broad category of misunderstandings arises where children either fail to see, or positively mistake, the agent's intention in doing x. The consequences here can be worked out in much the same way as in the case of situations: x takes on an arbitrary aspect, or seems patently less likely to achieve A's (misinterpreted) intention than other possible actions x' or x''. The difficulty crops up in a variety of ways. Qualifications which A would attach to p can be ignored or misunderstood. The assumption that x or p is intentional *under those descriptions* might be wrongly made.[42] Even where intentions are described in some detail, it is easy for children to make false assumptions in order to fill in the inevitable gaps. Whereas a historian can build on a knowledge of what apparently like-minded men of the age found it possible to want, and on acquaintance with the habits of thought and conventions of diplomats or soldiers or miners or wool merchants, and so has some chance of getting near the truth in the absence of direct evidence, children can call on only limited knowledge even of their contemporary adult world. It has already been argued that the prerequisite for this exercise of the historical imagination is detailed acquaintance with the age, and that it is not a matter of 'feeling' or intuition but of rigorous supposition based upon evidence.[43]

It is also worth stressing the considerable difficulty of characterizing an agent's intention in such a way as to make it possible to judge whether a given course of action meets it or not. Jellicoe, for example, presumably intended to defeat the Germans at the battle of Jutland, or at least that his fleet give a good account of itself — but what ratio of losses between the two sides would count as this? How many ships could he afford to lose? What would compensate a given loss? Once again a mass of background material would be needed to give an answer to these questions, and it is clear that a precise answer is not possible. But then trying to follow Jellicoe in ruling out certain possible courses of action as not likely to meet his intentions becomes a complicated business.

There is perhaps a case for delineating a third area of

misunderstandings, although in some ways it is more satisfactory to regard it not as a separate area, but as another problem associated with understanding an agent's situation. Although I may know that a naval commander (A) turned his ships towards the enemy (x) when under torpedo attack, and I know that he wanted to avoid the loss of his own ships (p), I can still fail to see how x would lead to p, and so fail to understand why A did x. Here it is my ignorance of an underlying causal connection (no doubt analysable in covering-law terms) which is responsible for my puzzlement. I do not realize that a ship steaming towards oncoming torpedoes presents a very much smaller target than one moving broadside on, and perhaps I do not know that the tracks of the torpedoes are likely to be visible. In another sort of example the connection between x and p may be of a very different kind—where A's doing x is designed to get B to do y, which, under some other description, is p. Here it is possible for me to be confused because I do not know that, B having the goals he has, for A to do x is to give B a reason for doing y.

From A's point of view the probable outcomes of his alternative actions (and therefore the connections between x and p) are part of his situation. (Compare chess: 'The situation is this—if I move here, he goes there; if I take his rook, he can either check me or . . .'.) This means that any attempt to give a detailed account of S^a involves the specification of a wide range of alternatives which there are grounds for believing A may have considered. Here historians work on the basis of evidence about A's 'ways of thinking', and their evidence as to what A knew of other aspects of the situation.[44] Where this latter kind of evidence is missing, historians tend to oscillate between S^a and S^h, for the latter both suggests and circumscribes the range of alternatives A might have considered.[45] Even so, the range can be wide. The problem for children is formidable, since the less one knows, the wider the range may appear to be, and the more slender are the grounds for eliminating those which were not 'on' for the agent. There are no rules for the *generation* of alternatives, although their elimination can be systematic, given sufficient evidence. (Compare Piaget's experiments, in particular the one in which children are asked to combine colourless liquids to produce a yellow one.[46] There the alternative combinations could be arrived at on the basis of a rule, and by the same token subjects could ascertain when those possibilities had been exhausted. There is no parallel to this in history. Indeed even the elimination of alternatives is a very much more abstract task in history than in Piaget's experiments in physical science. It is not a matter of *observing* that such and such a possibility does not occur, but of deciding whether it meets certain criteria.)

This discussion of different kinds of misunderstanding of a given explanation can provide the basis for a preliminary sketch of criteria for picking out possible *levels* of understanding. First, we might take levels of understanding of an agent's intentions. At one end of the continuum children can fail so completely to see what the agent is trying to do that they are unable to hazard suggestions, except for wild guesses unsupported by anything in the given explanation. With a little more understanding mistaken suggestions will be made, until eventually we reach the point where we can say that the agent's intention in its simplest form is understood. A further step is taken when qualifications and conditions are attached, even if mistaken, and finally the point is reached where the agent's intention can be characterized in detail, with the necessary qualifications, and perhaps even articulated further by hypothetical illustrations of what would and would not meet it.

Second, there are levels of understanding of the situation in which the agent found himself. Assuming for the moment the identity of S^a and S^h (so far as logically possible) this understanding can be characterized in a number of ways. A child can understand that A saw his situation as being so-and-so, where the description would be couched in static terms and make no reference to possible futures. A further step would be to see that A saw a number of courses of action available in the situation, leading to various outcomes. Connected with this would be an understanding that in this situation A saw x as being the only/best thing to do (given that he wanted to achieve p), and therefore an understanding of A's grounds for ruling out alternative courses of action. Built into this would be a grasp of the connections A believed to exist between x and p, and also the connections between other alternatives and their outcomes.

The distinction between S^a and S^h is so fundamental, but so demanding, that it is hard in an *a priori* scheme of this sort to know how to classify it. In almost all cases of historical explanation by rationale the distinction would have to be made: in other words the assumption of the preceding paragraph could not stand. If the distinction is generally a prerequisite for understanding even a 'simple' action, in the case of quasi-causal chains it is without qualification a necessary condition. Here the historian (or the child following the explanation) must (at least) oscillate between the point of view of the agent and that of other agents, whose views are not known to the first, and are thus part of S^h, not S^a. Almost invariably, in order to explain a particular outcome, the historian will have to show how, *in spite of the intentions* of the various agents involved, and yet at the same time *because of them*, events followed a certain path. (See the discussion in Part I.)

An allied but less formidable step in understanding may be taken in cases where p fails to come about, not because of some other agent's intervention, but because in S^h as opposed to S^a, x is not (causally) connected with p—is not, in other words, a move towards p at all. (A government tightens up the money supply, reduces public expenditure and cuts the wages of public employees etc., in order to overcome a recession.) Here the child would again have to distinguish between S^a and S^h, since the relation between A's intention and what actually occurred would have to be mediated by the historian's knowledge of the relevant general laws (part of S^h). But to take such a step is to go beyond what is minimally necessary for understanding why A did x. Another level again is reached if it is also understood *how A* came to believe himself to be in that situation, rather than in the one we can now see that he was in (and there is a parallel level in connection with seeing how the agent came to have a certain intention). But this is to move even further away from what is *necessary* to understanding the given explanation of why A did x.

Finally, it is possible to bring together the various elements separately discussed here into a set of (tentative) categories for the analysis of children's understanding of individual action. This is set out below. (For an examination of the use of these categories in empirical research, together with examples of children's responses in the various categories, see Chapter 6 of this book, 'Understanding and Research' by Dickinson and Lee.

Level One
Category 1
Action treated as unintelligible. Failure coherently to grasp agent's intentions or situation. Direct contradiction of explicit information. This level is inherently unstable.

Level Two
Category 2
Action explained by reference to the agent's intentions and situation, where the former includes an important 'conventional' element, and no differentiation is made in the latter between the agent's view of the situation and the historian's view. The 'conventional' element is an amalgam of personal projection, stereotyped ascriptions of dispositions, and assumptions based on 'merely conceptual' understandings of intentions and situations. For example, the concepts *king* and *admiral* each suggest possible goals for individuals falling under those descriptions, independently of evidence for the intentions of particular agents. Similarly a *battle* is taken to indicate generalized goals for its participants — notably *winning*. The action of a combatant who breaks off an engagement may therefore at this level be explained by the agent's *cowardice*. Support for conventional explanations of this kind may be drawn from personal projection, without any recognition that such projection bears little resemblance to the agent's views. Where evidence is employed to arrive at the *particular* intention of the agent, the account is seldom qualified, and fails to reconcile conflicting goals where appropriate. Generally, a temporary equilibrium is achieved in this category by ignoring or failing to perceive problematic aspects of the action.

Category 3
Action not understood. The equilibrium achieved in Category 2 is upset by its own inherent contradictions and by the perception of problematic aspects of the action: the breakdown is typically indicated by the suggestion of alternative courses of action as more appropriate. These alternatives do not recognize what the agent could or could not have

known, and this failure to differentiate the historian's from the agent's view of the situation prevents the achievement of equilibrium at the next level. There may in this category be some unintegrated elements of the next level, and also some characteristics of the previous level.

Level Three
Category 4
Action explained by reference to the agent's particular intentions and his own view of the situation, but seen relatively locally in the context of the description under which the action requires explanation. The agent's intentions are understood and may be highly qualified, but not ramified in terms of further goals. Conflicting intentions are recognized and partially reconciled. The situation is not fitted into a wider context, but, despite this restriction, equilibirum is achieved in category four by making the fundamental distinction between the agent's and the historian's view of the situation. Temporary stability.

Category 5
Action not understood, since although the distinction between the agent's view of the situation and the historian's view is made, the wider context is not grasped. In the previous level (two) any reference to this wider context remained unintegrated, and failed to resolve the contradictions inherent in an undifferentiated view of the situation. At this level (three) recognition of the inadequacy of the equilibrium achieved in category 4 will be shown by an uneasy fluctuation between seeing that the agent had his reasons, and finding the action inadequate in comparison with other possibilities. Suggestions for alternative courses of action may be made, but more hesitantly than in category 3, and (with lapses which may even revert to level one) tend to maintain the distinction between the agent's and the historian's view. There may be explicit mention of the wider context, but such references will fail to relate this extra dimension to the narrower conception of the action. This may result in the reappearance at a higher level of difficulties in reconciling the agent's conflicting goals similar in some respects to those encountered at level two. In general understanding in this category is still unstable.

Level Four
Category 6
Action explained by reference to the distinction between the agent's view of the situation and the historian's, and seen in a wider context. The agent's intentions are understood and an attempt made to reconcile conflicting goals (if appropriate) by appeal to his own view of the situation and to further ramifications of his goals. An extended view of the situation will usually involve an understanding in dynamic (and hypothetical) rather than merely static terms. In general problematic aspects of the action arising *both* from a differentiated view of the situation *and* from the relations between the restricted and extended context will be integrated in

category 6. Where appropriate the *adequacy* of the action may be judged in terms of both sets of distinctions, since understanding is not to be equated with approval.

NOTES

1. Peel, E. A., 'Some Problems in the Psychology of History Teaching' in W. H. Burston and D. Thompson (eds.), *Studies in the Nature and Teaching of History*, Routledge and Kegan Paul, 1967, p. 182.

2. Burston, W. H., *Principles of History Teaching*, Methuen, 1963 (2nd edn., 1972) is a pioneering exception to the general rule that works on the teaching of history have virtually ignored explanation. Burston's treatment leans heavily on W. H. Walsh's account of explanation in terms of colligation, which is not without problems. (For bibliographical details of Walsh's work see note 33.) Honourable recent exceptions to the general neglect of explanation by historians are Elton, G. R., *Political History, Principles and Practice*, Allen Lane, 1970, Chapter 4; and Hexter, J. H., *A History Primer*, Allen Lane, 1972.

3. Hempel, C. G., 'The Function of General Laws in History' in P. Gardiner (ed.), *Theories of History*, The Free Press, 1959. See also Hempel's 'Reasons and Covering Laws in Historical Explanation' in S. Hook (ed.), *Philosophy and History*, New York University Press, 1963 (also in P. Gardiner (ed.), *Philosophy of History*, Oxford University Press, 1974); and 'Explanation in Science and in History' in W. H. Dray (ed.), *Philosophical Analysis and History*, Harper and Row, 1966. For a detailed discussion of a historical example, see Hempel's *Aspects of Scientific Explanation and Other Essays in the Philosophy of Science*, The Free Press, 1965, pp. 478-83. Nagel, E., *The Structure of Science*, Routledge and Kegan Paul, pp. 547-606, also discusses historical examples.

4. Dray, W. H., *Laws and Explanation in History*, Oxford University Press, 1957.

5. W. Dilthey, B. Croce, M. Oakeshott, and R. G. Collingwood might be called 'classical' exponents of the various 'anti-positivist' (sometimes Idealist) positions adopted in this area.

6. Dray, W. H., op. cit., 1957. See also his *Philosophy of History*, Prentice Hall, 1964; '"Explaining What" in History' in P. Gardiner (ed.), *Theories of History*, The Free Press, 1959; and 'The Historical Explanation of Actions Reconsidered', in S. Hook (ed.), op. cit. For an exceptionally clear discussion of explanation with reference to history see von Wright, G. H., *Explanation and Understanding*, Routledge and Kegan Paul, 1971. For detailed criticism of the covering-law model in history see Dray, W. H., op. cit., 1957; and Perry, L. R., 'The Covering Law Theory of Historical Explanation' in W. H. Burston and D. Thompson (eds.), op. cit. The assertion that the applicability of the covering-law account is limited should not be taken as a denial of any kind of 'generalizing' elements in historical explanation at various levels. It would be foolish, for example, to deny the existence of general connections between holding certain views and undertaking certain actions. But discussion of this would go beyond the scope of this paper.

7. In what sense we would even speak of 'opponents' here is an interesting question.

8. Collingwood, R. G., *An Essay in Metaphysics*, Oxford University Press, 1940, Part I.

9. For discussion of a wide range of issues connected with this point see the interesting chapter 'The Sown and the Waste', Hexter, J. H., op. cit., pp. 104-44.

10. This example is 'simple' only in the sense that the question refers to *Chamberlain's action*, under a description which allows us to treat it as deliberate, and not to the whole complex of events at Munich; and thus it is simple relative to explanations of a

wider kind which might cover that whole complex. (See the discussion of 'quasi-causal chains' on p. 79.)

11. Von Wright, G. H., op. cit., p. 107.
12. ibid., p. 117.
13. Why, it may be asked, is it necessary for historical explanations to be 'logically conclusive arguments'? The great strength of Hempel's early covering-law analysis (Hempel, C. G., 'The Function of General Laws in History' in P. Gardiner (ed.), *Theories of History*, The Free Press, 1959) derived from the fact that, given a general law (or laws) and a set of initial conditions, the event to be explained can be *deduced* from its explanation. This deductive structure might be illustrated by a (merely) schematic treatment of the Munich example (a genuine covering-law analysis would of course be much more complex but here all that is at issue is the *form* taken by explanation):
    (i) All weak democratic heads of state faced with a show of superior force from a determined foreign opponent, will, if war is not demanded by public opinion at home (etc. etc.), give way.
    (ii) Chamberlain was a weak head of state, etc. etc.
    (iii) Hitler was a determined foreign opponent, and war was not demanded, etc. etc. Therefore
    (iv) Chamberlain gave way (and signed the Munich agreement).
    If we make the assumption (purely for the sake of argument) that the law and the statements of fact are correct, what is explained here is why the event occurred, rather than did not occur: (i) (ii) and (iii) taken together *entail* (iv). Given the truth of the premises, the event could not fail to have occurred. (Strictly speaking this is not true of this crude example, because 'giving way' could have taken forms other than signing the agreement. While this may be a difficulty for covering-law accounts, it can be ignored for the purposes of this discussion.) Hempel in effect insists that explanations must meet certain logical standards if they are to be more than the *ad hoc* constructions of everyday life. Hence, whether they are aware of it or not, historians' explanations *presuppose* laws. For if sometimes weak democratic heads of state *do* give way to determined foreign opponents, and sometimes they *don't*, how can the fact that Chamberlain *was* a weak democratic head of state explain why on *this* occasion he gave way? (Its proponents maintain that this same line of argument can be employed against more serious and complex explanations until the point where a law is conceded.)
    This matter has been discussed by Alan Donagan ('The Popper-Hempel Theory Reconsidered' in W. H. Dray (ed.), op. cit., 1966). Donagan argues that the 'deductive requirement' is more important for history than for natural science, since merely statistical laws of the kind that Hempel allows in his later accounts of explanation (Hempel, C. G., 'Explanation in Science and in History', ibid.) cannot explain the occurrence of individual events. He therefore proposes a practical inference schema bearing some resemblance to von Wright's later suggestions (quoted on p. 75), and claims that it does indeed meet the 'deductive requirement'.
14. Edgley, R., *Reason in Theory and Practice*, Hutchinson, 1969, p. 124. Underlying Edgley's thesis are '. . . three conceptual truths: if from the fact that p it follows that q, then from the fact that p one can infer that q; if from the fact that p one can infer that q, the fact that p is a (conclusive) reason for thinking that q; and if the proposition that q is a practical proposition, e.g. that one ought to do x, then a reason for thinking that q is a reason for doing x. The connection stated in this last truth between a reason for thinking something and a reason for doing something, is the connection mediated by the possibility of an action's being consistent or inconsistent with a practical judgement' (loc. cit.). The explanatory role of reason can then be explicated in general terms: 'If the fact that p is a reason for doing x . . ., the fact that p must be capable of being

somebody's reason for doing x; and if it is somebody's reason for doing x it must be the case that that person does, did, or will do x because he thinks or thought that p' (ibid., p. 152).

15. Dray, W. H., op. cit., 1957, p. 123.
16. In view of his influence on the covering-law model, it is interesting to see how close some of Popper's work comes to the 'hermeneutic' position of Dray or Von Wright (and for that matter of Collingwood). His initial discussion of the 'logic of the situation' (*The Open Society and its Enemies*, Routledge and Kegan Paul, 1962, 4th edn., Vol. II, p. 97) has been extended in the paper 'On the Theory of Objective Mind' (in K. R. Popper, *Objective Knowledge*, Oxford University Press, 1972). For example (ibid., p. 179): 'By a situational analysis I mean a certain kind of tentative or conjectural explanation of some human action which appeals to the situation in which the agent finds himself. It may be a historical explanation: we may perhaps wish to explain how and why a certain structure of ideas was created. Admittedly, no creative action can ever be fully explained. Nevertheless, we can try, conjecturally, to give an idealized reconstruction of the problem situation in which the agent found himself, and to that extent make the action "understandable" (or "rationally understandable"), that is to say, *adequate to his situation as he saw it*. This method of situational analysis may be described as an application of the *rationality principle*.' (Popper's emphasis.)
17. Dray, W. H., op. cit., 1957, p. 124.
18. See Gallie, W. B., *Philosophy and the Historical Understanding*, Chatto and Windus, 1964.
19. ibid., p. 97.
20. It may be objected that any explanation of Chamberlain's actions at Munich must make reference to his 'weakness', which is not a matter of reconstructing a rationale. Explanations of Chamberlain's actions in terms of weakness are, however, less explanations than moral judgements. It is not obvious that Chamberlain was weak in the sense that he took the easiest course, or simply vacillated. He pursued a determined policy of extracting concessions from Czechoslovakia *before* Hitler made his claims. Chamberlain did not lack support, but equally he continued his policy in the face of opposition in the Foreign Office, among civil servants and cabinet ministers, and in the face of advice from abroad. If he is to be described as 'weak', it is because his views (i.e. his goals and his beliefs about the situation) led him not to 'stand up to' Hitler. But that is to say he ought to have held different views. Of course explanations *can* be in terms of weakness of character, and will then be analysable along lines resembling those suggested by Patrick Gardiner (*The Nature of Historical Explanation*, Oxford University Press, 1961): but it is not to be assumed that explanations which appear at first sight to be dispositional necessarily are so. Moreover, explanations appealing to dispositions still leave open the question why the agent behaved in accordance with some general disposition on *this particular* occasion.
21. See Henle, M., 'Deductive Reasoning' in P. C. Wason and P. N. Johnson-Laird, (eds.), *Thinking and Reasoning*, Penguin, 1968.
22. Quoted in ibid., p. 96.
23. ibid., pp. 97-106.
24. Watkins, J. N., 'Imperfect Rationality', in R. Borger and F. Cioffi (eds.), *Explanation in the Behavioural Sciences*, Cambridge University Press, 1970. Watkins quotes Hough, R., *Admirals in Collision*, Hamish Hamilton, 1959.
25. Watkins, J. N., op. cit., or Hough, R., op. cit.
26. Of course one might still want to know why Tryon overlooked the possibility of the order being misunderstood, and why in fact the commander of the *Camperdown* did fail to understand it. But such further questions as to *how* things come about have already been discussed; additional issues in this connection are examined below.

27. Compare Popper's *rationality principle*, (note 16 above) and Collingwood's frequent insistence that one must understand a man's 'question' before judging his 'answer' to it. For a brief discussion of related issues see Elton, G. R., *The Practice of History*, Sydney University Press, 1967, pp. 81-2, and p. 98.

28. Von Wright's distinction between hermeneutics and causal explanation (op. cit., Chapter 1, especially pp. 15-16) confines the term 'causal' to deductive-nomological (covering-law) models. It is used in this sense here—that is, it is specifically distinguished from and juxtaposed to explanation by the construction of a rationale or practical inference.

29. Any explanation of (say) why the torpedoes missed, would, so far as it rested on such laws, be an 'inductive' explanation. To that extent it would not, of course, meet the 'deductive requirement' referred to earlier.

30. It must be emphasized that these examples are intended to illustrate the form of certain statements sometimes found in history books and to show what sense can be made of them. It is *not* asserted, for instance, that an adequate account of the decline of the Liberal Party would attribute its demise as a major political force simply to the actions of Lloyd George. See also Elton, G. R., *Political History, Principles and Practice*, Allen Lane, 1970, pp. 137-52, and especially p. 155, note 35, where a particularly interesting example—the *communeros* hindering Charles V's efforts to stop Luther—is employed in a rather different analytical framework from the one used here.

31. *Quasi*-causal, because although one may talk of *A*'s action as being 'the cause' of *B*'s, *A* is in fact (in the kind of case under consideration) giving *B reasons* for acting in a certain way. In von Wright's terminology there is not therefore a *causal* (deductive-nomological) relation between *A*'s action and *B*'s.

32. See Dray, W. H., op. cit., 1957, pp. 141-2.

33. So intertwined that W. H. Walsh, developing Whewell's notion of *colligation*, at first attempted to employ it in explicating historical explanation (Walsh, W. H., *An Introduction to Philosophy of History*, Hutchinson, 2nd edition 1958, pp. 59-64) and then, abandoning much of his earlier thesis, argued that colligation was primarily involved in interpretation ('Colligatory Concepts in History' in W. H. Burston and D. Thompson (eds.), op. cit., pp. 65-84), but still failed to make explicit the relationship between them. For a discussion of this relationship, see von Wright, G. H., op. cit., pp. 132-5.

34. Interpretation in history is, of course, much wider than this. The debate on the 'Tudor Revolution in Government' is a useful illustration. What is at issue in that debate is not only the meaning (and significance) of administrative changes *for the participants*, but their meaning (or significance) *in the story*. That is, the part they play in—the way they fit into—the story of English government from the Middle Ages to modern times. (Hence the importance of changes during the Yorkist and later Tudor periods as set out by Penry Williams and G. L. Harriss in 'A Revolution in Tudor History?' in *Past and Present*, No. 25, July 1963.) And to be able to say conclusively what the significance of an event or a man—e.g. Thomas Cromwell—in a story is, one must consider how things might have gone if those events had not happened, or that man had not existed. (See Kitson Clark, G., *The Critical Historian*, Heinemann Educational Books, 1967, p. 44, for a discussion of this.) Here historical imagination (discussed below) comes into play: but in the nature of things such speculations, however carefully developed on the basis of evidence, are not conclusive, and so such debates are not easily settled. (For an interesting example of how misleading the 'scientific' view of history implicit in the covering-law model can be if taken too seriously, see Holloway, S. W. F., 'What History Is and What it Ought to Be' in W. H. Burston and D. Thompson (eds.), op. cit., pp. 1-25, in which Holloway castigates historians for being so confused as to imagine that in arguments about interpretation they are disagreeing about anything substantive at all.) In interpretation there is thus a partial analogy with explanation, in that the

historian oscillates between the agents' views of what is happening, and his own assessment of it.

35. See, for example, the curious placing of 'imagination' under 'Attitudes towards the study of history' in Coltham, J. B., and Fines, J., *Educational Objectives for the Study of History*, Historical Association (TH35), 1971, and the subsequent rather confused analysis. (This is discussed further in the chapter by Gard and Lee, '"Educational Objectives for the Study of History" Reconsidered', on pp. 32-3 of this book.)

36. See Hexter, J. H., op. cit., Chapter 8, for the illuminating comments of a professional historian on a wide range of issues connected with the notion on 'What it must have been like'. It is a pity that so perceptive a historian as Hexter does not take a more positive approach to the task of clarifying this aspect of history. He makes no consistent distinction between knowing what a particular historical agent 'was like', knowing 'what it would have been like to be' a particular agent, and knowing what a *situation* 'would be like' if one were a particular agent.

37. This is too narrow, for clearly theoretical reason is also important in history: men have reasons for believing things too. This chapter is not, however, the place for a discussion of the differences. (See Edgley, R., op. cit., for a detailed discussion.)

38. Once again this concept sheds light on objectivity in history. The last of the four statements may be offered as an interpretation of the significance of Bismarck's action in the story of recent German history, or as an interpretation in the other sense—i.e. as if Bismarck *meant* his action in this way. A historian who, having produced evidence for his interpretation in the first sense, slips into employing it in the second sense, is failing to meet one criterion of objectivity.

39. This latter is much wider than it appears, for once it is accepted that historical narrative cannot be 'plain'—i.e. free from partially explanatory characterization of actions, and free from organization in terms of the meaning of and connections between these actions—we can see that a child's capacity to follow a narrative depends upon his ability to understand explanations in terms of intentions. (For the notion of a 'plain' narrative, see Walsh, W. H., *An Introduction to Philosophy of History*, Hutchinson, 2nd edn., 1958, pp. 31-3; for a critical appraisal of it see Danto, A., *Analytical Philosophy of History*, Cambridge University Press, pp. 116-32.)

40. Such a practical inference would only very rarely be set out in anything approaching a formal way in written history, and not much more often, so far as one can tell, in history teaching.

41. A characterization of A's situation *exclusively* in these terms (i.e. A saw his situation as being one in which x was the only—or best—thing to do to achieve p) could only barely be said to explain anything, since an essential part of the rationale would be missing, and in an important sense one could not attempt to follow A's reasoning. This might be thought to be a weakness in von Wright's schema set out earlier. But von Wright's schema is just that—a schema—and explanations of this kind do not occur without content and in a vacuum, so in reality this kind of case does not arise in its pure form: there is always a story, or a fragment of a story, into which A's action fits, and hence A's situation is always characterized independently of its being simply S . If, however, S^a is only minimally characterized independently of S^x, difficulties may begin to arise. Not the least of these is the question whether there is independent evidence—independent of the fact that he actually did x— to distinguish S^a from S^h, and therefore to support the assertion that it was because he believed himself in *this* situation that A did x. In the absence of direct evidence it is easy to assume that S^a is the same as S^h (as far as logically possible—see Danto, A., op. cit., Chapter IX) but this can lead to a complete misconception of A's reasons. Hence the closed characterization S^x can conceal bad mistakes.

42. Historians sometimes assume, in the absence of independent evidence, that what an agent accomplished was what he intended, but this is naturally a dangerous procedure. Difficulties arise particularly when interpretations turn on whether an action or series of actions, described in similar but different ways, were, under those descriptions, intentional or not. (Eg. Bismarck and the unification of Germany, or Hitler and the origins of the Second World War.)

43. Of course historians are sometimes said to have a 'feeling' for an age. But this is not so much a matter of feelings which the historian has, as of his having evidence of such wide and varied kinds in mind that it would be impossible to set it all out in a rigorously precise way—even if that is what he wanted to do.

44. 'Ways of thinking' would include everything from the 'absolute presuppositions' of the age, to the detailed knowledge and beliefs of the agent.

45. 'Consideration' here does not necessarily imply careful calculations on the part of A—simply that he could be expected to have seen the situation, however fleetingly, as one which allowed a certain course of action.

46. Inhelder, B., and Piaget, J., *The Growth of Logical Thinking*, Routledge and Kegan Paul, 1958, pp. 107-22.

6. Understanding and Research

A. K. DICKINSON   P. J. LEE

INTRODUCTION

Our concern in this chapter is with the problems, possibilities and teaching implications of research into children's thinking in history, themes which we discuss with particular reference to our own pilot study. Although only a pilot, our work attempts something new in trying to derive its foundations in the first place from an analysis of history. Rather than attempt to cover the whole range of children's thinking in history, we confine our attention to a limited (if important) matter, namely some aspects of historical explanation and understanding. The present chapter begins with a sketch of the theoretical basis of past work (Part I). In Part II we describe our pilot study, and discuss some of the problems and possibilities of developing research in this area. In Part III we suggest some implications for history teaching.

PART I.   THEORY AND RECENT RESEARCH

We do not intend here to attempt a comprehensive survey of recent work, but only to discuss some general features of research on children's reasoning and judgement in history: in particular the theoretical foundations. We will also refer in passing to one or two aspects of experimental design.

The most outstanding characteristic of research into children's thinking in history has been a negative one: its lack of any autonomous theoretical basis. The two most important influences have been (inevitably) Jean Piaget, and, more directly concerned with history, E. A. Peel. Piaget has not examined children's thinking in history as such, and in recent years most of his work has been in the area of natural science. Even his interest in moral development has taken second place to experiments in which children manipulate physical objects.[1] Peel, on the other hand, has shown a continuing interest in history, and frequently uses historical examples in discussing his own categorization of thinking. Indeed, the only detailed general survey of the field (until fairly recently) was provided by Peel.[2]

The theoretical impact of Piaget and Peel is plain to see. For example, in R. N. Hallam's list of criteria for the assessment of 'the operational level' of subjects' answers, we find in the 'concrete operational' stage: 'able to *forecast* a result from the evidence available'. In the stage 'Intermediate between concrete and formal operational thinking' we have: 'Going *outside the known data* in the story to form hypotheses, but not too successfully; beginning to relate different *variables*'. And under 'Formal operational thinking': '*Holds certain factors constant* and *varies others systematically* to discover which explanations are true . . .' (our emphasis).[3] In A. Rees' 'Criteria for evaluating responses within a category system' we have: (Category A) '. . . a comprehensive judgement that . . . involved . . . probablistic inference . . . which necessitated going beyond the information given: the inference or inferences acted as explanatory principles or *generalizations* which served to organize the information systematically' (our emphasis). In Category B, responses did not '. . . weave *all* the variables into a full combinatorial analysis . . .' (Rees' emphasis).[4] D. Thompson, who is particularly concerned to produce more genuinely *historical* categories, nevertheless in his Domesday Book test links them directly with those of Piaget and Peel: '. . . answers stating the information [given in the passage] indicated concrete or describer thinking whereas those that suggested [William I's] reasons for wanting the information were thinking at a formal or explanatory level'.[5]

Anyone acquainted with their work will recognize from these quotations that the influence of both Piaget and Peel is considerable; those concerned with history may wonder how far that influence is justified. It will be useful to take Piaget and Peel in turn and examine some of their central features in relation to the particular problems of history.

1. Piaget

What are the main characteristics of a typical piece of Piagetian research on the growth of logical operations? It is convenient to examine the basic components of such research: the tests, the protocols recording subjects' behaviour during the tests and the categories employed in evaluating subjects' thinking.

Three important characteristics of Piagetian *tests* can be picked out. Firstly, the tasks set for the subjects are mainly concerned with the manipulation of physical objects and the observation of the results of such manipulation.[6] (The manipulation need not actually be physical — the subjects can sometimes solve the problem 'in their heads' — but physical manipulation is nonetheless generally possible, and of course this is not accidental, but reflects an important tenet of Piagetian theory.)

Secondly, in an important sense the evidence required for the solution of the problem is all in: the subjects do not need extraneous information about the behaviour of the apparatus. Manipulation of the present apparatus should provide the answers sought. The subjects must bring certain schemes with them if they are to be successful, but in most cases not specific extra information.[7]

Thirdly, the solution of the problem requires the statement of a regularity or series of regularities: subjects are asked to explain what happens by appeal to a covering law.[8]

These characteristics of the tests partly account for the next components of a typical Piagetian experiment, the detailed *protocols* recording individual subjects' attempts to come to grips with the problem. Questions will be asked with the intention of discovering the 'working' involved in any particular subject's solutions: the attempted solution may tell us nothing of how it was arrived at. Since the subject's thinking is to be analysed in formal logical terms, this is of considerable importance. The experimenter may suggest moves for the subject, and ask what would happen if they were made. He may pose questions which show up ambiguities in the subject's thinking, or even force the subject to reconsider his solution. In this sense the experimenter is frankly manipulative and interventionist.[9]

Finally we have the third component, the *categories*. The categories into which subjects are fitted have a logical basis, and which subjects go into which category depends on a logical analysis of their handling of the problem (not simply on the logical coherence of their final solution). The categories, and their logical basis, are closely related to the material of the tests, which is drawn from the physical sciences. For example, among the criteria which serve to differentiate the main categories we find the schema 'all other things being equal' translated into 'each factor must be varied independently and the others held constant'.[10] Concepts such as *equilibrium* and *reversibility* often have a direct counterpart in the physical operations performed in the tests.[11] As already mentioned above, this is a connection which Piaget exploits in arguing that mental operations are in some sense internalized physical operations.[12]

This outline of some features of the experiments in *The Growth of Logical Thinking* is necessarily highly selective, but it provides a valuable contrast with the problems of theoretical and experimental work on thinking in history. To begin with, there is no equivalent in history to the carefully planned apparatus of a Piagetian experiment.[13] This is partly because, obviously enough, the subject-matter of history does not consist of experimentally manipulable objects, accessible to direct inspection. This means that children cannot *observe* the behaviour of objects under their own control, the consequences of manipulation. Another difference between Piaget's experiments and those possible in history is that the kinds of questions asked by the historian are radically different from those of the natural scientist. Of course a historian's evidence often takes the form of physical relics of the past, but he is not concerned to discover law-like relations between such objects. Hence, while Piaget's subjects were in effect asked to discover regularities in natural phenomena, the subjects of tests on children's thinking in history, in so far as they are asked to give explanations of action, must discover an agent's reasons for action. This involves detailed examination of specific events in particular times and places: a study of particulars. Whereas an experiment in *The Growth of Logical Thinking* provides (at least potentially) all the evidence required, if only the subjects will use it, it is simply not possible in history to develop a test in which 'all the evidence is in'.

All this means that it is much more difficult to get at a particular subject's reasoning in history than it is in natural science: there are no detailed protocols of the subject's thinking as he grapples with his problem.[14] Tests of thinking in history largely consist of *written* passages, questions and answers, so that while we have the subject's 'results', we do not have his 'working'. The latter has to be inferred from the former, a step fraught with difficulty, particularly with younger or less literate children.[15]

Finally, the categories in terms of which responses in history are assessed and classified cannot be borrowed ready-made from natural science. History is not concerned with 'variables', and, except in terms of very weak analogy, it is hard to see how 'each factor' *could* be 'varied independently and the others held constant'.[16] The explicit basis of Piagetian categories in formal logic (ultimately in certain elements of the propositional calculus) has been reflected only dimly in work on thinking in history; this is hardly surprising in view of the difficulties involved in the logical analysis of historical discourse.[17] The question arises whether, given the complexity of the logic of historical explanation, the propositional calculus is sufficient. It may be that in order to cope with thinking about action in history, future research will be forced to consider developments in tense-logic and in particular the logic of action, as exemplified in the work of G. H. von Wright.[18]

2. Peel

The central feature of Peel's analysis of thinking is the distinction between 'content-dominated' and 'possibility invoking' thinking.[19] Peel draws parallels between the former and description, and between the latter and explanation; while 'describer thinking' involves relating the parts of some phenomenon or problem, 'explainer thinking' goes beyond this to relate the phenomenon or problem to 'outside concepts, wider causes and generalizations'.[20] Peel's categories are very broadly defined in order to apply to a range of disciplines, and if at this general level it would be hard to dispute them, their application to *history* creates problems precisely *because* of their global quality. Three connected difficulties will be mentioned here.

Firstly, explanation in history is not the same as explanation in natural science. Peel recognizes this, but seems unable to shed basic assumptions derived from science. He describes historical change as '. . . a causal sequence of shifts between states in which human forces are more or less balanced', developing this view at some length.[21] But even if human societies *may* be viewed as 'systems' in equilibrium (and this is true only as an analogy) such an account would miss out the central role of *intentions* in historical explanation to which Peel himself draws attention.[22] History is not simply a matter of *forces* to be measured, but of *considerations* which agents have to bear in mind. Hence in tests of historical thinking children do not *observe* the effects of different *factors*, but must understand how things could be *considerations* for an agent. This is not a matter of forces, human or physical, but of rational connections. In history even a 'descriptive' narrative is already explanatory because it organizes events as manifesting *purposes* and *intentions*: historical explanation involves *internal* relations between actions.

Secondly, if historical explanation frequently rests on the discovery of internal relations, the characterization of 'explainer thinking' as relating problems to 'outside concepts' needs clarification. Peel quotes Runciman's fable, in which visitors to another planet observe the exchange of objects for pieces of metal and paper, learning to predict future occurrences, but failing to *understand*. Peel concludes from this that the understanding which is lacking is of 'independent and pre-existing concepts', namely money, value, barter, etc.[23] But the point of Runciman's example is *not* that 'outside' concepts be applied (our visitors might do that very successfully in terms of their own alien concepts) but that the actions to be explained *meant* something to the agents. The concepts required here would be those *in terms of which the agents saw their actions.*[24]

Finally, it would be a mistake to think of concepts functioning in history as they do in natural science. Peel seems to have in mind as a paradigm of 'explainer thinking' the application of powerful explanatory concepts of the kind found in natural science: thus for someone to *explain* climate he must refer to '. . . the principles of meteorology . . . and physics. These would include concepts of heat transmission, convection, radiation . . . and so on'.[25] But the explanatory power of these concepts is connected with their articulation in *general laws*, and as there are few of the latter available for history, the relation of a problem 'to outside concepts, wider causes, and generalizations' is misleading as a characterization of historical thinking.[26] If we assume that to have a concept is to understand a rule and to be able to pick out instances, we might say that in the case of scientific concepts an increasing range of instances come to be seen as cases of the *same* rule. In history new instances *expand* the rule: the latter is historically empty, being necessarily so vague as to mark out only a very general area of application. Alternatively it is so complex as to be nothing more or less than a description of all 'instances' so far known. 'Historical concepts' are in general everyday practical concepts in which the only specifically *historical* content is provided by particular instances.[27] When children are asked in a test of historical thinking to suggest a reason for William I's 'harrying of the North', they bring to the task a concept of *king* which has already embedded in it minimal implications for possible intentions.[28] But whether the concept is cashable historically will depend on the range of instances the children have met; relevant instances will be not just *any* kings, but medieval ones. Even this knowledge will be *faute de mieux*; what is really needed is particular knowledge of *William*, not of medieval monarchs in general. The same will be true of the *situations* in which agents act: 'merely conceptual' clues are second best; it is specific information which is required.

An example from our own work illustrates this. Subjects were given a passage on Henry II's expulsion of mercenaries and his destruction of adulterine castles, and after answering questions on these events, were asked: 'What sort of things do you think Henry would be aiming to do during his reign—not just about mercenaries and castles, but in general?' Here is the response of a boy aged fourteen years eleven months who had done no medieval history since primary school:

> He will be trying to get the country up high with the big nations e.g. build a big army, Navy etc. Make bigger industries in England to make larger exports to make more money. But first he would get his place as king fixed in people's minds and protect this position with arms against any revolution groups which might arise. But most of all he would be giving speeches and talking with power to get confidence from the people.

This subject graded his answer 2 on a scale running from 'almost certain' (1) through 'quite likely' (2), 'possible' (3), to 'just a guess' (4) and indicated that his grade was given on the basis of evidence in the passage and additional information of his own. The conception of kingship which emerges here is a fairly complex one, but (not surprisingly) appears to be very much based on aspects of the role of a modern political leader. It is *not* that the subject's concept of *king* is at a low level or lacks articulation, but that he has *no specific historical knowledge*: his concept is historically impoverished through lack of instances.

PART II.   UNDERSTANDING IN HISTORY— A PILOT STUDY

The basis of our own work is a specific analysis of one aspect of historical thinking, namely, that part of historical explanation which involves understanding why some agent acted as he did. This analysis is discussed in Chapter 5 (pp. 72-93 of this book). The category system there tentatively proposed was employed in a number of pilot tests, one of the most substantial of which forms the subject of this part of the current chapter. It is worth stressing again that these tests are *not* intended to be general tests of historical thinking.

Our pilot work took two distinct but related forms. Firstly, we wanted to replicate certain features of current test passages, but to enquire more closely into children's ability to suggest explanations in the absence of anything approaching adequate evidence (which is frequently a characteristic of such tests). To this end we selected and simplified a passage from William of Newburgh on Henry II, and asked two substantive historical questions as to why Henry expelled the Flemish mercenaries, and why he destroyed adulterine castles. Subsequent questions were less orthodox: we were particularly interested in the degree of certainty which subjects would attach to their answers, and in the effect of a heavily emphasized invitation to say what additional evidence might be required. We also hoped to discover what notions of kingship were being brought to bear on the two substantive questions. All this involved asking subjects to comment on their own earlier answers. It will be obvious that such an approach raises exactly the questions broached in Part I: how do we get at subjects' 'working', rather than their 'results', and how far is it possible to justify an 'interventionist' approach in this kind of work? Analysis of these responses is not complete, and much of the test is only partially relevant to our concerns here; we will not, therefore, discuss the Henry test any further in the current chapter.[29]

Secondly, parallel to this line of inquiry, we developed a series of tests in which much more information than usual was offered to subjects. For this purpose we needed a relatively 'simple' historical situation, in which an agent or group of agents could be regarded as having a limited range of possibilities for action. After some preliminary testing we chose Jellicoe's turn away during the battle of Jutland as being particularly suitable for probing children's understanding.[30]

The Jutland test went through four basic versions, with several alternative sets of questions and instruction sheets. The version ultimately chosen is appended to this chapter (see Appendices I and II).[31] Three suburban schools were used for this pilot: one mixed comprehensive and one mixed technical high school each provided a second and a fifth form; the technical high and another mixed comprehensive provided an upper-sixth form each.[32] The first comprehensive had an unusually small history upper-sixth that year but supplied eight lower-sixth subjects. Altogether 57 second-year, 40 fifth-year, and 34 sixth-year responses were collected. The test was administered to ordinary class groups in normal history periods, usually before a school break (to provide extra time if required).[33] Each subject received the pamphlet and instructions, and in addition a brief questionnaire to ascertain his or her prior knowledge of the subject, whether from school or other sources. (This covered background knowledge as well as Jutland itself.) Our verbal instructions drew attention to the general written introductory instructions, and indicated that it was primarily the *test* which was under investigation. It was explained that we were interested in the problems posed for pupils in understanding why things happened in history. The questions (see Appendix III) were administered separately, one at a time: thus subjects on their first reading of the pamphlet would have before them only question one (although it is important to remember that they would also have the general instructions).

An examination of the questions in Appendix III will show why this procedure was necessary: they constitute a series in whch knowledge of the later ones could affect answers to earlier questions. So, despite some inconvenience, a new question was presented to each subject as he finished the previous one. *Question One* asked simply *why* Jellicoe turned away. *Question Two* allowed subjects to show how far their first answer really represented their understanding. Too often it is assumed that a confident, unqualified answer to a question where the evidence does not allow such an answer indicates a relatively low level of thinking.[34] It may often do that, but it may also indicate that children know teachers *expect an answer*, and preferably a definite one. The typical question-and-answer pattern of classroom talk often trades on precisely that assumption: the teacher expects pupils to reason through to the next stage in *his* (the teacher's) argument on the basis of a limited set of clues.[35] The same assumption that teachers want straightforward answers may have another unfortunate effect, in concealing the confusion felt by the pupil (or test-subject). Comparisons of answers to Questions One and Two revealed that apparent understanding of Jellicoe's situation and intentions in Question One frequently gave way to puzzlement and confusion in Question Two. (See Appendix IV, Examples 1 to 4. Future reference to 'Examples' will be to the numbered responses in that Appendix.) *Question Three* pressed harder, looking for the kind of assumptions which so easily remain hidden in children's attempts to understand historical action, and which, left undisturbed, can make much history arbitrary and unintelligible.[36] Almost all subjects suggested alternative courses of action for Jellicoe, some showing signs of irritation that Jellicoe had 'irrationally' ignored obviously superior possibilities. Such irritation was often already apparent, together with spontaneous — uninvited — suggestions for 'more sensible' actions, in answers to Question Two. (Examples 2 and 4.) We now feel that Question Three is redundant in the many cases where subjects already have some alternative in mind, and presses too hard on other subjects, perhaps leading them to volunteer alternatives purely for our benefit. (See Example 5 for this. More genuine suggestions are made in Examples 6, 7, 8, and 15.) Both parts of *Question Four* attempted to discover whether or not subjects were distinguishing between the *agent's* view of the situation, and the *historian's* view which the information in the pamphlet enabled them to take.[37] In (a) a 'static' description would suffice, but in (b) a 'dynamic' characterization in terms of possible outcomes was demanded.[38] (Examples 9, 10 and 11.) There was an opportunity in the latter to rule out any alternative courses of action which had been suggested in answer to Question Three, and this was often taken. (See Example 11. This subject's answer to Question Three is too long to quote, and includes a detailed diagram.) Finally, *Question Five* was intended to overcome the limitations of Question One. As usually set in tests of historical thinking, a 'why' question like Question One might legitimately be taken by subjects to require a treatment in which the *details* of the situation are seen as problematic: it cannot be assumed from answers of this kind that subjects are unable to go beyond the immediate situation.[39] Question Five therefore sought to discover if subjects *could* relate the turn away both to some ramified statement of Jellicoe's intentions and to a broad grasp of the situation, whether implicitly or explicitly. (Examples 12 and 13.)

The category system used to evaluate the responses is set out in abstract form in Chapter 5 of this book (especially pp. 86-8). There are six categories, grouped into four levels. The set of five answers completed by each subject was treated as one overall response, and scored as such. (Where, therefore, an example from Appendix IV is referred to as being in a certain category or level, it should be taken as *exemplifying* that category or level as typically manifested in a *single answer*.) We will examine the categories one at a time in relation to the examples in Appendix IV.

Level I comprises solely category one responses, which often treated the turn away as unintelligible. In their efforts to make sense of the situation, subjects in this category misconstrued it in elementary ways.[40] Thus in Example 15 the subject confused British and German action, and (less basic) seems to have believed that the turn took place at night. The subject in Example 14 found the turn unintelligible through failure to grasp certain *physical* relationships and the outcomes of action consequent upon those relationships: the subject could not see that the turn away reduced both the effective speed of the torpedoes, and the size of target offered by each British ship. Example 5 ignored the specific statement in the passage that the British did not believe a simultaneous turn away possible.

Level II consists of categories two and three. Subjects in category two produced an explanation of the turn away, but in doing so failed to distinguish between the agent's and the historian's point of view. A frequent feature of category two responses was the conventional nature of the understanding displayed: the evidence in the passage was not used to uncover Jellicoe's particular intentions in his particular situation, but instead 'merely conceptual' clues, stereotypes and personal projections were employed. Jutland was a *battle*, so Jellicoe wanted to *win*, to 'blow the Germans up'. There were elements of conventional understanding in Example 12, and it was clearly present in Example 16. Good indicators of such thinking were explanations of the turn stressing the preservation of Jellicoe's own and his men's lives, rather than of the *fleet*, and attributions of cowardice or stupidity. Not all category two responses were conventional: some exhibited a clearer awareness of the evidence available in the passage. (See Example 9.)[41]

Subjects whose answer to Question One was evidence of category two understanding often revealed considerable puzzlement in later answers as a direct result of inability to grasp that Jellicoe simply did not know what *they* knew. These responses were classified as category three. In general responses in Level II revealed mistakes of hindsight (knowledge of consequences), and over-estimated Jellicoe's ability to discover what was happening. Example 9 (category two) had Jellicoe knowing the precise number of torpedoes launched against him, one of several common indicators of Level II; Example 6 (category three) complained of his listening to the Director of Naval Intelligence. Example 2 (category three) ignored the torpedo danger already given as the explanation of the turn (in Example 1). Taken by itself Example 1 had one or two signs of the distinction between the agent's and the historian's view (e.g. 'As it happened . . .') which would have put it in category four; considered together with Example 2 and subsequent answers (not quoted here) it was clear that the overall response was in category three.

At Level III, categories four and five, subjects were able to qualify Jellicoe's intentions in turning away: for instance the turn was often seen as a temporary move to preserve the fleet for further action, and the possibility of forcing another action by steaming between the Germans and their bases was discussed. (Examples 7 and 8 — both category five.) More important, at this level subjects distinguished Jellicoe's view of the situation from the historian's view, often stressing the poor visibility, the lateness of the day, and the fact that Jellicoe had been (wrongly) led to expect that the German torpedo tracks would be concealed. (Examples 3 and 10 were both illustrative of category four.) Some took the latter point a step further and recognized that Jellicoe might have expected many more torpedoes if he had turned towards the Germans. The differentiation made at Level III resolved some of the typical category three problems of the previous level, where subjects had suggested alternative courses of action open only to someone with their knowledge of what was going on. There was often still a measure of uncertainty about an explanatory equilibrium at Level III (achieved in a category four response), derived mainly from an inability to see Jellicoe's action in a wider context than the events of the battle. Thus answers to Question One which seemed to be evidence for category four could be followed in Question Two, Three and sometimes Four and Five by answers which revealed a certain amount of confusion. Such responses were classified as category five. A category five response was typically similar to one in category three in suggesting alternative courses of action, but unlike the latter, more or less maintained a distinction between Jellicoe's point of view and the historian's; this led to more tentative suggestions, sometimes ruled out and reasserted in the same answer. (Example 8 showed something of both these features.) Sometimes there was mention of the wider context, usually concentrating on the need to destroy the German naval challenge in order to maintain British command of the sea: half understood in this way, without Jellicoe's concomitant need to preserve his fleet, the wider context seems to have been an important factor in shifting subjects away from a category four explanatory equilibrium.

At Level IV the difficulties of category five were resolved, subjects seeing the rival considerations which demanded Jellicoe's attention in the wider context, and integrating them successfully. Category six responses (the only category at this final level) *explained* the turn away from the Germans, maintained the distinction between Jellicoe's and the historian's view of the situation, and gave a qualified and ramified account of Jellicoe's intentions. (Example 13 illustrated this level as it typically appeared in the final question.) In this category there were occasionally elements of critical appraisal of the action *as it had turned out*, but not at the expense of the explanation.

We regard subjects whose responses are in even-number categories as having achieved an 'explanatory equilibrium', and those whose responses are in odd-number categories as in a state of 'disequilibrium'.

'Equilibrium' as we use it is a much less sophisticated concept than Piaget's, but there are nevertheless some analogies. Subjects may achieve an explanatory equilibrium in our tests at different levels, and the *field*, understood as the range of descriptions under which actions may be subsumed, will be wider at Level IV than at Level II.[42] In Example 12 (part of a Level II response), Jellicoe's action was seen simply as winning a decisive battle, and getting rid of the German fleet once and for all. In Example 13 (Level IV) this description was just one of a number of possible descriptions, each at a higher level of intention. Thus Jellicoe was seen as protecting imports, and continuing British naval supremacy. In terms of *mobility* between the 'considerations' which may have been borne in mind by Jellicoe, there is also an analogy with Piaget. A subject at Level IV was more likely to move from one such 'consideration' to another than a subject at Level II. It is also possible that a higher-level equilibrium may exhibit greater *permanence* and *stability* than a lower-level one (although at this stage this must remain a conjecture).

Another, perhaps safer, analogy can be made with the work of Turiel.[43] In particular Turiel's description of *disequilibrium* would fit our categories closely: 'Judgements made during this phase were characterized by a great deal of inconsistency, conflict, and internal contradiction'. Disequilibrium in Turiel's account is characteristic of movement from one level to another, and this is likely to be the case in our work. It would *not* however be true of our category system that 'responses are not classifiable' while in disequilibrium.[44]

Our series of questions frequently produced a progression within each response as subjects were forced to consider Jellicoe's position more closely. The effects of Questions Two and Three in rendering unstable an apparent equilibrium in the answer to Question One have already been mentioned. Some subjects never 'recovered', failing to resolve their puzzlement in Question Four (particularly (b)) and Question Five. On the other hand many subjects, considering Jellicoe's situation carefully in Question Four, eventually ruled out the alternatives they had previously suggested. Where such a rejection was complete, it was taken as conclusive evidence that the subject had achieved an explanatory equilibrium (except in the rare case of uncertainty in, or conflict with, answers to Question Five). If rejection was only partial, answers to Questions Two and Five were examined against the answer to Question Four, with the purpose of ascertaining just how far the grounds of puzzlement or confusion still lingered. Where clear indications of uncertainty remained, the response was scored in the relevant odd-number category. Decisions as to whether explanatory equilibrium had been achieved or not do not, of course, affect the allocation of responses to *levels*.

We set out below the age, school, sex and level of response of the subjects who did the Jutland test. Table 2 shows that the majority of responses from the second year were at Level II, the majority of those from the upper sixth were at Level III, while those from the fifth year were almost equally divided between Levels II and III. The χ^2 result derived from Table 4 indicates the existence of an association between age and level of response in the particular population from which the sample is drawn; the contingency coefficient of 0.45 represents the degree of association and shows that it is significant. The X^2 value for Table 3 indicates that there is not significant evidence for an association between level attained and school attended. It should be remembered that with a sample of this size and composition statistical results allow only very limited conclusions.

TABLE 1: Distribution by Age, School and Sex of the 131 subjects (66 boys, 65 girls) who answered the Jutland test

Year	School	Sex Distribution Boys	Girls	Total of Subjects	Chronological Age Range	Mean Chronological Age
2nd	Comprehensive A	11	16	27	12:4 to 13:3	12:11
	Technical High	14	16	30	12:6 to 13:6	12:11
5th	Comprehensive A	12	7	19	15:7 to 16:6	16: 0
	Technical High	8	13	21	15:8 to 16:6	16: 1
Lower 6th	Comprehensive A	5	3	8	16:8 to 17:6	17: 1
Upper 6th	Technical High	8	5	13	17:5 to 18:5	17:10
	Comprehensive B	8	5	13	17:6 to 18:6	18: 1

TABLE 2: Distribution by Level and Age of scores on the Jutland test

Year	Age Range	Level (score for a subject's total response) 1	2	3	4	Total
2nd	12:4 to 13:6	9	35	12	1	57
5th	15:7 to 16:6	1	17	18	4	40
6th	16:8 to 18:6	—	4	20	10	34
		10	56	50	15	131

TABLE 3: Distribution by Level and School of scores on the Jutland test

School	Level 1	2	3	4	Total
Comprehensive A	4	27	16	7	54
Technical High	6	27	27	4	64
	10	54	43	11	118

$X^2 = 3.21$. For 3 d.f. at the 5 per cent significance level $X^2=7.82$. Therefore the calculated value is *not* significant.

TABLE 4: Distribution by Level and Age of scores on the Jutland test for subjects in Comprehensive A and the Technical High School

Year and Age Range		Levels 1 and 2	Levels 3 and 4	Total
2nd	12:4 to 13:6	44	13	57
5th	15:7 to 16:6	18	22	40
6th	16:8 to 18:5	2	19	21
		64	54	118

$\chi^2 = 30.39$. For 2 d.f. at the 0.001 significance level $\chi^2 = 13.82$. Therefore the calculated value is significant beyond the 0.001 value.

$C = 0.45$.

(The levels shown in Table 4 distinguish between those who could and could not qualify the agent's intentions and differentiate between his view of the situation and that of the historian. Levels 1 to 4 have been conflated in this way in order to meet the requirements of the χ^2 test as described by Siegel, S., *Non-Parametric Statistics for the Behavioural Sciences*, McGraw Hill, 1956, p. 178.)

Clearly the test here described is relatively crude, and open to a number of criticisms. *Some* 'interventionist' characteristics are necessary to probe behind children's answers, but Question Three appears to go too far, producing misleading signs of disequilibrium as subjects try to please by inventing alternatives. The questions are clumsy—Question Four in particular provoked occasional protest as being 'childish'—and a few subjects complained that they were repetitious. This was true only if crucial distinctions were ignored, but in any case the excision of Question Three should ease the problem. The passage is long, and we were probably partly testing ability to hold in mind and relate large amounts of evidence. Some cuts can be made, but too short a passage would produce worse problems.[46] Finally the language in the passage is only roughly simplified, and demands systematic attention.

Development of research in this area seems to require progress on two fronts: large-scale testing to obtain valid statistical data; and detailed investigation of *how* children come to achieve explanatory equilibrium. The first approach involves more precise and more varied test instruments, and we are currently constructing tests based on passages of modern diplomatic history and of Anglo-Saxon law, hoping later to widen the scope of our work to include children's understanding of quasi-causal chains.[47] This kind of testing, of course, also requires measurements of intelligence and reading-skills in order to establish possible correlations.

The second approach is in some ways more interesting. We have on tape a spontaneous discussion which arose after some fifth-year pupils had done the Jutland test, and which gives us reason to believe that a great deal of useful evidence as to the processes of children's thinking can be gained from systematic exploitation of small-group discussion. Children's efforts to thrash out together an explanation of some historical action may provide something analogous to a Piagetian *protocol*, and give us important clues as to how children's understanding may best be developed.

PART III. TEACHING IMPLICATIONS

Is it possible to say anything about teaching from the work done so far? Peel has warned that children bring to the classroom relatively little knowledge and experience which will help them to understand the sort of things they are likely to study in history. Our empirical work has produced further evidence to support this assertion: we have found that a great many of the children who had little or no prior knowledge of the topic examined our material and then offered explanations based on conventional and conceptually stereotyped views. Of course we must not write off their experience, but clearly there are good grounds for expecting children, at least initially, to have difficulty in understanding historical situations and grasping the intentions of historical agents.

The least convincing of Peel's suggestions for coping with this problem is that it can be avoided to a great extent because (with younger children) actions 'can be described without need to refer too much to their *intentions*'.[48] Coltham makes a similar suggestion when she claims, 'the same content can well be used with different ages, the younger looking mainly at what Collingwood calls the "outside" of events and the older at the "inside".'[49] These suggestions fail to make certain connections explicit. In the first place, to describe an agent's action is already to state his intentions at some level. Intentions cannot be left out without making history senseless, and are minimized only at the expense of reducing it to an arbitrary concatenation of events.[50] In the second place there are important connections between understanding an agent's intentions and understanding the situation in which he was acting.[51] Our empirical work so far suggests that *situations* cause more problems for children than intentions. The latter can be understood at various levels, but the simplification of situations involves leaving things out. An acting-situation may be indefinitely complex, even before the agent's point of view is introduced. When children have to oscillate between different conceptions of the already confusingly open array of items which make up such a situation, it is not surprising that problems arise. Moreover *these problems cannot necessarily be predicted in advance.* This is not only a consequence of the extreme complexity of any acting-situation, but also because one cannot know how a particular child is going to see it, and what 'second record' he will bring to it.[52] The child who, having read a detailed description of Alfred's problems in trying to bring the mobile Danish raiders to battle, suggested that his best solution would be to dig large pits across the chalk uplands, cover them with leaves, and wait for the Danes on their stolen horses to fall in, was revealing the sort of misconceptions which have to be dealt with *as they arise.* By the same token, the teacher who snubbed a boy's suggestion that the Mutiny Act of 1689 was a waste of Parliamentary time (because if the King wanted to he could raise an army and destroy his opponents before a year was out), was simply throwing away precious opportunities.

In these circumstances what is required is teaching methods which *allow* children to bring out their misconceptions and false assumptions, without fear of adverse reaction from peers or teachers. This is not to say that such misconceptions should go uncorrected, but that teaching should be open enough to encourage pupils to talk, and to listen to each other. There must be room for difficulties to be talked through (by pupils) until pre-conceptions become conscious and puzzlement is raised to the level of questions.[53]

The development of history games is potentially important here.[54] History games are not to be justified as *simulations* or *models* except in a loose and minimal sense.[55] Their strength is that they force assumptions into the open. If the 'workers' win the game of Harvest Politics, what have they done that the labourers of the 1840s would not have done?[56] What have the 'mill-owners' assumed? Why has the 'government' given way so easily to every little threat? Departure from the real course of events is not a failing of the game, but part of its justification. If the 'government' concedes enough in the General Strike game to make Baldwin turn in his grave, the teacher has a real chance to promote some understanding, because he will have some clues as to what pupils have been thinking.[57] The pupils talking in the transcript below had been the 'government' of 1926: they had tried to be modern politicians, ruling by consent. (They were unaware at the time that they were being taped.)[58]

Pupil One: We were more concerned with solving it — getting a situation where everybody was reasonably happy. Obviously everybody can't have everything they want but we wanted a happy medium. . . .

Pupil Two: I was just thinking about how we could solve the point — solve the problem. . . .

Teacher: When you say 'solve the problem', which problem is this?

Pupil Two: Well — get the miners back to work, get the mineowners and mineworkers onto a happy agreement and let everybody be happy again.

Pupil Three: And we all lived happily ever after!

Pupil Two: Sounds a bit corny but that's what you want. You've got to resolve it somehow. And you can't just say right you are going to do so and so because people just don't agree to that kind of thing. . . .

The teacher's work is *not* in making the game (*per impossibile*) like 'the real thing'. His work comes *after* it, in going *beyond* the game, which is for him both diagnostic of his pupils' understanding and a means by which that understanding may be advanced.

Everything said in this chapter points to a much more serious attitude towards imaginative work in history. Lamont has stressed that imaginative work is harder, not easier, than marshalling 'hard facts', and that our standards must be *more*, not *less*, austere.[59] Everything in our work confirms this view. Coming to see a situation from the point of view of the agent, and to distinguish what he could know and the way he could see it from what we *now* know and the ways in which we *now* may see it, is a difficult and complex task. It is also one of the most interesting and worthwhile tasks in history.

NOTES

1. The major work on moral judgement is Piaget, J., *The Moral Judgement of the Child*, Routledge and Kegan Paul, 1932. For experiments involving the manipulation of physical objects see Inhelder, B., and Piaget, J., *The Growth of Logical Thinking*, Routledge and Kegan Paul, 1958.

2. Peel, E. A., 'Some Problems in the Psychology of History Teaching' (in two parts) in W. H. Burston and D. Thompson (eds.), *Studies in the Nature and Teaching of History*, Routledge and Kegan Paul, 1967.

3. Hallam, R. N., 'Logical Thinking in History' in *Educational Review*, Vol. 19, 1967, p. 185. See also the same author's 'Piaget and Thinking in History' in M..Ballard (ed.), *New Movements in the Study and Teaching of History*, Temple Smith, 1970. Both articles are based on his *An Investigation into Some Aspects of the Historical Thinking of Children and Adolescents*, unpublished M Ed thesis, University of Leeds, 1966.

4. Rees, A., *Teaching Strategies for the Assessment and Development of Thinking Skills in History*, unpublished M Phil thesis, University of London, 1976, p. 72.

5. Thompson, D., 'Some Psychological Aspects of History Teaching' in W. H. Burston and C. W. Green (eds.), *Handbook for History Teachers*, Methuen Educational, 2nd edn., 1972, p. 32. It is not yet clear how far Donald Thompson has succeeded in devising categories which marry historical criteria with those of Peel, but it is encouraging to see that evaluation of 'how well the pupil had been able to think himself into William's situation' is to play some part.

6. Inhelder, B. and Piaget, J., op. cit. See for example pp. 46-66, or pp. 164-81.

7. loc. cit.

8. loc. cit.

9. See the experiments in Piaget, J., 'Les notions de mouvement et de vitesse chez l'enfant', quoted in Flavell, J. H., *The Developmental Psychology of Jean Piaget*, Van Nostrand, 1963, p. 323.

10. Inhelder, B. and Piaget, J., op. cit., p. 46.

11. Not always: see ibid., p. 131 for example.

12. ibid., see p. 6 or p. 273, for example.

13. ibid., *passim*.

14. One of the strengths of Hallam's work is the use of interviews based on standardized questions; it seems to us that criticism of Hallam's work has not always paid sufficient attention to this.

15. See pp. 99-101 of this Chapter, and note 46.

16. Inhelder, B. and Piaget, J., op. cit., p. 46.

17. For a summary of the logical basis of Piaget's 'concrete' and 'formal' categories see ibid., pp. 272-333.

18. See, among numerous works, von Wright, G. H., *Norm and Action*, Routledge and Kegan Paul, 1963.

19. Peel, E. A., *The Nature of Adolescent Judgement*, Staples, 1971, p. 26.

20. ibid., pp. 26 and 28. Also Peel, E. A., 'Conceptual Learning and Explainer Thinking' in E. A. Lunzer and J. F. Morris (eds.), *Development in Learning, Vol. II: Development in Human Learning*, Staples, 1968, p. 307.

21. Peel, E. A., 'Some Problems in the Psychology of History Teaching', I and II, in W. H. Burston and D. Thompson (eds.), op. cit., p. 186 and also pp. 162-3.

22. ibid., p. 160.

23. ibid., p. 183.

24. Note that an appropriate question here is: 'What are they doing?', which on the face of it calls for a *description*, but in reality is asking for an elucidation of internal relationships between actions. The original discussion is in Runciman, W. G., *Social Science and Political Theory*, Cambridge University Press, 1963, pp. 12-16. For an examination of some connected issues, see Winch, P., *The Idea of a Social Science*, Routledge and Kegan Paul, 1958.

25. Peel, E. A., op. cit., Staples, 1971, p. 29.

26. Few laws available *for* history, because most of the possible candidates are borrowed from other disciplines.

27. What is historically important in the concept *fascist*, for example, is not some atemporal rule of application, but the content provided by knowledge of what fascists have *been* and have found it possible to *do*. Some concepts employed in history *do* operate as Peel suggests, but they are precisely those which have been borrowed from other disciplines (economics and sociology, for example).

28. See Hallam, op. cit. in *Educational Review*, Vol. 19, 1967, pp. 198-9.

29. The Henry II test was administered to 127 second, fourth and lower-sixth subjects divided (roughly) evenly between a West London grammar school and a mixed comprehensive school in the Dagenham area.

30. See Chapter 5 of this book (p. 74 and note 10) for this sense of 'simple' situation. (Roughly speaking Jellicoe could have (i) continued his course, (ii) turned towards the Germans, (iii) turned away, (iv) split his fleet and engaged in some combination of (i) to (iii), and (v) combined (i) to (iii) in some *temporal* arrangement.) Other tests covered the German decision to begin unrestricted submarine warfare in the First World War, and Chamberlain at Munich.

31. Earlier versions were tested with 55 subjects aged from 12 to 16 years, from four suburban mixed comprehensive schools.

32. The schools were selected on the basis of their tradition of co-operation with the University of London Institute of Education, and while adequate for a pilot, are clearly not sufficiently representative for full scale research.

33. Double periods of 60 or 70 minutes were used. A few subjects required extra time, and eight responses were discounted as incomplete (some subjects having had to leave early for dentists' appointments etc.!). These do not appear in the totals given in the text.

34. This is a possible problem in Peel's short tests. See, for examples, his *Nature of Adolescent Judgement*, Staples, 1971, pp. 31-6.

35. See Chapter 4 in this book, particularly pp. 66-7.

36. See Chapter 5 of this book.

37. See Chapter 5, Part II, for this stipulative use of 'historians' point of view'.

38. Chapter 5, p. 85.

39. For a professional historian's treatment of the turn away, where the wider considerations are taken as obvious, and the details of the situation as problematic, see Marder, A., *From Dreadnought to Scapa Flow, Vol. III, Jutland and After, May 1916-Dec. 1916*, Oxford University Press, 1966, pp. 110-22. But of course the whole work is concerned with the wider issues.

40. There are two possibilities here: the subject (i) *feels* he understands the action, (ii) *in fact* understands—i.e. does not *misunderstand* the situation, the agent's intentions etc. In general, only if (i) is *false* does the response fall in the relevant odd-number category, (see below p. 103) but category one includes some cases where (i) is true.

41. This leads us to think that the category system set out by Lee may need modification in the light of the pilot: Level II could be split into two separate levels, the first containing categories for understanding and failing to understand at a conventional level, and the second a pair of categories for responses in which evidence is used to attempt to get at the particular circumstances, but there is no distinction between the agent's and the historian's view. This expansion will have to await new tests: the present one does not provide a sufficiently clear picture of subjects' thinking to differentiate so closely.

42. See Flavell, J. H., *The Developmental Psychology of Jean Piaget*, Van Nostrand, 1963, pp. 241-4 for the criteria used here.

43. See Turiel, E., 'The Development of Social Concepts: Mores, Customs, Conventions', in D. J. De Palma and J. M. Foley (eds.), *Contemporary Issues in Moral Development*, Lawrence Erlbaum Associates, 1974. We owe this reference to Dr John Versey.

44. Mention of Turiel, of course, appears to connect our work with that of Kohlberg. Again any links are limited to *analogy*, except for the basic similarity that we have tried to analyse the thinking characteristic of a particular form of knowledge. Obviously any comparison shows our work to be so far extremely primitive. (See Kohlberg, L., 'From Is to Ought', in T. Mischel (ed.), *Cognitive Psychology and Epistemology*, Academic Press, 1971.)

45. A further χ^2 test showed no significant evidence of association between level attained and sex of subject.

46. We refer here to the guesses made by subjects in the absence of adequate passage evidence. Responses to our Henry II test in which subjects were asked to grade their answers and to criticize them, suggested that many children were well aware of the lack of evidence for their answers, but still felt it necessary to say something definite.

47. See Chapter 5, pp. 79-80.

48. Peel, E. A., 'Some Problems in the Psychology of History Teaching, I' in W. H. Burston and D. Thompson (eds.), op. cit., p. 161.

49. Coltham, J., *The Development of Thinking and the Learning of History*, Historical Association, Teaching of History Series No. 34, 1971, p. 35. Such a claim makes nonsense of Collingwood.

50. See Part I of this chapter.

51. See Chapter 5.

52. See Hexter, J. H., *The History Primer*, Allen Lane, 1972, Chapter 4, for this notion. It is discussed in Chapter 1, on pp. 10-12 of this book.

53. This is further discussed in Chapter 4, pp. 66-8 of this book.

54. See, for example, Barker, B., Boden, R., Birt, D. and Nicol, J., *History Games*, Longmans Resources Unit, 1973. Barker discusses related issues in Chapter 7 of this book.

55. This kind of justification figures prominently in the work of D. Birt and J. Nicol, sometimes in the context of games which do little to bear out their claims. See Nicol, J., 'Simulation and History Teaching—Trade and Discovery, a History Game for Use in Schools', in *Teaching History*, Vol. II, No. 7, May 1972. For a critique of games see Milburn, G., 'Simulation in History Teaching: Promising Innovation or Passing Fad', in the same issue.

56. Barker, B., *et. al.*, op. cit., 1973.

57. ibid.

58. This recording was made with the co-operation of Bernard Barker and some pupils at Sir Frederic Osborn School, Welwyn Garden City.

59. Lamont, W., 'How Far Beyond Beginnings?' in W. Lamont (ed.), *The Realities of Teaching History*, Chatto and Windus, 1972, pp. 168-9.

APPENDIX I

Instructions

1.   Read through the pamphlet carefully.

2.   If you don't feel you completely understand any words or sentences anywhere in the pamphlet *please ask about them.*

3.   When you answer the questions, try to explain as fully as you can *why* you think the way you do.

   Above all: If you think you need more information before you can give any definite or proper answer

   (a) give an answer as far as you can;
   (b) say what extra information you would need to give a *proper* answer;
   (c) explain what is doubtful in the answer you gave, and how the extra information would have made the difference.

   (b) and (c) are the most important parts of the test.

4.   If you have any doubts about what these instructions mean, or want anything cleared up, *ask.*

Thank you for your help.

APPENDIX II

The Battle of Jutland
31 May–1 June 1916

During the First World War the British had a much bigger navy than the Germans. Britain needed more fighting ships than Germany because she depended on so many important things brought by ships from overseas: in particular food, but also the *raw materials* which kept her industries going. The navy was needed to protect the ships which carried all this from attack by German warships. It was also necessary to guard British colonies abroad, to protect supplies sent to the army fighting in France, and above all, to protect Britain itself from invasion.

The Royal Navy had a long tradition of fighting and winning *decisive battles.* In the First World War, too, it hoped to meet and destroy the German fleet in a *pitched battle.* The Germans knew their fleet was weak in numbers, and planned to avoid an all out battle unless they could first sink enough British *battleships* to make the numbers more even.

In 1916 the German plan was to lure the main British fleet into the North Sea past German *submarines* waiting several miles outside the main

British *naval bases* to sink as many ships as possible with *torpedoes*. To do this they steamed out into the North Sea themselves, so that the British would seize the chance of a decisive battle. The British did take the bait, but left port at night and the German submarines failed to sight them in the darkness: so the trap failed. At about 2.30 in the afternoon of 31 May the leading British ships sighted part of the German fleet about 100 miles off the north Danish coast.

The first stage of the battle began at about 3.45 p.m. and mainly involved the *battlecruisers* in each fleet. The British were horrified when two of their ships blew up early in the fighting, but eventually (about 6.30 p.m.) the whole German fleet (chasing the British battlecruisers) came upon the main part of the British fleet, and were so badly punished by the massed guns of the British that they had to turn and escape into the late afternoon mist. (The Germans had practised turning all their ships round together at the same moment, something the British thought was impossible because of the danger of ships colliding and sinking each other. So the British were amazed that the German fleet disappeared so quickly.)

Admiral Scheer, in command of the Germans, then tried to by-pass the British and head for home, but his ships misinformed him about the position of the British fleet, and he steamed straight into it for a second time at about 7.10 p.m. (see Map One). Again his fleet was in a desperate situation, since only the ships leading the German line could fire, and then only with their forward guns, while the British could bring almost all their guns into action (see Diagram One). Once again the Germans were badly mauled, and once again all his battleships turned away together (see Map Two). This time his *destroyers* delivered a torpedo attack and at the same time laid a smokescreen, but because the British destroyers counter-attacked the Germans were unable to launch their torpedoes at close range. Twenty-one torpedoes were launched towards the British fleet at a distance of about 7,500 yards.

Admiral Jellicoe, in command of the British fleet, temporarily turned it away from the torpedo attack, so that it was steering south-east for about 12 minutes. At least eleven torpedo tracks were seen crossing the line, and they were all avoided. Some time before the battle Jellicoe had been told by the *Director of Naval Intelligence* that the Germans had successfully concealed their torpedo tracks, but this turned out to be false information.

The turn away shocked some of the officers in the fleet, and many people criticized Jellicoe afterwards. One Admiral said he was 'horrified' at the decision:

> I felt instinctively that here was the sad climax of all our long discussions about *defensive tactics*. The [British] fleet was about to break off the action and probably to lose the best chance it ever had of achieving a decisive victory. I remember thinking then that I was witnessing a regrettable movement which I should remember to the end of my days, and though now 44 years ago, I recall that scene vividly today.

After the turn away no more contact was made with the Germans before darkness, and Jellicoe tried to put his fleet between the Germans and their bases. During the night the German fleet, heading for home, accidentally came upon the tail end of the British fleet, which was mainly made up of destroyers. Some damage was done on both sides, and in the darkness and confusion the Germans passed by the British lines and by daybreak were nowhere to be seen. They reached port the same day, and the battle of Jutland was over.

People have argued about who won ever since. On one hand the British lost more ships and men than the Germans. On the other hand many German ships were damaged, and although repairs were soon made, they did not challenge the British again for the rest of the war. Whatever the verdict, there is no doubt that the British were badly disappointed that their much larger fleet had not finished off the German navy once and for all.

Glossary

Raw Materials: Anything needed to make something with: for instance metals like iron and copper for making ships, tools, and all kinds of metal goods, chemicals for making explosives, cotton for making clothes and so on. They are 'raw' materials because no one has worked on them to turn them into any sort of finished article.

Decisive Battle: A decisive battle is one in which one side gains a clear victory. Usually a decisive battle at sea settles once and for all which fleet can sail freely over the oceans of the world, and which has to be very cautious even about leaving port.

Pitched Battle: An all-out-battle in which both sides fight to the finish.

Battleships: The biggest, most heavily armed, and best armoured ships in the two fleets. They carried between eight and ten guns firing shells between 12 inches and 15 inches in diameter. (The usual 13.5-inch gun fired a shell weighing 1250 lbs. Maximum range for a 12-inch gun was about 11 miles, and 15 miles for a 15-inch gun.)

Submarines: Ships which can dive and attack other ships from under water. Their under-water weapon was the torpedo.

Naval Base: The home port or ports of a fleet. They were very well protected, and once in its base, a fleet was almost completely safe against any attack by other ships.

Torpedoes: Steel tubes with explosive warheads which, once launched, were propelled just below the surface of the water by compressed air, which left a trail of bubbles. A single torpedo could cause severe damage even to a battleship; two might easily sink it. They could be used by quite small ships like destroyers or submarines.

Battlecruisers:	Designed partly as the scouts or lookouts of the battle fleets, they carried thinner armour and less of it, and so could steam faster than the battleships. But they still usually carried eight 12-inch or 13.5-inch guns.
Destroyers:	Fast small ships with no armour, carrying guns big enough only to deal with enemy destroyers. In a major battle their main task was to make torpedo attacks on enemy battleships, or prevent enemy torpedo attacks on their own fleet.
Director of Naval Intelligence:	The head of the naval department at the Admiralty in London whose task was to collect information about the enemy.
Defensive Tactics:	'Tactics' means ways of fighting a battle — for instance, should your ships sail in a line, or bunched together? 'Defensive tactics' are ways of fighting which help you defend yourself, or let you get out of danger, if you are being attacked.
Short Visibility:	If there is 'short visibility' you can't see very far or very clearly. 'Visibility' means 'seeing conditions' — obviously the weather makes a great deal of difference to how well you can see, but in a naval battle smoke from guns and ships' funnels affects visibility too.

(One half-tone plate was included in the test, but has had to be omitted here. It depicted the Grand Fleet in action at Jutland, and showed something of the smoke and mist present. See the Imperial War Museum photograph pack *Naval Warfare 1914-18*, photograph No. 7.)

APPENDIX III

Questions

1. Why did Jellicoe turn the fleet away from the Germans? Give as many reasons as you can.

2. Does anything puzzle you about Jellicoe's turning away at this crucial stage of the battle? If it does, explain why.

3. Can you suggest anything else Jellicoe might have done which you think would have been more likely to achieve what he wanted?

4. Imagine you are Jellicoe talking to a sympathetic listener the day after the battle.

   (a) Explain in as much detail as possible what the situation was at the moment the Germans launched their torpedoes.

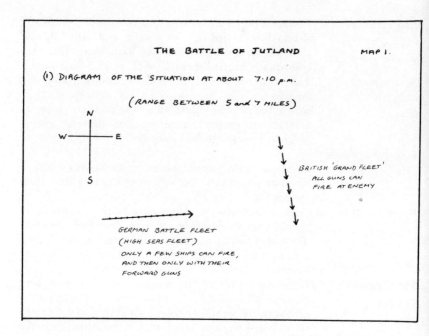

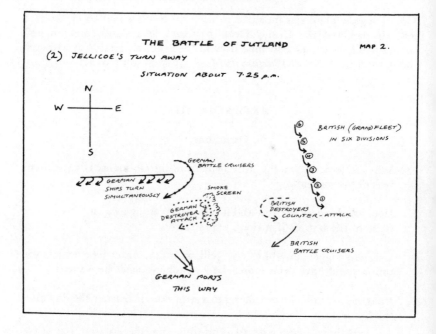

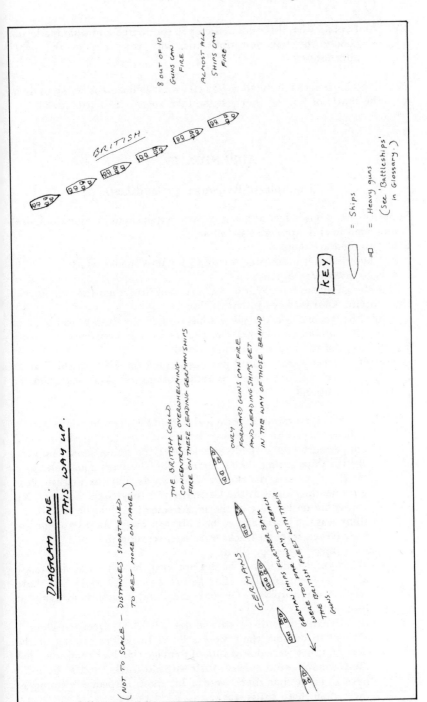

DIAGRAM ONE.
THIS WAY UP.

(NOT TO SCALE — DISTANCES SHORTENED
TO GET MORE ON PAGE.)

THE BRITISH COULD
CONCENTRATE OVERWHELMING
FIRE ON THESE LEADING GERMAN SHIPS

ONLY
FORWARD GUNS CAN FIRE
AND LEADING SHIPS GET
IN THE WAY OF THOSE BEHIND

GERMANS

GERMAN SHIPS FURTHER BACK
WERE TOO FAR AWAY TO REACH
THE BRITISH FLEET WITH THEIR
GUNS.

BRITISH

8 OUT OF 10
GUNS CAN
FIRE.

ALMOST ALL
SHIPS CAN
FIRE.

KEY

⬭ = Ships

⊏□ = Heavy guns
(See 'Battleships'
in Glossary.)

(b) Explain what different actions you considered and what made you choose the one you did, and why you rejected the other alternatives.

5.   Explain in as much detail as you can what Jellicoe was trying to do at the Battle of Jutland (not just the turn away — the battle itself).

APPENDIX IV

Examples of Responses (Jutland Test)

Subjects' prior knowledge (as given in their responses to the questionnaire) is indicated in this Appendix as follows:
S = studied at school
K = knowledge from outside school (TV, films, books, etc.)
O = no knowledge or study.
Knowledge of the First World War is coded first, then the war at sea, then specific knowledge of Jutland. Thus:

S/SK/SK   means that the subject has studied the First World War at school, and knows (from both school and outside) something of the war at sea and Jutland.

S/O/O   means that the subject has studied the First World War at school, but claims to know nothing of naval operations or Jutland.

1.   Boy, 12 years 6 months, technical high, O/O/O, Question One:
Jellicoe turned his fleet away temporarily so that his ships would not get hit by the torpedo attacks. Also the smoke screen stop the British ships seeing the Germans. The Germans could not have hit the ships at a distance of 7,500 yards, but the English ships were heading right at the Germans and they could not see what was going on because of the smoke screen, so Jellicoe did what I think was the wisest and turned his fleet away. As it happened at least eleven torpedo tracks were seen crossing the line.

2.   Same subject, Question Two:
What puzzles me is that he did not turn the other way and chase after the German ships. The British army [*sic*] could then have tried to catch up with German ships and attack them again at broadside.

3.   Girl, 13 years 2 months, technical high, K/O/O, Question One:
He had to because there were a lot of torpedoes coming at the fleet and they were doing a lot of damage. He had been told that the Germans could conceal their torpedo tracks, and so he must have thought that there were a lot more torpedoes coming at them than there really was.

4.   Same subject, Question Two:
      Yes, it does. He had a much larger fleet than the Germans, and
      I've just read that they wanted to destroy the German fleet very
      much, and he could have easily destroyed the whole of the German
      fleet if he had stuck at it, even though many of his own ships
      would have been damaged or destroyed. I don't think he could
      have really wanted to destroy the fleet or he would have stayed.

5.   Girl, 12 years 10 months, comprehensive, O/O/O, Question Three
      (the answer to Question Two had been simply 'No'):
      Jellicoe could have used submarines or do what the Germans had
      done.

6.   Girl, 16 years 6 months, technical high, O/O/O, Question Three:
      I think that in order to prevent his fleet being destroyed he should
      have stayed and finished the Germans off. And also he shouldn't
      have taken any notice of the Director of Naval Intelligence.
      Jellicoe could have also tried to surround the Germans thus
      preventing them getting away; because Britain had the advantage
      it was a mistake them turning back.

7.   Boy, 16 years 6 months, comprehensive, SK/SK/SK, Question
      Three:
      In my opinion Jellicoe could have continued pursuing the
      Germans instead of turning away at 7.25 p.m. He could have
      pursued with his main fleet with the destroyers shielding the
      Battleships from torpedo attack, at the same time (as he did) he
      sent Beatties Battle cruiser squadron to block the German
      entrance to their ports. So by Jellicoe could have forced the
      German fleet out to sea (where his superiority in numbers would
      tell) prevent torpedo attacks, and block the German escape route
      back to their ports.

8.   Boy, 15 years 9 months, comprehensive, SK/SK/SK, Question
      Three:
      As stated above [Question Two] he could swing to the south but
      risk getting fired upon by the destroyers. If he went northwards he
      could not block off the German entry into their home ports. The
      present situation as given on Map 2 is that he runs a risk of
      splitting up the fleet and having some of his battle cruisers
      knocked-out by the German destroyers. There does not seem
      anything possible for Jellicoe to do although he seems to be in the
      stronger position.

9.   Boy, 16 years 6 months, technical high, K/O/O, Question Four (a):
      When the Germans fired their torpedoes from a range of 7,500
      yards their battleships after a great deal of damage had been
      inflicted on them turned around. The German destroyers at
      the head of the fleet fired at us with 21 torpedoes of which 11 came
      near us and at the same laid a smoke screen [*sic*]. Immediately
      I saw these torpedoes I decided to get the ships out of their line.
      This we did successfully and we were on a south east course for

about 12 minutes after this time we no longer made any contact with the Germans.

10.   Boy, 15 years 11 months, comprehensive, SK/SK/S, Question Four (a):

To give a proper answer I would need to know Jellicoe's point of view and what other opportunities were realistically open to him. 'When the Germans launched their torpedoes I could not clearly see what was going on because of the smoke screen. I was also afraid that we wouldn't see the torpedoes as the Germans could cover the tracks. I didn't know how many torpedoes were coming towards us and how accurate they might be.'

11.   Boy, 12 years 10 months, technical high, K/K/K, Question Four (b):

I thought of following them, but with a smokescreen in front it was dificult to see. I also considered sending in my destroyers, but they were heavily committed in driving back a German torpedo attack, and without destroyers to protect my ships sending in my Battleships etc. would have been suicide.

12.   Girl, 16 years, comprehensive, S/S/S, Question Five:

Jellicoe was trying to win a decisive battle and to get rid of the German fleet once and for all. I can't explain it in detail because there is no detailed notes on what he was trying to do.

13.   Girl, 17 years 6 months, comprehensive, O/O/O, Question Five:

Jellicoe was trying to sink as many of the German ships as possible, after successfully avoiding the German trap. The Germans ran into the British by mistake, but once there were going to pay for it by taking the full punishment of the British guns. This was just the situation Jellicoe wanted, the maximum destruction of the German fleet with the minimum risk from the German guns, or torpedoes. As it was important that the British sustain as little damage as possible, enabling them to continue their protection of imports, and their naval supremacy.

Jellicoe also wanted to block the German entrance to their base so that once they had been seen they had little alternative but to fight.

14.   Girl, 13 years 2 months, technical high, K/O/O, Question Two:

Yes. I don't see *why* he turned away. If someone was firing at him surely it would have been better for him to have returned fire, not just, as it were, turn his back on the danger.

15.   Boy, 12 years 6 months, comprehensive, K/K/K, Question Three:

Jellicoe had already set up smoke screens and it was at night so therefore he could have gone into the German lines and surprise them.

16.   Girl, 13 years, comprehensive, O/O/O, Question One:

I think Jellicoe turned his fleet away to avoid the torpedoes and save his fleet and mens lives. I think also he did it to show the Germans if we wanted to bomb and blow them up we could have and we still can.

7. Understanding in the Classroom

B. BARKER

Teachers are naturally concerned to develop the ability to reason about historical events and evidence but have been hindered by the intractability of their material. How can thinking be at the centre of a history lesson when there is so much to know and understand before you can formulate even quite simple generalizations? There is the apparently insuperable task of organizing evidence and information so that children with a restricted vocabulary can nevertheless perceive problems of explanation and motivation and think through solutions for themselves. The difficulty is evident from the following example. Suppose the teacher is required to devise a lesson on the industrial revolution. He opens the textbook which informs him that. . . . 'The demand for cloth led to shortages of yarn for weavers. So a machine to spin yarn faster was invented, the Spinning Jenny. Soon the weavers could not keep up with the amount of yarn produced, so weaving machines were invented. At first, these were powered by water-mills, and as they were expensive they were set up by merchants in factories.'[1]

Although couched in simple language the extract involves a number of concepts not easily presented for mixed-ability groups. Most teachers will hesitate before beginning a discussion about the role of the entrepreneur, the laws of supply and demand or the function of technological innovation. It is likely that the industrial revolution would disappear beneath several layers of explanation. The pedagogic options are horribly restricted. A worksheet might pose questions like: 'Why did merchants build factories?' Less-able pupils could be offered the alternative of drawing a picture of a factory, perhaps aided by an illustration from the book. Gifted children might be set an essay: 'Describe the industrial revolution'. Alternatively, the teacher could talk about the factory system, perhaps enlarging on the conditions of work or some other more tangible aspect of industrialization, leading into an 'Imagine you are a mill-hand type of writing. A film-strip might be shown as a stimulus for the mill-hands before they start describing 'their' lives. Such a pattern of learning depends on literary skills to quite a disproportionate degree. Children do not write about 'innovation' or 'technology' or 'entrepreneurs' with any ease or fluency, and it is difficult for the teacher not to conclude that a limited vocabulary involves restricted understanding. Nor can the teacher readily devise an escape from his dependence on flows of language. He can simplify, eliminating polysyllables; he can select concrete images, preferring Doré's portrayal of social conditions to an account of *laisser-faire* capitalism; he can emphasize factual description or narrative. Learning comes to rely on imitation, repetition and literary expertise, and teachers reluctantly acknowledge that most children cannot think historically.

This is not to deny the importance of a developing facility with language for the formulation and expression of historical ideas. But the concept of free trade does not begin with *laisser-faire* and teachers have assumed too readily that a failure to master words must imply a similar failure to perceive relationships or manipulate meanings. Very often, however, the problem is the gap between the everyday language of concrete objects and the language, or even shorthand, used to evaluate past life. The slowest child can appreciate betting odds or the principles of the football pool. He would not buy dear and sell cheap. Economic problems should therefore be within the range of his understanding. It is not merely a question of simplifying vocabulary but of establishing that the connections and meanings developing in the pupil's own experience and language are transferable to situations with which he is, as yet, unfamiliar.

The history teacher must therefore consider how to devise thought-provoking exercises dealing with past events, yet drawing on transactions present in daily life or easily recreated in the classroom. His starting point will be the recognition that abstract connections can be made concrete and specific, that description is not the only way to shape images and structures with which children can engage. Active involvement is the essential prerequisite for effective learning in history. The materials used must demand some activity other than imitation or memory from the pupil, enabling him to reconstruct the past, discovering in his own relationships and experience tangible parallels with seemingly abstract historical issues. Problems and events should be presented so that students can readily identify with them and enter into their complexities. Children enjoy games and competition, and with careful calculation classroom exercises can be designed to incorporate those features which most promote involvement in the past. The most natural device is to ask children to imagine themselves confronted with the same problem or decision as people in history. They should be asked not just to 'imagine' themselves mill-hands but how they will eke out such wretched earnings, or how they feel about fluctuating bread prices. There is no formula or system by which real understanding may regularly be achieved. It is simply a question of devoting time and ingenuity to devising exercises which involve children and encourage a thoughtful response.

Many are unfortunately inhibited in their efforts to build exercises on these principles by the suspicion that open-ended speculation and classroom re-creations may falsify the past, straying from what is commonly understood as the proper task of historians; establishing what *actually* happened. Might not response-oriented materials lead to anachronism or travesty? The answer is that it is not sufficient to describe the past to understand it. History is as concerned with interpretation, explanation and motivation as with establishing a sequence of events. An understanding of the 'why' in history depends on a willingness to consider the balance of possibilities in any given situation. Unless some thought is applied to what might have happened the unique features of historical events will remain elusive. If children are to think about history they must be led inside precise, tightly-defined situations and given an opportunity to explore alternatives and options for themselves. On the other hand, classroom exercises should be structured to ensure reasonable, realistic responses. Many of the pupil's ideas should be shaped by the arrangement of the material presented. The careful examination of an incident accurately grounded in historical sources is quite different from the vague openness of 'Imagine you are a mill-hand'. A more conventional approach does not necessarily yield more precise results. The narrative observation 'The demand for cloth led to shortages' risks inaccuracy and distortion as much as any open exercise. The danger of history appearing as an inevitable and irresistible tide of events is probably greater than that of pupils being misled by the fertility of their own imaginations.

The volume of detailed knowledge required for mature historical thinking can only overwhelm the child, whose need is for working information organized to assist him in its manipulation. Children do not easily perceive problems of explanation or interpretation in a chronological sequence. Events should be broken down and structured so that different possibilities and outcomes are visible in a clearly delineated situation. It will be readily accepted, without thought, that expensive water mills are put in factories unless the alternatives are presented for discussion and the pupil's own ideas are considered. The traditional criteria for selecting subject matter (e.g. period, reign) have been too insensitive to their own content to assist in the choice of events for study or in the preparation of materials for classroom use. A more promising possibility is for teachers to construct their own patterns or concepts, selecting events, topics or themes likely to communicate the variety and significance of human experience in the past. For example, a concept like Government could be approached through Feudalism and the American Revolution; or Belief through Monasteries and Islam. A history department can develop a strategy about the *kind* of things it is important for children to know about. But this will not in itself enable us to devise and design teaching materials.

What the teacher needs to do is identify a central event, turning point or otherwise important moment, using source materials to focus attention on the main features. This provides a structure for experiment and investigation derived from real human situations properly observed. Pupils should see a number of possible outcomes and freely speculate about the relationship of different elements in a crisis or event. Historical incidents are unique, and there is no intention to foster a search for the laws of history. But each event has a discernible structure and it is this the teacher must reveal for his students, reducing the essential working information to a minimum. Wherever possible this underlying pattern should be adapted to its likely classroom use. A diplomatic incident, for example, can be reconstructed in the form of negotiations; military or political events might be focused on a key decision taken by a principal figure.

The following examples have been selected to illustrate how various techniques may be employed to involve students in historical issues and problems. Five examples deal comparatively with developments in Britain and France from 1760 to 1835 and show how the approach argued above may be sustained in specific class exercises. Although originally designed for a third-form course, all the examples except the first have been used with sixth-formers. Open-ended problems can be used with a wide age range, for while the quality and maturity of response varies greatly, the essential information and questions remain to demand explanation and prompt thought.

1.   French Peasant/English Wage Labourer

One teacher takes the part of George, another Jacques. The class is invited to imagine itself making a TV programme (e.g. 'Man Alive') about the lives of peasants in France and labourers in eighteenth-century England. The 'characters' will only speak in answer to direct questions about themselves. Following the interviews, each pupil is expected to produce a written report comparing the life-styles of George, Jacques and their families, and should be encouraged to keep notes throughout.

2.   Louis XVI's Budget

You are an accountant called in to assist Louis XVI with his annual budget. Total the figures and write a report for the King recommending measures he might take. Explain the reasons for each of your proposed remedies and estimate its likely financial consequences. The following are points to consider:

Raising Taxes
Reducing Armed Forces
Economizing on Court Expenses
Trimming Civil Spending
Paying off some of Royal Debt
Redistributing Tax Burden

(Budget statement provided on p. 125.)

3.   Rebellion in the Countryside

A nobleman returns from Paris to his country home to find all the windows smashed, the servants missing, the barn doors open and all the grain taken. Nailed to the door is the following notice:

Oh petty tyrants placed at the heart of the provinces to hold sway over their destinies! Oh proprietors of seigneurial estates who demand the most crippling and servile exactions! . . . be so good as to glance at those unfortunate men whose muscles are only occupied in working for you! What do you see in our villages, in our fields? A few enfeebled men, whose pale faces are withered by poverty and shame . . . each child wearing rags.

(from *Cahiers de doleances* 1789)

Suggest what has happened in his absence and explain the behaviour of the people involved.

How do you think the villagers described in the extract will react to an increase in the gabelle or feudal dues?

How do you suppose the nobleman will respond to a Royal appeal for help in the present dire financial crisis?

What will happen if the King is unable to pay the interest on the debt?

4. Cotton Entrepreneur
(Tables provided on pages 127-9.)

The game comprises 13 rounds (1760, 1775 etc.) in which players work in pairs, taking investment decisions as entrepreneurs (businessmen) in the British cotton industry.

(Rules and Questions on p. 126.)

figures in livres (= 5p approx.)

INCOME		*EXPENDITURE*	
Direct Taxation		Defence	
Poll Tax — per head	60,000,000	Cost of American War 2,000,000,000	165,500,000
Taille — tax on wealth	90,000,000	Civil Expenditure	146,000,000
Vingtièmes	40,000,000	Interest on Royal Debt	318,000,000
total		Royal Household	42,000,000
Indirect Taxation		total	
Gabelle — salt tax	100,000,000		
Traites — internal customs	70,000,000		
Aides — customs duties	75,000,000		
total			
Benevolences — usually granted by the clergy	100,000,000		

LOUIS XVI'S ANNUAL BUDGET

Rules for Cotton Entrepreneur

(a)   At the beginning of each round the teacher reads figures from the Teachers Table (p. 127) giving the cost of raw cotton (per lb), spinning and weaving costs, and sale price (per lb) prevailing in that year. Players are warned that these figures will fluctuate from year to year and that it is up to them to detect any pattern or trend. Each pair is issued with a balance sheet (pp. 128-9) where costs and prices entered each year. All decisions and calculations are shown on the sheet.

(b)   Players add their costs (raw cotton, spinning and weaving) and subtract the total from the price per lb to obtain the profit per lb on that year's operations. They must then decide whether or not to purchase one of Crompton's mules. A decision to buy is recorded on the balance sheet with a tick for each machine in the space provided. A maximum of 2 machines may be purchased per round. Each machine reduces spinning costs in the year in which it is acquired and in each round thereafter by 3. The profit per lb will be correspondingly increased. Machines may have the cumulative effect of reducing spinning costs to 0, which reflects the overall effect of mules on wage rates. Costs cannot, however, become a negative factor, i.e. fall to −1. If no machinery is purchased total profits are multiplied by 10 for that year. (The purchase price of machinery is held to be the loss of this multiplier.)

(c)   All calculations must be entered on the balance sheet; 8 minutes should be allowed for decision-taking and arithmetic in 1760; between 2 and 5 minutes thereafter.

(d)   From 1820 Power Looms are available on the same terms and with the same results as mules, only it is weaving costs which are reduced. A maximum of 2 looms may be bought per round, each reducing weaving costs by 3.

(e)   The winning pair have the highest overall aggregate profit.

Post-play discussion is an important part of the game and the following questions should direct responses and prepare students for *Wage Slaves* (see below, p. 130).

What was the policy adopted by the winning group?

What was the effect on the cotton industry of the rapid introduction of spinning mules?

Why were wages in handloom weaving so high before 1820?

What was the effect of the power loom on wages?

Why do you think the price of cotton (finished cloth) fell so sharply towards the end of the game?

Did high profits mean high wages?

Do you think cotton workers should have been treated better?

Why do you think businessmen were so swift to take up the mule and power loom?

Date	Cost per lb raw cotton	Wage cost per lb		Price per lb
		Spin	Weave	
1760	15	12	12	48
1775	12	12	15	48
1785	24	12	24	72
1790	21	10	18	60
1795	24	12	36	96
1800	24	8	16	54
1805	12	12	24	72
1810	17	7	36	96
1815	19	6	24	72
1820	9	4	24	48
1825	9	2	12	48
1830	7	2	7	30
1835	9	2	5	30
1840	6	2	3	24
1845	5	2	2	18

COTTON ENTREPRENEUR: TEACHERS' TABLE

[Using this table the teacher announces Costs
and Prices at the start of each round]

COTTON ENTREPRENEUR: BALANCE SHEET

Raw Cotton per lb

Tick if machine purchased.

Spinning costs per lb (reduce by 3 if power
loom owned or purchased this year).

Weaving costs per lb (reduce by 3 if power
loom owned or purchased this year. Applies from 1820 only).

Total costs per lb

Price per lb

Total profit per lb

Multiply × 10 if no machinery purchased
this year.

Notes:
Crompton's Mule
Companies may purchase at the rate of 2 per annum.
Reduces spinning costs by 3 per machine.

Power Looms
Available from 1820 onwards only.
Reduces weaving costs by 3 per machine.
Only 2 purchases p.a.

Costs
May not fall below 0 in any year.

1760	1775	1785	1790	1795	1800	1805	1810	1815	1820	1825	1830	1835

Total profit per lb is multiplied by 10 in those years in which machinery is not purchased.

** The figures in the game are historically accurate (except for wages before 1815, which are conjectural), and are expressed in pre-decimal pennies.

5.   Wage Slaves

You own several of the factories described in the following extract.

Thirty or forty factories rise on the tops of the hills I have just described. Their six stories tower up; their huge enclosures give notice from afar of the centralisation of industry. The wretched dwellings of the poor are scattered haphazard around them. Round them stretches land uncultivated but without the charm of rustic nature, and still without the amenities of a town. . . . Heaps of dung, rubble from buildings, putrid, stagnant pools are found here and there among the houses and over the bumpy, pitted surfaces of the public places. . . . On ground below the level of the river and overshadowed on every side by immense workshops, stretches marshy land which widely spaced ditches can neither drain nor cleanse. Narrow twisting roads lead down to it. They are lined with one-storey houses whose ill-fitting planks and broken windows show them up, even from a distance, as the last refuge a man might find between poverty and death. None-the-less the wretched people living in them can still inspire jealousy in their fellow-beings. Below some of their miserable dwellings is a row of cellars to which a sunken corridor leads. Twelve to fifteen human beings are crowded pell-mell into each of these damp, repulsive holes.

(Alexis de Tocqueville on
Manchester in 1835)

The newspapers report that Lancashire is on the verge of a boom in sales of cotton piece goods to the Far East. There are many competitors whose products are cheap enough to worry you. Explain how you would invest the profits from previous operations, considering the options listed below.

Improve the wages of your workers.

Invest in new machinery (e.g. Crompton's mule), likely to cut costs of production.

Purchase or build additional mills to increase your capacity during the boom.

Install fences and machine-guards to protect the many small children in your employ.

Build a substantial mansion for yourself and your family.

Offer higher piece-work rates to domestic outworkers who can be laid off when the boom collapses.

Finance your wife's growing social life, important for your own advancement in the neighbourhood.

Increase the hours worked in your mills.

Invest on the stock market.

Demolish the 'wretched dwellings' described by de Tocqueville and construct model industrial dwellings for your employees.

An essential feature of these exercises is their variety; *George and Jacques* uses a dramatic, team-teaching presentation to stimulate note-taking, questions and comparisons. *Louis XVI's Budget* is a problem-solving activity based on figures. *Rebellion* involves empathy and imaginative writing. *Entrepreneur* is a competitive game, while *Wage Slaves* requires careful judgement, decision-making and report-writing. Together they should demand a wide range of historical thinking.

The 'Situations' deal with the major issues and principal connections between economic and social trends in late eighteenth-century Britain and France, but aim to suggest various techniques for devising exercises rather than provide a self-sufficient treatment of the period. With most secondary-school history groups the analysis and discussion arising from the exercises should lead to more active involvement and a developing understanding of historical questions. The additional resources, reading, information, class discussion and note-taking used with the 'Situations' will depend on individual teachers and the character of the group working with them. Formal exposition of the main events of the French Revolution or of technical innovations in England may greatly assist some students with these exercises and set them in a wider context. Sixth-formers may find some items a useful introduction to extensive reading. With mixed ability classes it might be preferable to use the materials as they stand, clear and uncluttered with narrative.

George and Jacques provides teachers with an opportunity to introduce a wide variety of information, from taxation (the gabelle, window tax, poll and land taxes) to food, and they should be prepared as if for a straightforward lesson on social history. The other exercises should be presented in the form indicated here. But pupils should not be simply issued with printed sheets and left to sort out the problems for themselves. The teacher should read through the exercises, explaining terminology and procedural difficulties. The rules for 'Monopoly' would dumbfound many who have played it with great enjoyment for years. The written instructions, as in (2) and (4), have to cover every eventuality, and should be considered as addressed to pupils and teachers together. The basic working materials — the budget sheet in (2), the list in (5) and the balance sheet in (4) — are, however, presented as clearly as possible, and in practice have proved readily comprehensible by second and third-year mixed-ability classes.

The problems and concepts have been defined and arranged within each situation so that they are as accessible as possible. The design of the lesson materials, particularly the use of a 'stimulus' item to draw pupils into the key questions, is more important in creating this accessibility than simple language. Easy monosyllables no more meet the needs of a mixed-ability class than complex phrases. Pupils aided by a teacher can cope with most ordinary language encountered in history provided the items are properly structured.

The comparative presentation by Jacques and George (1) is designed as an introduction, showing incidentally how even essentially descriptive, expository material can be usefully incorporated in a more thoughtful approach. The teachers become historical characters, and the pupils have to ask questions if they are to obtain sufficient information for their report.

The comparative dimension ensures that thoughtful contrasts are made; Jacques and George answer alternately. This inversion of the familiar classroom relationship, together with an element of role-play, stimulates the children to participate, yet it is possible to communicate a good deal of background information useful in later exercises to an unusually attentive audience.

The game (4) is focused on essential features of the Lancashire textile industry, chosen for its central role in British industrialization. Investment, technical innovation, business cycles and the role of the businessman are examined while the pupils compete to make a profit. Many different types of game can be devised (cf. *History Games*, Longmans Research Unit, 1973) involving committee work, negotiations, decision-making or planning. But whichever technique is chosen the point of simulations is the same; to involve a class in exploring an historical process and investigating its difficulties for themselves. The comparison of the outcome of the game with real events and the discussion and analysis of differences is essential.

Rebellion (3) and *Wage Slaves* (5) are examples of the very wide range of written assignments with which teachers can develop the insights and involvement derived from a game or team-teaching presentation. Each exercise seeks to focus a historical situation through a map, picture, document, table of figures, list of alternatives or some other arrangement of the necessary information, ideas and options. The aim is to encourage pupils to think and argue from historical evidence.

Louis XVI's Budget (2) gives the pupil the role of royal accountant and presents him with the central problems of the *ancien regime*; finance, taxation, noble resistance, war debt etc. Once pupils have an understanding of the situation and have responded to it with their own ideas for reform they are asked to consider the likely consequences. In *Wage Slaves* (5) the role of the entrepreneur is carried into a written exercise, where the options facing him raise a wide range of issues, e.g. factory safety, the causes of poverty. In both (3) and (5) open-ended speculation and debate are encouraged although the activities are directly related to particular documentary evidence.

These examples cannot solve all the difficulties confronting teachers whose interest is encouraging understanding. They do, however, revive confidence in the possibility of school children thinking about history. The wide-ranging generalization and the detailed factual survey may have to be sacrificed, but the gain should be more active, intelligent and genuinely experienced reactions, as well as a less literary understanding of human life in the past.

NOTES

1. Knox, D., *The Industrial Revolution*, Harrap, 1974, p. 6.

8. The New Examinations: Servants or Lipservers of Historical Understanding?

A. K. DICKINSON

INTRODUCTION

Too many people, Malcolm Muggeridge is alleged to have said, regard the Commandments as an examination paper testing ten abilities, of which they should attempt to satisfy just eight. Critics of history examinations have argued with less wit but great conviction that too many compilers of these examinations believe that historical understanding subsumes a number of abilities of which they should examine just three, comprehension, factual recall and communicative powers. The last decade, of course, has been a time of major changes. These have included changes in social behaviour (which have reinforced Muggeridge's assertion) and changes in examinations intended to bring about significant improvements in the examining of history, including a reduction in the incidence of examinations testing a very limited range of abilities.

There is general agreement about the *identity* of the changes in examinations: new examinations at 16 + , 17 + and 18 + , growing concern to test candidates' understanding of the historical mode of inquiry, the introduction of various examining techniques intended to increase reliability and validity, and greater emphasis on teacher control. But there is no consensus of opinion about the *reception* which these changes merit. W. Lamont has welcomed CSE examinations on the grounds that they have challenged the basic premise of the 'old' history that the purpose of teaching history is to impart information. He has claimed that they have moved closer to the academic criteria of the historian, thus reinforcing the new premise that the main purpose is to enable pupils to find out about the past and the discipline of history.[1] There has also been enthusiasm for the objectives specified by some Examining Boards in the belief that they publicize important cognitive abilities and increase the validity of the examinations. K. Dawson and R. Ben Jones, however, have emphasized the lack of pre-tested 'A' Level papers, implying that their reliability and validity remain in doubt.[2] P. J. Lee and A. Gard have indicated confusions in the Coltham and Fines' framework of objectives which has been very influential with certain Examining Boards.[3] And some examinations provide indisputable evidence that the old premise has *not* been repudiated universally, that there are still examinations which demand or produce 'an emphasis on the accumulation and memorization of historical information at the expense of almost everything else'.[4]

All this leads one to wonder about the efficacy of the changes. What evidence is there that the various changes have initiated significant improvements in the examining of history? Do the new examinations really assess historical understanding or do they merely offer lip service to this ideal? This chapter seeks to answer these questions by looking at the main characteristics of the new examinations and investigating their claim to be reliable and valid tests of historical understanding.

1.   CHARACTERISTICS OF THE NEW EXAMINATIONS

Three assumptions underpin the new examinations in history: that they should assess pupils' *understanding* of the products and procedures of historians, that a variety of techniques are required to assess such understanding, and that examinations should fulfil the role of servant, not master, with teachers having control over them in certain respects. These assumptions have not been totally absent from many traditional examinations but generally the new examinations can be differentiated from the old in terms of which abilities they examine, how they examine them and who makes the administrative decisions.

(a)   Teacher Control

It has been a feature of the CSE and CEE from their conception that teachers can decide whether their pupils will be examined by a syllabus and examination scheme defined by the Examining Board (Mode 1), a syllabus agreed by them and examined by the Board (Mode 2), a syllabus and assessment programme devised by them and moderated by the Board (Mode 3), or a mixture of the above (a mixed-mode examination). This affected GCE Boards. They accepted more Mode 3 and mixed-mode examinations. A further very important extension of teachers' power regarding administrative decisions has been achieved by the teachers who represent the professional associations and the schools and colleges which participate in each Board's examinations. They have extended their influence (or control) over the policies and examining processes of the various Boards.

Are the effects of the extension of teacher control likely to be predominantly beneficial? Some critics have questioned the desirability of this last extension on the grounds that it will bring about a divorce between secondary and tertiary education. Mary Warnock, for example, has argued that the Schools Council has been concerned only with secondary schools whereas the old Examining Boards were designed as Boards of the universities with some representatives of secondary education and were concerned not only with what happened in school but after school as well.[5] But the assertion that an effective marriage is breaking up is well founded only if there is evidence that the union was consummated and is about to end. There are some grounds for accepting that the old Boards *were* interested in secondary education; there is less evidence to support the assertion that one can write off the influence of higher education representatives on relevant committees, the pledge that the partnership between teachers and the representatives of LEA's, industry, commerce and higher education will be preserved, and the interest of teachers in the problems of tertiary education (all teachers have tertiary backgrounds!).

A more serious criticism of teachers' growing control of examining policies and processes is that a different policy, placing greater emphasis on advice and direction from centralized agencies, would have produced more improvements. Evidence will be presented later to support the assertion that progress *has* been made in specifying important objectives and devising effective tests. It must remain a matter of conjecture whether *more* would have been achieved by a different policy, but *prima facie* the present policy seems appropriate. I. Goodson has argued (in Chapter 3 of this book) that centralized projects for changing the curriculum may facilitate changes but not implement them and, therefore, that an effective strategy for curriculum change must envisage a central role for the classroom teacher in developing and analysing his work. Similarly one can argue that the pronouncements of those formally in authority may facilitate changes in examinations and classroom practice but that they are most likely to be *implemented* when those concerned with deciding the form and content of examinations are also closely involved in curriculum planning, teaching and research into examinations.

Is this expecting too much of teachers? The demands would be great and most teachers already have more than enough to do. But if teachers are not fully involved in such work it is likely that fewer of the suggested changes will be implemented successfully. If, on the other hand, arrangements are made to involve teachers in test construction and research their participation will increase their understanding of examining techniques, assist their analysis of classroom activities and should ensure some correlation in curriculum and examination changes. In short the policy most likely to achieve widespread, soundly based and complementary changes in the history curriculum and examinations seems to be one in which teachers are not simply exhorted and advised but given the opportunity to extend their understanding of examining procedures and to choose or construct assessment schemes which match their evolving criteria.

(b) Examining Techniques

Another characteristic of the new examinations is the variety of examining techniques they employ. The London/Middlesex 16+ feasibility study experimented with seven different techniques.[6] It used open-ended questions, a project, oral examinations, teacher assessment of effort and attainment, structured essays (with candidates being given questions to be answered within their essays or a plan in the form of a list of sub-headings), objective questions and short answer questions (with or without accompanying 'stimulus' material). Most of the new examinations use one of the many combinations offered by selecting three or four examining techniques from those available.

This range of techniques makes it possible for examinations to assess systematically candidates' understanding of both the procedures and products of historians. But this ideal will be achieved only when a great deal of expertise has been acquired. The problems facing examiners must not be under-estimated. The London/Middlesex working party intended that their oral examination would test various aspects of historical understanding but tape recordings confirmed that the examiners generally had failed to devise and marshall appropriate questions.[7] Although the examiners failed to achieve their main objective, their study added significantly to our understanding of the problems and potential uses of this technique in history examinations. They experimented with five approaches, including unstructured orals based on the candidate's course-work or particular interests, discussion of a project written earlier and a more structured oral based on visual material introduced by the examiner. Their report contains evidence which suggests that the most successful approach was a discussion based on a talk prepared by the candidate.[8] At present most Boards using oral examinations link them to the candidate's project or course-work, which may have been completed weeks earlier.

There have also been problems about making the best use of the project or personal topic, a form of assessment which potentially seems very well suited to the fundamental aims of the new history. Its advocates claim that it can be used to provide pupils with practical experience of some aspects of the historian's craft and to assess their use of evidence. These claims are attractive but there are inherent problems, problems for teachers, pupils and examiners.[9] The report of the London/Middlesex working party emphasized the fundamental problem, stating that it found little evidence of the successful use of primary or secondary sources, just extensive copying from books. This working party concluded that the project 'was beset by so many pedagogical and practical difficulties as to be best dispensed with'.[10] Other Boards have admitted to problems but not drawn the same conclusion. Clearly there is a need to communicate the purpose of the study and the assessment, and to specify the nature of the guidance to be given to candidates. When this is done and action taken against unwelcome practices such as plagiarism, the project can help to establish whether or not candidates have some grasp of certain of the presuppositions and procedures of the historian.[11]

Another examining technique which is a possible contender for use in the new examinations is the multiple-choice objective test. This form of assessment often appears alien to the new history because it is used so extensively to test factual recall. Its value had been debased by the use of items such as the following:

Deniken, Kolchak, Wrangel and Yudenich were all
A   rivals for supreme power in Stalin's last years
B   prominent figures in the Comintern
C   Russian generals in the Second World War
D   victims of the Stalinist purges and terror
E   White commanders in the Russian Civil War[12]

But multiple-choice items do have some virtues. They can test quickly and objectively knowledge necessary for understanding what is being studied. They are always pre-tested and could be used to monitor certain aspects of courses. Can they test more than factual recall? Certainly it is impossible to test some abilities by this method, including originality and clarity of expression. But it can be used to assess more than just factual recall. One item designed to sustain this claim had a man looking at a portrait and saying, 'Brother and sisters have I none, but that man's father is my father's son'. Candidates were asked whether the man was looking at (a) his father, (b) himself, (c) his son, (d) either himself or his son? The item below shows that it is possible in history to use items which not only test whether candidates have grasped some vital aspects of a topic studied but also encourage them to *use* their knowledge:

Hitler's actions after he came to power showed that he wanted Germany to have
A   communist leaders
B   democratic elections
C   economic self-sufficiency
D   intellectual freedom
E   racial toleration

Factual recall should be a necessary, not sufficient, condition of a correct answer. This item seeks to get candidates to match the policies given with their knowledge of Hitler's action and situation. They will have studied many aspects of Hitler's life and work and can draw on this knowledge to provide them with the necessary evidence of his actions, personality and situation on which to base decisions about his intentions. The advocates of multiple-choice objective tests usually concentrate on the benefits of quick and objective marking and wide coverage of the syllabus content. What is being suggested here is that multiple-choice items are not necessarily alien to the new history and that their inclusion makes it feasible to aim at a more comprehensive assessment of abilities. They should not be regarded as appropriate for just the semi-illiterate and the Americans. Their role will be supplementary because priority must be given to techniques which reveal the candidate's thinking in more detail. But they can be used to assess quickly and efficiently certain components of historical understanding.

Document questions are more conducive to the new history and have been a common feature of the new examinations. It is less easy to understand why they have been palpably misused on some occasions. One Board at least has set questions designed to assess 'the candidate's ability to understand and interpret historical evidence free from the need to have previous knowledge of the subject'.[13] Such an approach provides evidence for those who believe that what candidates are asked to do bears virtually no resemblance to the work of the historian. It ignores the fact that when the historian works on documents he aspires to know a great deal about the society which produced them and to be aware of all the primary and secondary material relating to that work. History is a public form of knowledge and those who hope to satisfy its criteria must show such awareness.[14]

When document questions are used to assess candidates' treatment of evidence they should encourage them to answer on the basis of the source material presented plus the relevant knowledge they themselves bring to the study. Item 1 on pp. 150-51 appears likely to satisfy this criterion because the instructions direct candidates to use both the evidence provided and their knowledge of Germany in the 1930s. Another pleasing feature of the item is that it employs a cartoon which is likely to arouse interest and will extend or reinforce their understanding of an aspect of Hitler's rise to power. But it misses the opportunity to assess systematically certain aspects of historical understanding. For example, the cartoon is necessary for answering just one of the seven questions set, and question 1(f) is a blunt instrument for assessing candidates' understanding of why Hindenburg and Papen assisted Hitler to power. If a candidate is to explain their action fully he must search for and present evidence of Hindenburg and Papen's view of the situation and their particular intentions. Ideally this search will cover the local context of the maze of intrigue in Berlin in 1933 and the extended context of the weaknesses of the Weimar Republic. Item 1 has some good features and was innovatory when compiled; but it is open to the criticism that it merely offers lip-service to the new history and the assessment of historical understanding.

The Associated Examining Board has experimented with the combination of a personal study in depth and a methodology paper to assess 'A' Level candidates' appreciation and use of the procedures of the historian. It has published a specimen methodology paper which includes 'unseen' documents and is said to test a variety of skills.[15] Item 2 on pp. 151-5 is concerned with a much more limited (though important) part of historical thinking. It is one of the author's early attempts to devise items which could be used with 16 + candidates to assess certain aspects of their *use* of evidence when faced with the problem of explaining why an agent (whom they will have studied) acted as he did (in an incident which they may or may not have studied in detail). The comments of Generals Halder and von Rundstedt are quoted to emphasize the problematical aspects of

Hitler's order: the questions are designed to establish *how* each candidate uses the evidence available to him (in the item and acquired in earlier studies). Does he use it to try to get at Hitler's particular view of the situation and intentions at Dunkirk and to integrate these intentions with his further military and diplomatic aims (notably the defeat of France and the collapse of Allied morale)? Such a strategy is necessary to achieve full understanding of such an action. Does he use a different strategy? Each candidate's set of answers will reveal how he has used his available evidence. It should be possible to assign each set of answers to one of the following grades: [16]

Grade E
Candidate consistently contradicts or misconstrues the evidence available. Consequently he fails to grasp Hitler's intentions or situation and is likely to treat his action as unintelligible.

Grade D
Candidate much less likely to contradict or misconstrue the evidence. The main feature now is that the candidate draws almost exclusively on his own (conventional or anachronistic) view of what a commander is likely to do and fails to look for evidence of Hitler's particular intentions and view of the situation. The candidate makes virtually no reference to relevant information beyond the points mentioned in the questions.

Grade C
Candidate employs much more of the evidence available to him. But he fails to use it to elicit information about Hitler's particular intentions and view of the situation. 'Hitler launched a great attack on May 10th. His army was very successful and drove the British, French and Belgian troops back towards Dunkirk. Hitler stopped the advance on May 24th because the enemy were cornered.'

Grade B
Evidence employed to get at Hitler's particular intentions and view of the situation. Candidate recognizes what Hitler could and could not have known. (Pointers to this level include appreciating that when Hitler made his decision he could not have known for sure that weather conditions — and the activity of the RAF — would hamper the efforts of his Air Force so much.) But candidate fails to integrate Hitler's action at Dunkirk into the wider context of defeating France, reducing Allied morale, setting up the attack on Russia etc.

Grade A
Candidates not only uses evidence as in Grade B but integrates the action to be explained into the extended context.

Candidates' handling of the evidence may or may not improve as they tackle questions 2 and 3, which demonstrate deliberate intervention.

Question 2 is designed to encourage them to think about the situation from Hitler's point of view, to give those who need it a further chance to show that they appreciate the need to use their evidence to elicit what the agent could and could not have known for sure. Question 3 is intended to give a lead which may result in their explaining the action in an extended context.

Collectively the answers to such questions should provide sufficient evidence for certain aspects of candidates' handling of evidence to be graded accurately. But this sort of item is demanding in terms of time. Is it possible to assess the same (limited) aspects of historical thinking as effectively but more quickly? One alternative is to use a different type of question, one which focuses essentially on understanding either intentions or the situation and can be answered relatively quickly.

Question 4.   What was Hitler trying to do when he stopped the advance on Dunkirk on 24 May? Read the suggestions below and give *each* of them a mark out of 5 to show whether Hitler is likely to have thought them important or not.

1 = very likely indeed—this was probably one of his main aims
5 = he almost certainly would *not* have wanted this at all.
Put a circle round the number you choose.

A   Hitler's intention was to allow all the British, French
and Belgian troops to escape with their equipment   1   2   3   4   5
B   Hitler's intention was to ensure that the German Air
Force met some stern opposition from British planes   1   2   3   4   5
C   Hitler's intention was to let his Air Force play a major
part in defeating the British, French and Belgians at
Dunkirk   1   2   3   4   5
D   Hitler's intention was to preserve as many of his tanks
as possible for the attack on the main French armies   1   2   3   4   5
E   Hitler's intention was to save the lives of his best
troops   1   2   3   4   5

One could not sustain a claim that an objective set of marks is attainable, but there are good grounds for claiming that it is possible to pick out different sorts of assertions here and that the set of marks awarded by each candidate will indicate whether he has made this differentiation. In other words, each set of marks will reveal whether a candidate has differentiated between suggestions which really get at the agent's particular intentions (C and D), those which are likely to have weighed less heavily with him (E), and those which contradict the evidence (A and B).

Question 5.   What was Hitler's view of the situation when he stopped the advance on Dunkirk on 24 May? Read the statements below and show whether you think they are probably true or probably untrue.

1 = he probably *did* believe this when he stopped the advance
2 = he probably did *not* believe this when he stopped the advance
Put a circle round the number which shows your decision.

A   Hitler believed that his panzer divisions would no longer be
    able to make such good progress   1   2
B   Hitler was sure that it would be easier for his Air Force to finish
    off the enemy if the panzer divisions stopped outside Dunkirk   1   2
C   Hitler believed that it was important to preserve his panzer
    divisions if Germany was to defeat France quickly   1   2
D   Hitler was sure that the Royal Air Force would severely trouble
    German Air attacks on Dunkirk   1   2
E   Hitler believed that it would be easy for the British and French
    to escape to England because the sea was smooth   1   2

Collectively a candidate's answers will indicate whether or not he has consistently used the evidence available to get at the agent's particular view of the situation. Sceptics will point out that a candidate can simply guess at each of the answers. This criticism can be countered by the assertion that he is unlikely to guess right five times out of five. Of course there are other relevant criticisms and questions such as these are more likely to win acceptance as useful teaching devices than as good examination items. Some ticking of boxes can be justified but we must remember that the thinking it assesses is a necessary but not sufficient condition of the construction of a significant historical narrative. In *some* ways essay questions are much closer to the activity of the historian.

We must make a difficult decision. A good deal of time is required to assess even a few components of historical thinking systematically by conventional techniques. Consequently we must use some non-essay items, or settle for the traditional form of assessment, with its inherent strengths and weaknesses, or devote much more time to assessment than is usual at present. But first we must decide what we wish to examine.

(c) Abilities Examined

The traditional examinations have been accused of testing mainly the accumulation, memorization and recall of historical facts, explanations and interpretations and the ability to express them clearly. Is this criticism fair and what do the new examinations test? Do the new examinations simply pay lip-service to the new emphasis on historical understanding and treating history as a means of finding out about the past or are they really promoting and assessing these ideals? The section above contains some evidence that it is *not* mere lip-service, that the new examinations *are* endeavouring to assess candidates' appreciation and handling of some of the procedures of the historian. It also contains evidence that further changes are required if the new examinations are to achieve their aims in full.

One problem to be overcome is that some examinations include a few questions which are in tune with the new history but overall place so much emphasis on factual recall that they maintain the tradition of treating history as essentially a body of information to be received and recalled.

A second problem is that some of the new examinations overlook the fact that history is a mode of study with shared understandings, standards and procedures. As mentioned earlier, one Board at least has set questions designed to assess candidates' ability to understand and interpret historical evidence 'free from other sources and the views of other authors'. Such an examination ignores certain important features of the historical mode of inquiry, notably that it is a public form of knowledge, that the historian works within a framework of established facts and interpretations. Traditional 'O' and 'A' Level examinations have been appreciative of this framework. They have employed questions, particularly at 'A' Level, which have encouraged candidates to reflect on it in certain ways. Their strength has been their emphasis on the framework; their weakness has been their neglect of the way it is established and employed by historians.

A recent small-scale study revealed that a high proportion of the pupils questioned had a false view of the very foundations of history.[18] The pupils generally agreed that primary sources added to their understanding of the past (by providing 'extra detail', 'atmosphere' and a 'second opinion to that of the textbook') but they were divided equally between those who believed that history books presented the 'real facts' of history while sources provided extra detail, and those who considered that primary sources were to be trusted more because they were 'first-hand knowledge'. Very few pupils showed any awareness of the problems associated with source material or the real relationship between the textbook and (primary) source material. These findings were the result of a study in a single school (where source material was used regularly to provide detail and a sense of the reality of events). But they merit reporting because they emphasize a fundamental misunderstanding, because source material is widely used in this way (though often less effectively), and because the same misconceptions were evident among the pupils interviewed by M. Booth in his research.[19] School children cannot be transformed into trained historians but teachers can do much to eradicate these misconceptions, and examinations can reinforce their efforts. For example, early work on a topic can include the question, 'How do we know anything about this particular topic?', while later the teacher can ask 'What particular sources have proved useful?', 'What further questions might one ask?', and 'What would count as evidence if one wanted to answer them?'. Examinations can reinforce such work by examining candidates' appreciation of the historian's use of evidence. Candidates could be asked to explain which sources have been useful for a particular topic, which questions they helped to answer and which further questions they raised.[20]

Much more can be said about the abilities which the new examinations are endeavouring to assess and the problems of matching them to examining techniques, but already enough has been said to indicate that some of the changes are very welcome whereas others cast doubts on the validity of the new examinations. Therefore these issues will be looked at further in the context of answering the vital question 'How reliable and valid are the new examinations?'.

2. THE RELIABILITY AND VALIDITY OF THE NEW EXAMINATIONS

(a) Reliability

A great many teachers over the years have been sceptical about the validity of public examinations in history (that they measure what they are designed to measure) and their reliability (the accuracy and consistency of the mark or grade awarded to a candidate). Doubts about their reliability were derived from their dependence on essay-type examinations offering a choice of questions and marked by a host of examiners, and were reinforced periodically by newspaper disclosures of wide discrepancies in the grades awarded to the same pupils by GCE 'O' Level and CSE Boards. Long periods of silence by the Boards regarding their procedures did not allay this scepticism.

Although there is much evidence to support doubts about their reliability there is also an increasing amount of evidence which suggests that history examinations are now generally reliable measuring instruments. High reliability estimates were recorded for two traditional 'O' Level history examinations in a recent Schools Council research project, *GCE Examining at Ordinary Level*, directed by A. S. Willmott (1970-1973). The project analysed 29 GCE examinations worked in 1970 and 1971. Reliability estimates ranged from 0.70 to 0.93 and included 0.80 and 0.84 for history.[21] The median value for history (0.82) was the same as the overall median. The median values for all CSE subjects investigated equalled or exceeded 0.85, but this study did not include history. A. S. Willmott and D. L. Nuttall assert that on the basis of the evidence available to them it can be said that CSE and GCE 'O' Level examinations are 'equally reliable and that the level of reliability attained is as high as might reasonably be expected'.[22] They report that the margin of error in terms of a five-point grading scale is one grade in either direction for the grade actually awarded and conclude optimistically that their work 'has shown that public examinations at 16+ are convincingly reliable as measuring instruments'.[23]

Willmott's reliability estimates for the two essay-based 'O' Level history examinations are quite high and refute the belief that essays cannot be a component of a reliable examination. They also mean that these examinations satisfied one of the conditions of validity, a valid test being one which measures what it claims to be measuring *and* is reliable. But the values will not allay all the fears of teachers. Statisticians may find them acceptable but most teachers will feel that they emphasize the need for care in interpreting grades and for further efforts to secure reliability. The margin of error reported by Willmott for the 1970 history examination meant that candidates had to differ by at least 12 marks, probably 24, before fairly firm conclusions could be made as to their real differences in attainment in history.[24] In other words, all that can properly be said about a candidate awarded a grade 4 on a 5 grade scale is that his 'true' grade could be as high as a grade 3 or as low as a grade 5.[25]

Clearly care is needed in interpreting grades and improving reliability, but the evidence does encourage some optimism because the new examinations are likely to be more reliable than the traditional ones. Inter-examiner reliability has been improved by introducing objective-type tests and carefully moderating the marking of essay questions. The Boards have tried to increase content reliability by using more pre-tested and unambiguous questions. The new examinations are generally longer and the longer the test the more reliable it is likely to be (although candidates might prefer not to be convinced of this). Also it is likely that a method other than an internal consistency test is needed to do justice to the reliability of many examinations, particularly the new examinations which employ several types of questions designed to assess a variety of abilities.[26] Thus there seem good reasons for assuming that the new examinations in history are reasonably reliable and consequently satisfy one condition of validity.

Reliability on its own, however, is an empty achievement: there is no point in improving it if validity is in doubt. How far do history examinations measure what they claim to measure?

(b) **Validity**

Public examinations in history are intended to assess candidates' attainment rather than to predict their future performance. Therefore their validity depends on the extent to which they sample the objectives and content of a given course. A precise statement of these is needed so that the extent of this content validity can be established by comparing the specification with what the examination papers actually assess. The growing tendency among Examining Boards to provide clear statements of syllabus objectives and content indicates their concern to satisfy this requirement. The statement issued by the London GCE Board before their 'O' Level multiple-choice paper became operational is in some ways a model for this sort of specification. It provided details of the abilities to be tested, syllabus content and weighting.[27] Each of the examinations, it said, would aim to test the abilities to recall significant factual knowledge, to understand significant historical information, to perceive historical relationships and/or to analyse and evaluate historical information. These abilities plus the syllabus content and weighting for each examination were summarized in chart form (see following page).

Such specifications not only contrast with the traditional very limited statements about content and objectives but suggest a precision which has encouraged the belief that the new examinations may have a very strong claim to content validity. Unfortunately this strong claim cannot be sustained in some instances because objectives have been wrongly specified or imperfectly matched with examining techniques. The distinction above

Syllabus B
English History, 1902-1955 and European History, 1904-1954

	A *English* Central political, economic and social history	B *European* Central political history	C Inter- national relations	D Cultural, ideological, scientific history	Weighting %
1. Factual recall					25
2. Understanding					50
3. Perception, analysis and evaluation					25
Weighting %	35	30	30	5	

between the ability to understand significant historical information and to perceive historical relations cannot be sustained because understanding significance already implies grasping relations. The statement's claim to precision is further undermined by the fact that the ability to analyse and evaluate historical material subsumes a number of activities. Its greatest weakness, however, is the fact that such a taxonomy cannot be used to specify exactly what each item will assess. When biology, physics and geography specialists were asked to decide whether each part of some 'O' Level questions was testing knowledge, comprehension, application or analysis and evaluation (i.e. another modified Bloom taxonomy) the only consensus was on items presumed to be testing mainly knowledge.[28] The same thing happened when physics teachers were asked to classify eighty items on two Nuffield 'A' Level multiple-choice papers.[29] The teachers were given clear instructions and a document explaining the modified Bloom taxonomy but they were bound to disagree because the taxonomic content of an item is a property of the learning experience of the candidate rather than the question itself. This being the case it is very difficult, if not impossible, for an examiner to write an item which will test the same ability in all the candidates, and anyone who claims, on the basis of such a taxonomy, to be able to specify accurately the ability which any given item is testing is claiming a spurious precision unless he is going to ask each candidate to explain how he arrived at his answer.

Can public examinations in history achieve a very high level of content validity? In theory they can if behavioural objectives are stated much more precisely, but there is little evidence to suggest that such a specification will soon be available in history. Coltham and Fines have produced the most detailed specification at present available but it contains errors and imprecision (see Chapter 2 above). Given that it is very unlikely that anyone in the immediate future will be able to translate the complex forms of historical understanding into precise sets of observable behaviours it appears that the most we can do is to sustain a less ambitious claim to validity. We can support those examinations which state objectives which honour the new history courses and are based on an analysis of the discipline of history and on empirical investigation. We can support those which select examining techniques to match these objectives, which get at the process as well as the product of candidates' thinking, and which are revised in the light of further philosophical and empirical work. The strengths and limitations of the new examinations' claim to validity are exemplified by the AEB Pilot Scheme in 'A' Level History.[30] The decision to assess candidates' understanding of the methodology of the historian by means of a dissertation, plus oral and essay questions to be answered by reference to the dissertation, indicates concern to match stated objectives with examining techniques. It also suggests a strong claim to validity. But this claim could be strengthened. The AEB list of course objectives includes 'to elicit from the student empathetic response to historical material'. It elucidates this objective by saying 'while they should bear in mind the work of later historians,' students should be encouraged to appreciate a situation as seen through the eyes of a contemporary'. It then suggest that it is unexaminable, presumably in the mistaken belief, inspired by Coltham and Fines, that such activity is essentially conative, not cognitive. In fact there are good grounds for asserting that understanding a situation in history involves grasping the agent's view of it, the historian's view based on additional evidence *and* differentiating between them, that all this is essentially a cognitive activity[31] and that it *can* be tested.[32]

Are the new examinations likely to achieve high content validity? There are many obstacles to be overcome, including the need to make a comprehensive list of the important components of historical understanding, to make informed decisions about what should be examined at 16 +, 17 + and 18 + respectively, and to agree on matters of weighting. It is unlikely that Clio will soon be able to claim that precision is a characteristic of her examining technique, but at least decisions are being based increasingly on the analysis of relevant information instead of tradition and intuition.

3. CONCLUSION

The burden of the argument above is that welcome changes have been made in public examinations in history but that many problems remain. The old 'O' and 'A' Level examinations offered only a minority of pupils a real chance of gaining a Certificate of Education, they appeared to many teachers to be more concerned to direct teaching than to follow it and were rarely defended as valid or reliable tests of historical understanding. Now the majority of pupils are offered the opportunity to gain formal recognition of their learning ability: 86.3 per cent of all sixteen-year-olds entered for at least one public examination in Summer 1974, with 79.1 per cent sitting English and 38.6 per cent history. Further opportunities to gain certificates are offered by the 17 + and 18 + examinations. Teachers have the opportunity to select or design examinations which serve their syllabuses. More teachers than ever before are aware of the principles of educational measurement due principally to their involvement in Mode 3 and mixed-mode examinations. Progress has also been made in establishing what constitutes historical understanding, which components pupils can be expected to master and how they can be examined. Consequently the new examinations reward a greater range of abilities and it is increasingly unlikely that a candidate's grade will be decided by performance on a single terminal test. All these changes encourage optimism. But if the optimism is to be sustained, further changes must be made, particularly in areas where fairly limited progress has been made so far. In 1969 Connaughton's review showed that research findings had little influence on established examination practices.[33] Research still has not exploited fully the interest and abilities of teachers or always asked the right questions. Research is needed which involves teachers more and provides them with more and quicker feedback in terms of which components of historical understanding are proving difficult for candidates, the likely causes of misunderstanding and evidence regarding effective teaching materials and techniques.

Many people will not share the author's conception of the millenium, including those who argue for the abolition of examinations, those who reiterate the ideal stressed in the Norwood report of examinations conducted by teachers at their school on syllabuses and papers framed by themselves,[34] and those who think progress would be swifter if the traditional rights of teachers to control the curriculum were ended. These views cannot be given the detailed attention here which they merit. Space permits just three comments: public examinations provide an important check on standards; the existing checks ensure that bad schemes can be exposed; and a detailed national syllabus could not be justified at present on the grounds of optimizing pupils' learning potential, because no one possesses sufficient understanding to decide all the issues associated with such a programme, and there would in any case be considerable problems about implementing it.

Those who do share the author's assumptions about ends (that public examinations in history should assess important components of historical understanding in a valid and reliable way, involve teachers at all stages, provide them with considerable feedback about their courses, and cater for the majority of pupils in an age group) are likely to agree with the judgement that appreciable progress has been made towards the millenium. They are also likely to agree that among the main reasons for this progress were the decisions by central government to establish the Schools Council and the CSE. There may be less agreement about likely future trends given problems such as identifying a common core syllabus and achieving an appropriate administrative structure for examinations at 16 + , 17 + and 18 + . But it was reassuring to hear the Secretary of State for Education, in a speech marking the opening of the Great Education

Debate, state that the freedom of the teacher in the classroom is 'one of the splendours of the English system'.[35] Further significant improvements in the examining of history are possible: they are most likely to be achieved if there is no reversal of this and the other policies which have nourished the recent changes.

NOTES

1. Lamont, W., 'The Uses and Abuses of Examinations' in M. Ballard (ed.), *New Movements in the Study and Teaching of History*, Temple Smith, 1970, pp. 202-3.
2. Jones, R. Ben and Dawson, K., 'History and the Eighteen-plus' in R. Ben Jones (ed.), *Practical Approaches to the New History*, Hutchinson Educational, 1973, pp. 204-5.
3. See Chapter 2 of this book.
4. Thompson, D., 'Some Psychological Aspects of History Teaching', in W. H. Burston and C. W. Green (eds.), *Handbook for History Teachers*, Methuen, 1972, p. 35.
5. *New Society*, 11 March 1976.
6. University of London University Entrance and School Examinations Council/Middlesex Regional Examining Board, *History: Feasibility Studies concerning a single examination or system of examining at 16 +*, Eyre and Spottiswood, 1975, particularly Chapter 2. 1975.
7. ibid., p. 29.
8. loc. cit.
9. There is a brief discussion of the different sorts of claim made regarding children's use of sources and some of the problems associated with those claims in Chapter 1 of this book.
10. London/Middlesex Regional Examining Board, op. cit., p. 22.
11. The Associated Examining Board's 'O' Level World History examination contains a project which satisfies these criteria. The strategies which the Board devised to ensure that the project was well used are described in some detail in Chapter 3, pp. 47-50 of this book.
12. London/Middlesex Regional Examining Board, op. cit., p. 38.
13. Oxford/Southern Regional Examinations Board, *Joint Feasibility Study into a Common Examination in History at 16 + : Report of the Working Party on the First Examination, 1974*, Oxford Delegacy of Local Examinations/Southern Regional Examinations Board, 1975, paper 2A.
14. The theme that history is not something undertaken privately but is an ongoing public form of knowledge is discussed in Chapter 1 of this book.
15. This specimen paper is published in full in *Teaching History*, Vol. IV, No. 15, May 1976, and is one component of the AEB 'A' Level history pilot scheme.
16. See Chapter 5, Part II, and note 41 to Chapter 6, for discussion of the theoretical basis of these grades. Item 2 has not been extensively pre-tested. The author is kite flying and could not claim at present that responses to the item could be graded with the accuracy and reliability appropriate to public examinations. For a well illustrated and generally detailed account of the BEF's retreat through Belgium and the evacuation from Dunkirk see Barker, A. J., *Dunkirk: The Great Escape*, J. M. Dent, 1977. For a more detailed explanation of Hitler's actions at Dunkirk (setting-out possible political and humanitarian considerations as well as military ones) see Shirer, W. L., *The Rise and Fall of the Third Reich*, Simon & Schuster, 1960, pp. 731-6 and Toland, J., *Adolf Hitler*, Doubleday & Co., 1976, pp. 609-11.
17. See, for example, the Joint Matriculation Board's *General Certificate of Education Regulations and Syllabus 1978* which states that 60 per cent of the marks will be allocated to testing 'the candidate's knowledge of a given body of factual material'. Even

the new examinations, based on the Schools Council Project: *History 13-16* and operated jointly by the Southern Universities Joint Board and the Southern Regional Examinations Board place considerable emphasis on factual recall. See paper 1 which accounts for 40 per cent of the total marks.

18. I am indebted to Carola Terraine for these insights. A key question she used was 'How useful is it to use source material (things written at the time or pictures drawn at the time) when studying history?'

19. Booth, M. B., *History Betrayed?*, Longmans, 1969. See, for example, p. 63 and p. 67.

20. See Part III of Chapter 1 of this book for further comments on the use of evidence in the classroom.

21. Reliability coefficients can range from 0 to 1. Values approaching 1 indicate negligible error of measurement. Values in the range of 0.8 to 0.9 are considered acceptable for examinations which cover a limited range of ability (e.g. GCE and CSE). For details of the results reported here and the methods and formula chosen, see Willmott, A. S., and Nuttall, D. L., *The Reliability of Examinations at 16 +*, Macmillan Educational, 1975, Chapter 3. Willmott, A. S., and Nuttall, D. L., *British Examinations: Techniques of Analysis*, National Foundation for Educational Research, 1972, give a full discussion of the ways of estimating reliability and the particular problems associated with examinations which consist typically of a number of different components, each designed to assess different attributes (e.g. the new examinations).

22. Willmott, A. S., and Nuttall, D. L., 1975, op. cit., abstract.

23. ibid., p. 57.

24. ibid., pp. 12-13.

25. ibid., p. 58.

26. Although examinations now usually consist of a number of tests of different abilities, and reliability estimates are of internal consistency (i.e. the extent to which the questions in an examination all measure the same thing) these estimates cannot be dismissed at present. We just do not know how far 'different' skills and abilities are correlated. But the current trend does make it imperative to investigate the feasibility of estimating reliability at the most basic level possible, for example, a group of questions examining a specific ability. Such a study would also shed light on the feasibility of reporting results in terms of a profile instead of a global figure.

27. *Teacher's Booklet (for the multiple-choice objective test): History — Syllabus B Ordinary Level,* University of London University Entrance and School Examinations Council, 1972, pp. 4-5.

28. Willmott, A. S., and Hall, C. G. W., *'O' Level Examined: the Effect of Question Choice*, Macmillan Educational, 1975, Chapter 6.

29. Fairbrother, R. W., 'The reliability of teachers' judgement of the abilities being tested by multiple choice items', in *Educational Research*, 17, June 1975, pp. 202-10.

30. A statement of the objectives and examination structure was published in *Teaching History*, Vol. IV, No. 15, May 1976.

31. See Chapter 2 of this book, particularly p. 23 and pp. 32-3.

32. See Chapter 6 of this book, particularly Part II.

33. Connaughton, I. M., 'The validity of examinations at 16 +' in *Educational Research*, 11, 1969, pp. 163-78.

34. *Curriculum and Examinations in Secondary Schools*, HMSO, 1943, reprinted 1962, p. 140.

35. *The Times*, 23 October 1976.

Item 1 Topic: HITLER
Writing Time: 30 minutes

THE TEMPORARY TRIANGLE
Von Hindenburg and Von Papen (*together*)
'FOR HE'S A JOLLY GOOD FELLOW,
FOR HE'S A JOLLY GOOD FELLOW
FOR HE'S A JOLLY GOOD FE-EL-LOW,
(*Aside:* 'Confound him!')
AND SO SAY BOTH OF US!'

1. Question 1 refers to the cartoon above. This cartoon appeared in the English magazine *Punch* in January 1933. It illustrates an important stage in Adolf Hitler's rise to power. Use this cartoon and your knowledge of Germany at this time to answer the following questions:

                                                                    Marks

    (a) What is the emblem on the banner in the right back-   (1)
        ground?

    (b) What office did Hitler secure in January 1933?   (1)

    (c) What office was held by Hindenburg at this time?   (1)

    (d) The men in uniform in the background belonged to   (3)
        the SA. How did they assist Hitler to come to power?

    (e) How did Papen assist Hitler to come to power?   (2)

    (f) Why did Hindenburg and Papen assist Hitler to come   (4)
        to power and why might they have been doubtful of
        behaving correctly in doing this?

    (g) Describe the events between January 1933 and August   (8)
        1934 by which Hitler was able to secure further power
        in Germany.

(Cartoon and question reproduced by kind permission of *Punch* and the University of London University Entrance and School Examinations Council respectively.)

Item 2

Time: 1 hour

Read the passage below and then answer *all* the questions.

The German Attack of May–June 1940

Hitler had plans for expanding Germany eastwards, mainly at the expense of Russia, and to the west, mainly at the expense of France. On 10 May, 1940, he launched a great atack in the west. German aeroplanes and panzer divisions, each containing about 250 tanks, were used to attack vital objectives. The main body of the army followed them, establishing full control over the conquered areas.

The German attack was very successful, the panzer divisions doing their job particularly well. The Dutch were defeated after four days of fighting and a large army of British, French and Belgian troops was forced back into the area around Dunkirk. This area was crisscrossed with canals, ditches and flooded areas: the troops were hemmed in by the sea and the advancing German forces. On 24 May the chasing German tanks and heavy guns came in sight of Dunkirk. The enemy were cornered. Hitler discussed the situation with Göring, commander of the German Air Force, and General von Rundstedt, commander of Army Group A. The same day Hitler ordered the panzer divisions to stop

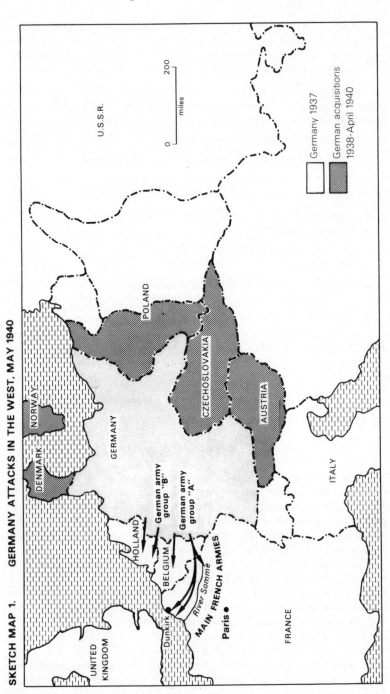

SKETCH MAP 1.   GERMANY ATTACKS IN THE WEST, MAY 1940

on the canal line outside Dunkirk. The Air Force and Army Group B, which had virtually no tanks, were to deal with the enemy troops.

Most of the soldiers in Army Group A were amazed at the decision. So were some of the generals. General Halder wrote in his diary, 'Our left wing, consisting of tanks and heavy guns, will thus be stopped dead in its tracks on the direct orders of the Fuehrer. Finishing off the encircled army is to be left to the Air Force.' On 26 May he wrote, 'These orders from the top make no sense. The tanks are stopped as if they were paralysed.' Another general, talking after the war about what happened, said, 'If I had had my way the English would not have got off so lightly at Dunkirk. But my hands were tied by direct orders from

SKETCH MAP 2.   SITUATION ON MAY 28TH

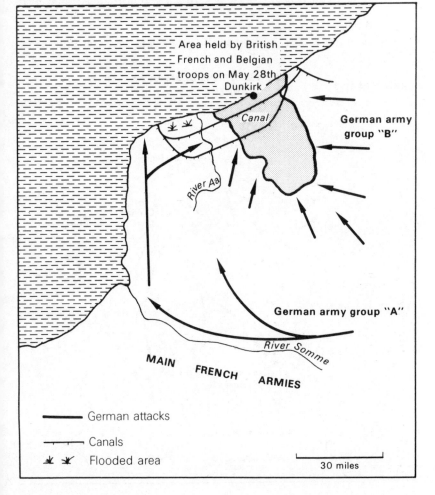

Hitler himself. While the English were climbing into the ships off the beaches I was kept uselessly outside the port unable to move.'

Göring told Hitler that the German Air Force could finish off the British, French and Belgian troops. But bad weather prevented the planes from flying some of the time. When they could fly they met, for the first time in the war, stern opposition from British planes. The British planes suffered heavy losses but they did destroy many German bombers.

On the evening of 26 May Hitler gave a new order. The tanks were to attack. But the British, French and Belgian troops had hastily built some defences around Dunkirk. Plans had been made to get the troops away sea. Calm weather meant that the sea was smooth and between 27 May and 4 June nearly 340,000 British, French and Belgian troops were rescued from the beaches by 850 boats of all sizes, including fishing boats and holiday yachts. On 4 June the Germans broke through and captured the 40,000 French troops still there.

Most of the British, French and Belgian troops were saved but nearly

SKETCH MAP 3

PROGRESS OF THE GERMAN ARMIES IN FRANCE 1ST–22ND JUNE

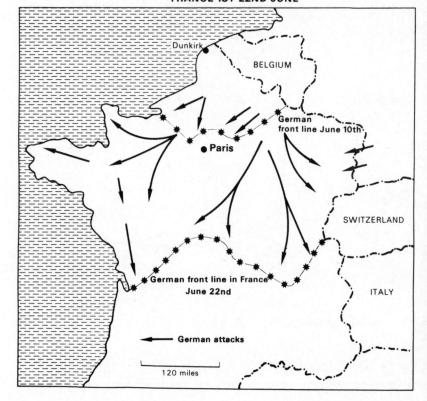

all their equipment was lost. The Royal Air Force had been weakened considerably, losing 474 planes. Hitler's next move was to attack the French armies along the river Somme. He thought that their defeat and the capture of Paris would mean the collapse of French resistance. He used his panzer divisions to lead the attack. On 5 June the German attack on the Somme began. Paris was captured on 14 June and eight days later the French Government made peace on Hitler's terms. Hitler was soon making final plans for attacking Britain and Russia.

People have argued whether Dunkirk was a deliverance or a disaster: British losses included 243 ships, 63,879 vehicles and 68,111 soldiers killed, wounded or taken prisoner. Most historians agree that it was both a great deliverance and a great disaster — and that some of the time it looked as if it would be just a great disaster.

Question 1.   Why did Hitler order the tanks to stop advancing on Dunkirk on 24 May? Give as many reasons as you can.

Question 2.   What different actions do you think Hitler considered on 24 May? Why did he reject those alternatives?

Question 3a.   Explain what Hitler was trying to do in May and June 1940.

Question 3b.   Do you think what happened at Dunkirk fitted into this plan?

9. History After School

ASA BRIGGS

The relationships between university teaching of history and school teaching of history are complex ones. Universities are involved in the setting of syllabuses, but do not dictate them, and since the setting up of the Schools Council they have been involved less. University entrants wishing to study history from schools or technical colleges usually carry on their studies of history without a break, bearing the trail of their 'A' levels with them. Teachers of history in schools include new history graduates straight from their university studies — and with more of them possessing postgraduate qualifications in the subject — but such new graduates are always in a minority. Books and other materials used in schools — and they are not standardized — are often written or edited by university teachers, sometimes, but not always, in cooperation with teachers of history, but far more (including the latest types of learning materials) are prepared by teachers in the light of developing classroom experience. Such relationships are capable of quantification in terms of numbers, ratios, throughputs and feedbacks, as has been shown — if then incompletely — in the United States. But most people in this country would be satisfied with Professor Elton's basic quantitative statement 'there have never been more historians in the world at work than there are today'.[1]

Since university courses vary as much as school syllabuses and are subject to frequent revision — there is no university core curriculum — it is not easy to pass from quantitative analysis to qualitative assessment. Even the effects of the continuous study of history on the part of students and of the study of particular university history syllabuses on the part of the teacher, are matters of gossip or folklore not of careful comparative scrutiny; and there has been no detailed examination of the strength in the secondary school classroom of the pulls of the past experience of pupils in primary schools and of the teacher's own experience of history through the university. The clues are scattered through *Teaching History*, an invaluable publication which first appeared in May 1969.

Looking more generally at history after school, it is plain, of course, that the relationships between school and university teaching are not the only factors influencing national attitudes to history as a subject. History books have always been widely reviewed in this country, far more widely than in most countries, and during recent years history as 'entertainment' has grown immensely in volume and impact as a result of the development of the mass media. It is indeed often difficult to separate the entertaining and the educative, and some of the presentations, making use of new techniques, have been highly sophisticated.[2] Likewise, history as a collective 'leisure pursuit' for adults has grown in importance, again, sometimes but not always, as a consequence of the activities of the media. A number of small working groups have deliberately set out to remain uninfluenced by the media, preferring active participation to passive viewing and working with people they know to seeing or listening to people they do not. They have been particularly active in fields like local history or industrial archaeology, sometimes pioneering new kinds of exploration. The idea of the 'history workshop' has attracted considerable interest; and while the first number of *History Workshop: A Journal for Socialist Historians* claimed that its editorial collective was concerned at 'the narrowing of the influence of history in our society and at its progressive withdrawal from the battle of ideas',[3] there is no country in the world which devotes more time to the interpretation — highly pluralistic — of anniversaries, jubilees and centenaries. The present is always calling the past to the rescue.

In noting recent tendencies and trends, it is useful to turn back for a starting point to a detailed survey of university history courses in this country relating to the year 1968, a year of considerable importance in the history of the universities themselves and something of a watershed.[4] In a lively immediate comment on the conclusions of the survey Dr Brian Harrison began by noting that the evidence suggested that during the previous decade a 'revolution' had occurred in 'the structure and scope of university history courses'.[5] A new pattern of degree syllabuses had been introduced, many of them involving combinations of history and other subjects. In many universities there had been a growing pressure 'not only for modernity but for contemporaneity'. Moves, sometimes tentative, occasionally ambitious, were being made towards the study of world history. The domination of political history had been shaken, above all in the 'new universities' which Dr Harrison saw as the main centres of change. So, too, had the domination of mediaeval history (always exaggerated). The historiographical dimension was also receiving more attention although there was little to suggest that 'philosophical' (or methodological) questions relating to history were being taken particularly seriously. He did not mention quantitative history, although a neighbouring article in the same volume of *History* included a review by E. H. Hunt of Robert W. Fogel's *Railroads and Economic Growth* (1964), sub-titled *Essays in Econometric History* and hailed by one of its first reviewers as 'a revolution in economic history'.[6]

Dr Harrison also discussed in his article significant changes in the methodology of teaching and examining. In a few universities, not all of them new ones, 'theses' had become part of the degree requirement — Harrison did not employ the now familiar term 'project', already familiar long before 1968 in what were then Teachers' Training Colleges—and in many universities seminars, organized in place of or in addition to lectures, were fostering a 'history workshop' atmosphere which 'broke through the textbook approach' and gave students the feeling that they and their teachers were engaged in a 'joint inquiry'. The result of all this ferment was that history students were being offered a 'wealth of new opportunities' in 1968. Yet Dr Harrison recognized that 'the formal provisions of a syllabus can give only a faint indication of its real character, and a conventional course well taught can be far more stimulating than a novel course badly taught'.[7] His article ended, moreover, with a cautious reference to possible 'counter-revolutionaries'. 'Those who feel that historians have a perspective or method sufficiently distinctive to justify separate cultivation,' he suggested, 'may fear that such changes will gradually eliminate any distinctive arrangements for the teaching of history at universities'.[8]

The caution came out not only in the thought itself but also in the guarded expression of it—the use of the word 'gradually' and the phrase 'may fear' rather than 'fear'. Others were more forthright then and since, yet there has been no general alarm. After at times fascinating, at other times exasperating, arguments inside universities—buried away already in a mass of ephemera—the single-subject honours course has maintained its primacy since 1968, and there are still more standard three-hour examination papers of the 'traditional' variety than there are 'projects'. Lectures are still given and are well attended, and a few universities have been backward in developing seminar techniques even for post-graduate students.[9] The new universities are not all centres of innovation. There have been changes in the content of the syllabuses—and they are still being made every year—but there is far less, if any, of a sense of ferment.

One of the most interesting effects of the changes which have taken place is that history graduates have now usually 'covered less ground' than they used to do. This, however, has been less an effect of the development of combined subject degrees or of new general course patterns than of the increasing popularity in most universities of 'thematic' or 'problem' history in which a 'vertical' theme or a problem is studied 'in depth' rather than a 'horizontal' period. Sometimes thought of as a way of pulling history students away from the 'false security' of 'A' level syllabuses, such courses have not always succeeded in giving them a sense of freedom to range widely through time. The best of them, however, have familiarized history students with the conditions of effective time travel. 'Project work' has also reduced coverage. The projects have tended to cluster around 'fashionable' preoccupations (for example, urban history or labour history) and have often had a local slant because of the nature and availability of the materials used as evidence. The best of these too, however, have fostered a commitment to independent, detailed study and to an exploratory approach to issues and problems, even to chronology. They have certainly served as a useful link between undergraduate work and graduate work in history. Their effects on classroom teaching, like those of 'thematic' history are less certain, although project work has figured prominently there for decades.

It is the argument of this footnote to the recent academic history of history after school that institutional re-arrangements in universities have come to figure less prominently in thinking about the future of history as a subject than a number of far-reaching intellectual changes in the study of history itself which have taken place in this country and others since 1968. We have to look outside departments or schools to appreciate these. Yet there is one notable exception. The development of history courses at the Open University, which did not take in its first students until 1971, has been exciting and influential.[10] It has also taken fuller account of the wide range of possible historical interests and ventures than most universities. Four features have stood out—first, an 'Introduction to History' course which, like the older Sussex introductory course,[11] is concerned not with particular facts about particular periods, but with the methods of history; second, the use of extended 'case studies', of which one in particular, part of the Foundation course—'industrialization'—is explicitly designed (with well chosen supporting materials) as a common course to 'integrate the historical approach with those of other humanities disciplines'; third, the subsequent pursuit within the cluster of single-discipline courses of the study of subjects which had not hitherto figured prominently in existing university syllabuses, notably 'War and Society', a 'thematic' course, drawing examples from 'the entire span of human society' and 'bringing in' art, literature, music, science and technology; and fourth, a pioneering course, brilliantly contrived, on 'historical data and the social sciences', which has gone further than any other course at the undergraduate level in Britain to wrestle with the methods and problems of quantitative history not only in relation to economic history.[12]

The strength of the Open University has depended not only on such willingness to think afresh about syllabuses and curricula—with the needs in mind of students who have never studied history seriously or at an advanced level at school—but on learning methods with the emphasis placed on learning rather than on teaching. The printed materials are of a high quality and are intelligently ordered and illustrated. The visual is used functionally and not decoratively. The correspondence texts are historiographically sophisticated: they do not purvey facts and opinions, but encourage the student to argue and to probe just as he would do in a tutorial. 'Media' also are used to probe, not to entertain. Thus, there are sixteen film compilations forming a television component in the War and Society course. Once again the visual, counting for more and more in daily life, is used directly to stimulate observation and criticism. One of four sub-themes in 'Sources and Historiography' is economic and technological change, and the characteristic feature of this course is that up to one half of the student's time is taken up with a private 'research project', usually, but not necessarily, concerned with local history. It is not examined by mini-thesis, however, as it would be in most universities. Instead, the student is asked in his final examination paper to discuss his research project 'with particular references to the sources used, and with an evaluation of their usefulness or otherwise, the most important discoveries you have made, the problems you have encountered, and the relationship of this project to the broader perspectives of the course as a whole'.

It has been argued persuasively that within human knowledge the contribution of history to understanding should be 'perspective'. If so, the Open University course provides it deliberately and explicitly. The course also meets the demands of those who argue that historical study rests on an identification, dissection and criticism of 'evidence' and that 'the crucial element (for the historian) is present evidence and not the fact of past evidence'.[13] In this way, the course provides an up-to-date version — up-to-date in its recognition that evidence can be of many different kinds — of the late-nineteenth century ideal of the Oxford History Schools and of *Quellenkritik* — 'exact testing of authorities, scrupulous verification of citations, minute attention to chronology, geography, paleography, and inscriptions' — although it is doubtful whether Professor Marwick, keenly interested as he is in the values which shape historians, would share what Frederic Harrison cited as the final Oxford comment on such historical education, 'when all these are right, you cannot go wrong'.[14]

Intellectual changes — and the values directing them — within the study of history itself have had a bigger impact on the teaching of history after school since 1968 than such important institutional changes, even though the example of the Open University is being followed in some other universities and polytechnics.[15] It would be impossible to understand fully the approach of the Open University itself without taking account of some of the intellectual changes from outside which have influenced the course-makers. They have created 'a new kind of history', although the extent of its newness is often exaggerated: indeed, it was as long ago as 1949 that this phrase was used — and then by no means for the first time — by Lucien Febvre in his review of Marc Bloch's *Apologie pour l'Histoire*.[16] The 'new kind of history' with which this chapter is concerned is not by any means restricted in appeal to this country. Indeed, French historians, notably those of the *Annales* school, are often taken to be its inventors.[17] Their direct influence in Britain is often greatly exaggerated, but then, so too, is the direct influence of some of the recent American quantitative historians or Cliometricians.[18] Perhaps more important than direct influence is the creation of an atmosphere or a climate, and it has certainly changed markedly since 1968.[19]

Two main intellectual changes are considered in this chapter out of many which have taken or are still taking place, and a third which has developed less rapidly than might have been expected is also considered briefly. The chapter concludes with a statement about how these changes may influence institutional developments at a later date. The case of slow development is the study of world history: as a Scandinavian historian has put it, 'there are many new and important advances in historical research; but exceedingly few have to do with broad-scale studies and interpretations of the course of Western history' and without such studies it is difficult to pass to world history.[20] The two cases of rapid development are the study of social history, which has already been reflected institutionally in the setting up of a Social History Society in this country in 1976. The cultivation of this field raises many questions about the relationship between history and the social sciences, with one *simpliste* view maintaining that history is simply one dimension of the social sciences.[21] Similar questions are also raised by the second case of rapid development—the identification of non-documentary evidence, including quantitative evidence.

'Sociology', Professor Hugh Trevor-Roper remarked in a 1969 lecture, 'entered historical study in the eighteenth century. . . . It has remained within it, strengthening its position in it, ever since. Today, I cannot conceive of good history without a sociological dimension.'[22] Yet sociology has still had relatively little influence on the writing of social history and there has been at least as much borrowing by sociologists from social historians as the other way round. Nor has there been much detailed study in this country of the relationship.[23] Economic history has been far more strongly influenced by economists—with one rather neglected book published by a distinguished economist during the period suggesting a number of fascinating themes for further study.[24]

As far as quantitative history is concerned—economic, social or political—there have been many significant advances since 1968, when British economic historians, according to G. R. Hawke, were far more hostile than favourable to Professor Fogel's study of American railways.[25] There has also been an interesting shift in Professor Fogel's own philosophy of history following his work with Stanley Engerman on American slavery leading up to the publication of the controversial *Time On The Cross*, heavily criticized not least by other quantitative historians. Professor Fogel has come to believe that 'the final synthesis' in history lies beyond the realm of the social sciences. 'The task which historians set themselves cannot be achieved through the social sciences alone. Because historians aspire to comprehend the totality of human behaviour, their concerns transcend the subject matter of the social sciences and enter moral and aesthetic realms.' 'We have come to realize,' they have written more recently, 'that history is, and very likely will remain, primarily a humanistic discipline. We now believe that the issue raised by historical quantifiers is not whether history can be transformed into social science but the realm of usefulness of social science disciplines in a humanistic discipline.'[26]

It is interesting to set such a *credo* alongside what has proved to be a far more influential *credo* in Britain—that of Edward Thompson in his massive study *The Making of the English Working Class*, perhaps the most influential single book to appear among the social histories of the 1960s. 'I am seeking to rescue the poor stockinger, the Luddite cropper, the "obsolete" hand-loom weaver, the "utopian" artisan, and even the deluded follower of Joanna Southcott from the enormous condescension of posterity.'[27] Such history-from-below has had a far bigger appeal in Britain—and to some of Professor Fogel's left-wing critics in the United States—than any revolutionary methodology. In this book and elsewhere, however, Edward Thompson has set out what seems to him to be the limitations of theoretical sociology as an academic discipline, and his writings as a whole are very much within a humanistic tradition. Likewise, in the wittiest and liveliest general book on history published during the 1970s — and one which has been taken far too little into the reckoning in most universities in this country — J. H. Hexter has suggested that 'the historians who have invested most heavily in the enterprise of analytical history correspond very closely with the historians committed to the notion that history must be, and must be nothing else, but a social science. But to turn history wholly towards the social sciences is to fix its goal, its Holy Grail, on a point that lies outside the social sciences.'[28]

Before turning to some of the possible institutional implications of this statement — the last section of this chapter — it is necessary to point more precisely to a number of landmarks in the recent history of social history and to some of the varieties of evidence now considered relevant by historians and the methods of interpreting them. When a Social History Society was set up at Lancaster, a new university, in 1976 the event was rightly regarded as the culmination of twenty or thirty years of English scholarship, some of it concerned with fragmenting knowledge — perhaps 'specializing' would be a fairer term — and most of it trying to put together or synthesize, as Fogel and Engerman hoped that they were doing and as Professor Harold Perkin, the founder of the Society, had consistently attempted to do. The fragmenting was associated with the development, sometimes lush, of sub-histories, some with their own professional organizations — among them historical demography (a good subject for teamwork), industrial archaeology, labour history, urban history, local history (a good subject for linking 'amateurs' and 'professionals'), the history of science and technology, medicine, crime, leisure, houses, furniture and gardens. The organizations had different age and standing, and some had gone through boom periods, notably labour history and urban history.[29] The fact that most of the sub-histories were within the broad field of social history was a sign of how far social history had advanced since the publication during the Second World War of G. M. Trevelyan's *English Social History*. It was also interesting that almost all the sub-histories were concerned either with 'history from below' or with the visual aspects of a changing human environment. Local history involved both concerns, and already by 1970 half the increasing number of postgraduate theses were concerned with local history in one form or another.[30] Yet it too had to be saved from condescension, the kind of condescension expressed in a review by G. M. Trevelyan of the first volume of A. L. Rowse's *The England of Elizabeth*; 'ever since the publication of *Tudor Cornwall* I have believed that Mr A. L. Rowse had it in him to become a historian of high rank if he would lay aside lesser activities and bend himself to the production of history on the grand scale.'[31]

It is such history on a 'grand scale' (including social history) which has dropped out of fashion in recent years. Local history is often determinedly local even when it stretches out to comparison. Labour history looks at the people without names. Urban history deals with the every-day routines of life and reactions to them. Crime brings in the outcasts. Medicine deals with the infirm. Yet there are key concepts influencing the modes of interpretation — like 'community', 'class', 'cohort', 'pre-industrial', 'post-industrial'. There is a journal, too. *Past and Present* may be set alongside *Annales* or *The Historical Methods Newlestter*. Its language is less esoteric. The influence (not always direct) of anthropology on English historians has on the whole made them less pretentious than historians influenced by sociology. And they welcome immediacy, contact with life, freedom from pattern. Professor Richard Cobb, one of the most effervescent of teachers, has made the most of all these qualities, refusing to place himself in any school. It will not do, he says, to place himself alongside Lefebvre, Soboul and Rudé. 'Soboul and Rudé are Marxists, and I am nothing at all; the only thing we have in common is the type of document we use and a preoccupation with the Revolution and its personnel as seen from below rather than from government level.'[32]

By pointing to 'the type of document' as the common feature, Professor Cobb is directing attention again to the second main development of recent years — the use of new kinds of evidence (and machinery to assemble and interpret it). The tape-recorder, the photo-copying machine, the camera, the computer have all increasingly influenced historical scholarship, broadening the range of the record of the past. Just as significant as the setting up of the Social History Society or of specialist bodies before it, like the Society for the Study of Labour History (1960), was the drawing together in 1972 of a group of people (blessed by the Social Science Research Council) who were interested in 'oral history'. One of the speakers at their first meeting stressed that oral history was not a subject: it was better, he suggested, to speak of 'oral sources for the study of history'. Subsequently those sources have been subjected to careful criticism, with a very early paper by Paul Thompson clearly identifying some of the main issues.[33] Thompson has been keenly interested in the development of 'visual history' also; and visual records, whether in the shape of films or television on the one hand or paintings, objects and buildings on the other, have been studied more carefully in recent years than ever before. Among the by-products of the study has been an increasing interest in what librarians have called 'ephemera'. The kind of social history now being taught in universities and 'workshops' draws heavily on such materials: and many of them relate directly, of course, to 'history from below'. All things connect.

Social history should concern itself directly with the inter-connections. Yet it is easy to argue, as Peter Stearns, the editor of the ten-year old *Journal of Social History* has done in the United States — with a certain amount of disillusionment — that 'social history has been fettered by its service as handmaiden to established disciplines. Lack of generalized, and rigorous training, distraction from internal methodological and conceptual problems, plus the limitations on approaches to a broad synthesis as opposed to spinning off one sub-field after another — urban history being a case in point — all suggest the need to recognize social history as an independent discipline'. His conclusion that there should be a split between 'conventional' history and social history 'departments' is dangerous in principle and could be very dangerous in practice institutionally: in principle, since it is not so much that social history has spun off one sub-field after another as that sub-fields have found it necessary to come together through a still developing social history; in practice, since to segregate social historians from 'conventional' historians — a curious category — would be to lose the possibilities of moving towards the synthesizing that is still necessary. We would certainly lose much of the vitality of the last ten years if we were to accept Professor Stearns's view that 'only through recognition as a separate discipline with its own identity can social history fulfill its role as a vital part of the range of the social sciences, an essential approach to the understanding of the human animal'.[34] There are already far too many demarcation lines between different kinds of historian.

Nor is all the history that is not social history 'conventional' in character. Extremely interesting work is being done by literary scholars on aspects of changing historical experience and how they were perceived; and in one major field, psychological history or psychohistory — the hyphen went out during the 1960s — 'historians continue to be bothered by the nagging feeling that standards of valid explanation partake more of what they feel to be the mystery and idiosyncrasy of the psychoanalyst rather than of the rigor historians usually want to employ'.[35] There are doubts, too, about the nature and validity of the evidence. Yet William L. Langer claimed as long ago as 1957 that the use of psychology by historians was 'The Next Assignment'.[36] There is probably at least as much to be expected from social psychology, itself a neglected subject in Britain, as there is from psychoanalysis, but as a prominent American psychohistorian has said, so far there has been little progress: 'we cannot point to a single book by a historian and exclaim in hearty consensus, "that book really shows what a historian can do with psychology"'. The connections between development in this field and other recent aspects of development in historical scholarship are demonstrated by the fact that it was Fernand Braudel who wrote one of the most interesting recent articles on one aspect of this subject in 1972 — and one very close to the interests of the Oral History Society, 'Personal Testimony'.[37] How is such concern for personal testimony to be related to the broader historical interests of new generations of social historians in classes, professions, elites and other varieties of social groups?[38] It is certainly related to any effective development of world history, where some of the key problems in recent history (e.g. Hitler and Nazism) often receive curious or careful analysis by psychologists.

World history remains the great lacuna, as it was before the Harrisonian revolution. Indeed, it is interesting to turn back to Professor Barraclough's 1966 Jubilee Address to the Historical Association when he pleaded less for new methodologies in history than for a 'renewal of subject matter'.

Referring to Professor W. H. McNeill's *The Rise of the West*, he urged historians in this country to study more African and Asian history and quoted E. H. Dance, one of the Vice-Presidents of the Association most familiar with classroom teaching and its links with research, to the effect that 'in the world which can be circumnavigated in a week, it is quite as important for British children to learn the history of Europe as it is the history of Britain, and quite as important to learn the history of Asia as the history of Europe'.[39] Although when he spoke, there were some universities which were seriously engaged in world history — the University of Leeds was a pioneer when I was Professor there from 1955 to 1961 — most historians found the technical problems of researching and teaching in this field more difficult than the problems of physical circumnavigation; and even when there were developments in African and Asian history — with extremely interesting historiographical consequences — they did not always or even usually lead to a more active study of world history, but rather to new forms of specialization. There were, of course, links with the 'history-from-below' and a dependence on new methodologies.

The position remains more or less the same, despite the publication of Dr J. M. Roberts's masterly volume, very much an individual exploration;[40] the appearance of massive UNESCO volumes, very much a collective effort, but one imperfectly carried through;[41] the re-emergence of German *Universalgeschichte*;[42] and the Scandinavian 'Trends in Western Civilization' project which starts from the assumption that before there can be any world history there has to be a 'macro-history' of Western civilization first based less on original research than on the systematic assembly, classification and interpretation of existing materials. When Professor Rudeng, who is concerned with Professor Galtung in this last project, went on a historical tour of Western Europe in 1974 he met few major historians concerned with this field, and his observations are valid despite the fact that two very distinguished historians are each engaged in it — Dame Veronica Wedgwood and Professor Daniel Boorstin.[43]

Given the crucial relationship between social history and 'history-from-below' and the methodologies associated with it, it is clear that there is an equally crucial relationship between 'contemporary' history — now very widely studied in schools and researched in universities — and world history. As was pointed out by Professor Barraclough and remains valid: 'In the long run contemporary history can only justify its claim to be a serious intellectual discipline and more than a desultory and superficial review of the contemporary scene, if it sets out to clarify the basic structural changes which have shaped the modern world. These changes are fundamental because they fix the skeleton or framework within which political action takes place'.[44] Far more work needs to be done in universities before the skeleton or framework can bear flesh and blood . . . or even upholstery; and meanwhile there are many historians who share Professor Kaufmann's trouble in imagining a 'universal history' which does not suffer from 'anthropological presumption', 'the proud delusion that we can write about (or devise means for writing about) universal history without corroding the very structures of illusion which make our experience of membership in any intelligible human unit explicitly human and therefore historically resonant'.[45] The 'human animal' is not enough. Nor is the progress of science and technology. Nor is history viewed narrowly as a 'social science'.

If we are thinking of future institutional arrangements affecting the place of history in universities, it is a mistake to believe that it should be placed solely within the 'social sciences area'. There should be options and choices of the kind that were allowed for in Sussex when Dr Harrison was writing his first paper. Contexts matter as well as methodologies. There was more than common sense in the sturdy opinion of the late Dr Kitson Clark, speaking of G. M. Trevelyan — about whom he had many doubts — that he could do three things which the analysts among historians are sometimes unwilling (note 'unwilling', and not 'unable') to do — 'he could paint a scene, he could tell a story and he could describe a man'.[46]

NOTES

1. Elton, G. R., *The Practice of History,* Fontana edn., 1969, p. vii. For some of the key American figures, see Landes, D. S., and Tilly, C. (eds.), *History as Social Science,* Prentice Hall, 1971.

2. One of the most interesting explorations of recent years *The Long March of Everyman,* 'a major venture in audio' raised every kind of methodological issue. The 'internal' BBC papers relating to the project and its development, particularly those written by Michael Mason, the initiator of the venture, cover issues necessarily not touched on in the book based on the series, edited by Theo Barker, 1975. For a classic statement of the claims of Everyman, see Becker, C. L., 'Everyman His Own Historian' in the *American Historical Review,* Vol. XXXVII, 1931/2, pp. 221-36.

3. See *History Workshop, A Journal of Socialist Historians,* Issue I, Spring 1976, p. 1. For comments on this and the second issue, see my review in the *New Statesman,* 11 March 1977.

4. Barlow, G. (ed.), *History at the Universities,* Historical Association, 2nd edn., 1968.

5. Harrison, B., 'History at the Universities, 1968, A Commentary' in *History,* Vol. LIII, 1968, pp. 357-80.

6. North, D. C., 'Quantitative Research in American Economic History' in *American Economic Review,* Vol. LIII, 1963, p. 128.

7. Harrison, loc. cit., p. 357.

8. ibid, p. 380.

9. For the importance of the seminar, see Landes and Tilly, op. cit., pp. 92 ff., which begins with the words 'no innovation in the modern history of higher education is more important than the seminar'. Cambridge University with its 'classes' and London University with its continental-type professorial seminars were far in advance of Oxford University in developing this innovation, and even now there is a tendency in Oxford and a number of other universities to believe that the tutorial system is self-sufficient. Seminar methods have received relatively little attention.

10. For the history of the Open University, see Perry, W., *Open University,* 1976.

11. This course, first introduced in 1961, was designed for all arts and social science students and not just for those likely to major in history. It approached historical problems through the study of one particular historian, usually through one particular book (e.g. R. H. Tawney's *Religion and the Rise of Capitalism*). The course was intended not only to direct attention to the varieties of human experience but to the different ways of

interpreting it on the part of different historians and different generations. It had the same 'linking' intentions as Open University courses have had.

12. See Marwick, A., 'History at the Open University' in the *Oxford Review of Education*, Vol. II, No. 2, 1976, pp. 129-37. See also *Applied Historical Studies Newsletter, An Occasional Publication for Students and Staff*, 1975.

13. Landes and Tilly, op. cit., p. 6, make the point about perspective. For evidence, see Elton, op. cit., pp. 20 ff. He uses the point to argue for the 'autonomy' of history as a discipline. See also Barzun, J., *Clio and the Doctors*, University of Chicago Press, 1974, p. 43, where 'the unimproved historian's greatest strength' is said to be 'his regard for evidence'. 'What do I know? How do I know it?'

14. Harrison, F., 'The History Schools' in *The Meaning of History*, Macmillan, 1902, pp. 118-38. The article was first published in 1893 and should be compared with the prospectuses of the *Revue Historique* (1876) and *The English Historical Review* (1886). For Professor Marwick's views, see his book *The Nature of History*, Macmillan, 1970. His own interests and values have shaped Open University courses: for example, he has written a number of valuable books about twentieth-century war. Where there is no personal commitment behind new university courses in history, it is unlikely that they will either get off the ground or provide a stimulus to learners. J. H. Hexter in *The History Primer*, Allen Lane, 1972, p. 131, explains how he had given no 'credit line' to his own range of experience as an influence on his work.

15. The University of Strathclyde, for example, has created a Department of History and has pioneered both the history of science and technology, for which it was perfectly placed geographically and historically, and industrial archaeology 'when many doubted its integrity and some were openly hostile' (Professor S. G. E. Lythe, 'History's Special Obligations at Strathclyde', a note printed in an internal University of Strathclyde Bulletin, 1973).

16. The essay is translated and printed in Burke, P. (ed.), *A New Kind of History: From the Writings of Lucien Febvre*, Routledge, 1973. 'At the frontiers, astride the frontiers, with one foot on each side, that is where the historian has to work, freely, usefully.' (p. 31). For the use of the term 'new history' in the United States before 1914, see Higham, J., *History*, Prentice Hall, 1965, pp. 104-17.

17. There is an increasing volume of writing on this subject. See especially Aymard, M., 'The Annales and French Historiography' in *The Journal of European Economic History*, 1972, pp. 491-511; 'Historical Studies Today', a special issue of *Daedalus* (Spring 1971), which deals with 'history in depth — our economic, social and mental history'; and Hexter, J. H., 'Fernand Braudel and the *Monde Braudellien*', in *The Journal of Modern History*, Vol. XLIV (1972), pp. 480-539.

18. See Keith Thomas in *The New York Review of Books*, 13 Dec. 1973, for the relative lack of interest shown by *Annales* writers in what Febvre called *mentalités*, a subject of special interest to Thomas, and Berkhofer, R. F., *A Behavioral Approach to Historical Analysis*, Collier Macmillan, 1969. This was reviewed in the pioneering American publication *Historical Methods Newsletter*, Vol. IV, No. 3, 1971, pp. 84-8, a *Newsletter* then with few subscribers in this country. In the same number there was a review article 'The Rush to Violence in Social Analysis' (pp. 88-99).

19. In a brilliant obituary note of Georges Lefebvre in *Past and Present*, No. 18, 1960, Richard Cobb pointed out how difficult it is to trace direct influence.

20. Rudeng, E., *The State of Macro-History Today*, Working Paper, University of Oslo, 1974.

21. See, for example, a quotation from the French historian, F. Mauro in a Leicester inaugural lecture by Professor R. Davis, *History and the Social Sciences*, Leicester University Press, 1965: 'History is the projection of the social sciences into the past'. There is a balanced account of the issues in T. C. Cochran, *The Inner Revolution*, 1964.

22. Trevor-Roper, H. R., *The Past and the Present: History and Sociology*, London School of Economics, 1969.
23. See my article 'Sociology and History' in A. T. Welford (ed.), *Society: Problems and Methods of Study*, Routledge, 1962, pp. 91-9.
24. Hicks, J., *A Theory of Economic History*, Oxford University Press, 1969.
25. Hawke, G. R., 'Mr Hunt's Study of the Fogel Thesis' in *History*, Vol. LIII, No. 177, 1968, p. 19.
26. See Fogel, R. W., 'The Limits of Quantitative Methods in History' in the *American Historical Review*, Vol. LXXX, 1975.
27. Thompson, E., *The Making of the English Working Class*, Gollancz, 1963, p.12.
28. Hexter, op. cit., p. 179. On page 5 he writes that he 'is concerned with thinking coherently about history as a whole, not with effective participation in history as a professional activity'.
29. See Briggs, A., and Saville, J. (eds.), *Essays in Labour History, 1886-1923*, Macmillan, 1971, p. 1, for a brief account of developments in the study of labour history beginning with the foundation of the Society for the Study of Labour History in 1960 and the subsequent publication of the Bulletin. In 1963 H. J. Dyos began to circulate an *Urban History Newsletter* and in 1968 he edited *The Study of Urban History*. My introduction to this volume traces the early stages of the boom: the later stages are clear from the first *Urban History Yearbook*, Leicester University Press, 1974, edited by Professor Dyos.
30. Everitt, A., *New Avenues in English Local History*, An Inaugural Lecture at Leicester University, Leicester University Press, 1970. The needs of the writers was met by such publications as Emmison, F. G., and Smith, W. J., *Material for Theses in Some Record Offices*, Phillimore, 1973.
31. A *Sunday Times* review quoted by Finberg, H., *The Local Historian and his Theme*, a Lecture at Leicester University (1952). This was a pioneering contribution from a pioneering university in this field. Professor Finberg was also associated with the Standing Conference for the Study of Local History which brings 'amateurs' and 'professionals' together.
32. Cobb, R., 'Georges Lefebvre' in *Past and Present*, No. 18, 1960, pp. 52-67. See also his piece written along with Alun Davies, 'Georges Lefebvre et les Historiens anglais' in *Annales Historiques de la Revolution Française*, 1960, pp. 97-102.
33. Thompson, P., 'Problems of Method in Oral History' in *Oral History: An Occasional Newssheet*, No. 4, 1972.
34. Stearns, P., 'Coming of Age', reprinted in *Social History Society News Letter*, Vol. II, No. 1, 1977.
35. Schoenwald, R. L., 'Using Psychology in History' in *Historical Methods News Letter*, Vol. VII, 1973, pp. 9-24.
36. Langer, W. L., 'The Next Assignment' in the *American Historical Review*, Vol. LXIII, 1958, pp. 283-304.
37. Braudel, F., 'Personal Testimony' in the *Journal of Modern History*, Vol. XLIV, 1972, pp. 448-67.
38. See, for example, Hundert, E. J., 'History, Psychology and the Study of Deviant Behavior' in the *Journal of Interdisciplinary History*, Vol. II, 1972, pp. 453-72.
39. Barraclough, G., 'History and the Common Man', A Jubilee Address, 12 April 1966. He quoted the address of his immediate predecessor in 1964, 'Never have doubt and discontent about the subject been more evident than in these years of rapid growth'. This was still very much the mood among many historians. Cf. Plumb, J. H., *Crisis in the Humanities*, Penguin, 1964, p. 28, in which he complained both about 'the anarchy of professional activity' and 'spiritual nihilism'. The ferment had already started.
40. Roberts, J. M., *History of the World*, Hutchinson, 1977. It is interesting to note that

Dr Roberts's relevant personal experience had included, besides university teaching, travel and the editorship of a history magazine designed for large audiences.

41. See Steensgaard, N., 'Universal History for Our Times' in the *Journal of Modern History*, Vol. XLV, 1973, pp. 72-82. The UNESCO *Journal of World History* ceased publication in 1972. It had been in existence since 1954 and was replaced by *Cultures.*

42. See Schulin, E. (ed.), *Universalgeschichte* (1974) and Muller, G., 'Universalgeschichte in Unterricht und Lehre' in *Neue Sammlung*, Vol. IV, 1964, pp. 243-64.

43. See Rudeng, loc. cit.

44. Barraclough, G., *An Introduction to Contemporary History*, Watts, 1964, p. 9.

45. Note by Kaufmann, R. J., *First Thoughts on Universal History*, 1971.

46. Kitson Clark, G., 'G. M. Trevelyan as an Historian' in *Durham University Journal*, Dec. 1962, p. 4. See also Bullock, A., *Is History becoming a Social Science?*, Leslie Stephen Lecture, 1976.

Index